Electro-epilation

A Practical Approach

Second edition

eth Cartwright

Gill Morris

ichelle Severn

First published in 1995 by:
Stanley Thornes (Publishers) Ltd

Second edition published in 2001 by:
Nelson Thornes Ltd
Delta Place
27 Bath Road
CHELTENHAM
GL53 7TH
United Kingdom

05 / 10 9 8 7 6 5

A catalogue record for this book is available from the British Library

ISBN 0 7487 6376 7

Page make-up by Florence Production Ltd

Printed and bound in Scotland by Scotprint

Contents

FOREWORD

Hirsutism is by no means uncommon. In the 15–44 year age group it is present in one-third of women in the form of upper lip hair, and 6–9% have hair on the chin or side of the face. On rare occasions this may be indicative of endocrine dysfunction, but in the vast majority of cases increased facial hair must be regarded as a cosmetic or psychological problem.

The reaction may be variable and complex, but will depend upon a woman's racial and cultural background, as well as her perception of her body image. The idea that 'perfect women' have no facial hair is clearly ridiculous, and much time is spent in photographic darkrooms removing traces of facial hair before a picture can be printed in the glossy magazines.

The medical practitioner may frequently encounter the perceived problem of hirsutism, and can offer helpful and objective advice and information to the patient. In some cases the general practitioner will make a referral to a specialist, but in the vast majority of cases there is no underlying medical pathology and referral to a centre offering electrolysis is the usual outcome. The advice and treatment offered there should be sufficient to resolve any normal problem, and the result is usually a restored sense of confidence and wellbeing in the client.

R.M. Graham, MB, ChB, FRCOG
Consultant Obstetrician and Gynaecologist
The Nuffield Hospital, Leicester

PREFACE

This book has been written for all electrologists: tutors, students, recently qualified operators and experienced practitioners. The aim of the book is to provide a comprehensive description of up-to-date practical techniques and the associated theory of all methods of permanent hair removal: electrolysis, short-wave diathermy and blend. The theory and practice of blend epilation are described in detail.

The book has specific benefits for those teaching or studying for an award in electrolysis or for those sitting entrance examinations for a professional electrolysis body. Practitioners and employers who wish to keep up to date with changes in the profession will find this book an ideal source of reference, giving in-depth explanations of the latest practical techniques, hygiene requirements and training.

The text has been written in an easy-to-follow, logical format that encourages learning and understanding.

ACKNOWLEDGEMENTS

The authors and publishers gratefully acknowledge the following for their assistance in providing photographs and illustrations:

Corel – cover photograph
E.A.Ellisons
Hairdressing and Beauty Equipment Centre (HBEC)
House of Famuir – fig. 13.8(b)
Sterex Electrolysis International Ltd (photographs supplied by Liz Moore on behalf of Sterex)
St. John's Institute of Dermatology, London - figs. 1.10–1.14, 1.16–21
Woodford Medical, Danbury, Essex – fig. 15.2

Also many thanks to Marie Leatherland for her help and assistance in the preparation of this book.

INTRODUCTION AND OVERVIEW

Electrolysis is the permanent removal of unwanted hair. This simple phrase hides the pleasure and satisfaction that this treatment gives to all those who are involved with it. In the opinion of the authors, permanent hair removal is the most rewarding treatment one can provide.

The majority of your clients will be happy and well-balanced people with hair growth concerns that are purely 'cosmetic'; others may be self-conscious or even quite distressed when they take their first tentative steps through your door.

Those who choose to specialise in electrolysis will come across people with quite severe hair growth problems that demand skill, professionalism and empathy from the therapist. We hope that reading this book will help you achieve these qualities.

Galvanic or direct current was the first method of electrical epilation and one from which the term 'electrolysis' was derived.

Electrolysis as a means of permanent hair removal was first used and documented in the USA by an ophthalmologist, Dr Charles E. Michel, in 1875. Dr Michel treated ingrowing eyelashes (trichiasis) using a surgical needle, which he sanded down to achieve the desired diameter, and a 'wet' battery (like a car battery) from which he obtained his galvanic current.

This is generally accepted to be the beginning of electrolysis, although Dr Michel actually started his treatments some 6 years before this in 1869.

1875	The first recorded treatments were presented to the medical field by Dr Charles E. Michel in St Louis, Missouri, USA.
1886	Dr George Henry Fox published a booklet on galvanic epilation entitled *The Use of Electricity in the Removal of Superfluous Hair and the Treatment of Various Facial Blemishes*.
1895	The first training course in electrolysis was written by Daniel J. Mahler in Rhode Island, USA.
1910	Dr Plyms described his treatment and gave his direction as to practical application in the publication *Electricity and the Methods of Employment in Removing Superfluous Hair and the Treatment of Other Facial Blemishes*.
1916	Professor Paul N. Kree developed the 'multiple needle' technique, which allowed more hairs to be treated in a given time. This technique resulted in electrolysis becoming a practical, if slow, method of removing unwanted hair. More and more people were becoming involved in this fledgling profession.
1924	Dr Henry Bordier of Lyon, France, was the first to use short-wave diathermy (a high-frequency current also referred to as radiofrequency) and he extolled its benefits. Dr Bordier's views were well supported by many others around this time.

Late 1920s and early 1930s

During this period short-wave diathermy increasingly became the dominant modality. (In America short-wave diathermy is known as thermolysis.) Early short-wave diathermy equipment was, however, unreliable because the 'spark gap' machines were inconsistent and difficult to control.

Mid 1940s	New, more reliable, methods of producing the high-frequency alternating current were introduced and resulted in a dramatic rise in the use of short-wave diathermy.
1944	The Institute of Electrolysis was founded in Britain.
1945	Arthur Ralph Hinkel and Henri E. St. Pierre applied for a patent for the first blend, or combined current, epilator.
1947	Dr F. A. Ellis compared the effectiveness of short-wave diathermy and galvanic treatments in his paper *Electrolysis versus High Frequency Currents in the Treatments of Hypertrichosis – A Comparative Histologic and Clinical Study*. He concluded that galvanic treatment was more effective for permanent hair removal.
1950	The US Federal Communications Commission brought diathermy instruments under its control.
1957	The British Association of Electrolysists was founded.
1981	The world's first sterile disposable electrolysis needle was invented by Englishman John Heath.
1986–87	The American International Guild of Professional Electrologists won a court case against a manufacturer of 'no needle' high-frequency tweezers, preventing it from using the word 'permanent' in its advertising. Permanent removal of hair had not been proven to the court by the tweezer manufacturer.
Mid to late 1980s	Blend starts to become popular with British electrologists.
Present day	Electro-epilation has become more and more popular, not just in America, where it started, but throughout the world. In the UK there are over 220 colleges offering electrolysis courses. Treatment is rarely given by the medical practitioners who began the process, but by specially trained people: people who care, people who want to help others, people like you – electrologists.

Progress Check

1 Who pioneered electrolysis for hair removal and when?
2 Where was electrolysis first used?
3 What development in 1916 helped the electrolysis profession?
4 Who was the first person to use short-wave diathermy for hair removal?
5 Why were early short-wave diathermy machines unpredictable?
6 In which study was galvanic described as being more effective than short-wave diathermy?
7 Who invented the world's first sterile disposable needle?
8 When did blend epilation become popular in Britain?

Part I

Anatomy and physiology

SKIN

After studying this chapter you will be able to:

- describe the structure of the epidermis and dermis
- state the names of the layers of the skin and their contents
- understand the relationship between collagen and elastin
- understand the functions of the skin
- list the appendages of the skin and what they do
- describe and understand the structures in the dermis
- understand the formation and function of melanin
- recognise the terms used to describe skin diseases and disorders
- describe skin diseases and disorders and their causes.

The skin is one of the largest organs of the body and forms its external covering. The skin is constantly being worn away and replenished by new cells from below. It varies in thickness on different parts of the body, for instance it is thinnest on the eyelids and lips and thickest on the soles of the feet (plantar region), palms of the hands (palmar region) and buttocks.

Structure of the skin

The skin can be divided into two parts.

1 The outer layers of the skin are called the epidermis.
2 The lower layers of the skin are called the dermis.

Structure of the epidermis

The epidermis is the most superficial layer of the skin, and is mostly considered dead. It consists of five layers.

Stratum corneum/horny layer
- This forms the outer layer of the skin.
- Scale-like cells are continually being shed and replaced by cells from below rising to the surface.

Stratum lucidum/clear layer
- This layer consists of small translucent cells through which light can pass.
- The cells do not contain a nucleus.
- The cells contain drops of oily substance.
- The nails are a continuation of this layer.

Stratum granulosum/granular layer
- This layer is 1–3 cells thick.
- The cells look like very distinct granules.
- Keratin is produced in this layer, and is found mostly in the plantar and palmar regions.

> **REMEMBER**
> The active parts of the hair follicle are found in the dermis.

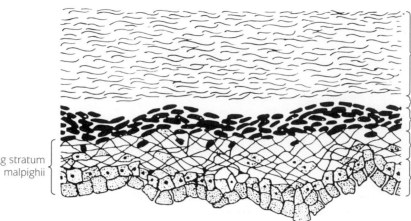

Figure 1.1 *Strata of the epidermis*

- These cells are almost dead, and as more keratin is laid down they undergo a change into a horny substance.
- Keratin helps keep the top layers of the epidermis waterproof and protects against weak acids and alkalis.

Stratum spinosum/prickle cell layer
- This layer is 3–6 cells thick.
- The cells have bridges running between them called desmosomes. These are made of keratin and allow substances to pass between the cells.
- These cells are constantly dividing.

Stratum germinativum/basal layer
- This consists of a single layer of cells.
- This is the layer responsible for the growth of the epidermis; the cells are produced by mitosis (cell division).
- As the cells move up and out they become keratinised (full of keratin).
- A typical cell takes 2–3 weeks to pass from this layer to the surface.
- This layer contains the skin pigment melanin, which protects the sensitive cells below from the destructive effects of ultraviolet rays.

Structure of the dermis
The dermis can also be called the true skin or the corium. The dermis forms the bulk of the skin and is made of tough resilient tissue that cushions underlying organs against mechanical injury.

Papillary layer
- This layer is thin and made up of widely separated, delicate collagenous and elastic fibres and numerous capillary meshes.
- It contains small cone-shaped projections of elastin tissue that point up to the epidermis; these projections are called papillae.
- Some of these papillae contain looped capillaries; others contain nerve fibre endings, called tactile corpuscles.
- This layer also contains some of the skin pigment melanin for protection.
- This layer of the skin forms the connective tissue sheath around the hair follicle.

> **REMEMBER**
> - The epidermis is composed of five layers.
> - The epidermis is mainly considered dead as there is no blood through it.

> **REMEMBER**
> The dermis is the true skin.

> **REMEMBER**
> Melanin protects against ultraviolet light.

Reticular layer

- This layer consists of dense, coarse, branching collagen fibre bundles.
- Most bundles are arranged parallel to the skin, but some are perpendicular to it, indicating the direction of the extensibility of the skin.
- The reticular layer of the skin of the areola and nipple of the breast, the penis and the scrotum contains smooth muscle fibres which wrinkle the skin on contracting.

The papillary and reticular layer are embedded in ground substance gel. The main structural feature of the dermis is the network of mechanically strong fibres, mostly collagen but with some elastin (these two substances are made of protein). The collagen and elastin fibres are embedded in ground substance.

Collagen

- Collagen is a white fibrous tissue which is made up of a group of proteins which are the most abundant proteins in mammals, constituting about 25% of the body weight.
- Collagen is a stiff, triple-stranded helical (spiral) structure.
- Each collagen strand is called an alpha (α) chain.
- So far seven genetically different alpha chains have been found. Type 1 is the most predominant in vertebrates, with some type 3 also being present.

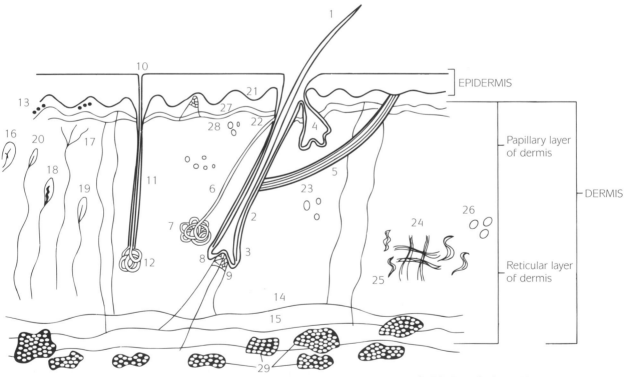

Figure 1.2 *Structure of the dermis: 1, hair shaft; 2, hair follicle; 3, dermal papilla in the dermis and at base of follicle; 4, sebaceous gland; 5, arrector pili muscle; 6, apocrine sweat duct; 7, apocrine sweat gland; 8, bulb of hair follicle; 9, capillaries in skin and at base of follicles; 10, sweat pore; 11, eccrine sweat duct; 12, eccrine sweat gland; 13, melanocytes; 14, vein; 15, artery; 16, Ruffini's end organ; 17, pain nerve ending; 18, Meissner's corpuscle; 19, Krause's end bulb; 20, Pacinian corpuscle; 21, mast cells; 22, histiocytes; 23, eosinophils; 24, collagen; 25, elastin; 26, fibroblasts; 27, venule; 28, arteriole; 29, adipose tissue*

Collagen gives the skin strength and the ability to resist deforming forces. Collagen gives the skin a plump youthful appearance.

Elastin
- Elastin is a yellow elastic fibrous tissue.
- Elastin fibres make up only about 1% of the dermis.

What is the function of elastin?

- Elastin fibres give the skin elastic properties, allowing it to recoil back to its original position after being stretched.
- Overextension can occur, for example in pregnancy or rapidly developing obesity, leading to rupture of the elastin fibre. This allows the collagen to become overstretched and even tear, forming characteristic linear scars within the dermis called striae (stretch marks).

Subcutaneous layer
This is a fatty layer found underneath the dermis, made of adipose tissue.

This layer is for protection as the fat offers insulation against temperature loss from the body and it acts as a good buffer against knocks and blows to the outside body.

Only the larger deeper hair follicles and sweat glands can be found in the subcutaneous tissue.

Functions of the dermis
- The main function is mechanical, i.e. when the skin is stretched the irregular three-dimensional network of collagen fibres gradually becomes reoriented into an arrangement of more parallel bundles.
- Because of the way the skin is made, it can adapt to local or general changes in size and contour, to allow for movement of the head and limbs and a very wide range of facial expressions.
- The functions of the skin result from the interplay of three factors:

1 **Tension**. This holds the skin in shape against deforming forces and is due to the presence of elastin fibres.
2 **Elasticity**. This is the ability of skin to resume its original position (shape) after the deforming forces have ceased to act and is also due to elastin.
3 **Tensile strength**. This is the degree to which elongation can take place before tearing occurs and depends mainly on the presence of collagen fibres.

> **REMEMBER**
> These functions are only of the dermis and not of the skin as a whole.

Progress Check

1 What are the two parts of the skin called and how many further layers are these two parts divided into?
2 Name all the individual layers of the skin.
3 What is melanin and where is it found?
4 What is keratin and where is it found?
5 What is the corium?
6 What are the main fibres in the dermis?

Functions of the skin

Protection
The skin provides a waterproof coat which protects the body from dirt, minor injuries, bacterial infection and chemical attack. The first barrier is the layer of sebum and sweat produced by the skin, forming a slightly acid film over its surface (acid mantle). The acidity, pH 4.5–6, discourages the growth of bacteria. Sebum is also slightly fungicidal and so helps prevent fungal growth.

The second barrier is the stratum corneum, which acts as a filter against invading bacteria. Any organisms passing through the barrier may be attacked by wandering phagocytic cells (cells which scavenge particles and other cells by engulfing them) in the dermis. Finally, melanin protects the underlying tissues from damage by ultraviolet light.

The subcutaneous layer protects against mechanical injury, i.e. knocks and blows.

Sensation
The skin acts as a sense organ to detect changes in heat (Ruffini's end organ), cold (Krause's end bulb), touch (Meissner's corpuscles), pressure (Pacinian corpuscles) and pain (pain corpuscles). The skin informs the brain of changes in the environment through its sensory nerve endings. The nerve endings responsive to touch and pressure are situated near the hair follicles.

Heat regulation
By the dilation of superficial blood capillaries in the skin when we are warm, and their constriction when we are cool, we can help to maintain the body temperature at 37°C. At the more extreme body temperatures we sweat to lose heat and shiver to make heat. The subcutaneous tissue under the dermis also acts as an insulating layer to prevent too much heat loss.

Excretion
Perspiration from the sweat glands is excreted from the skin. Waste products such as lactic acid and urea, water and salt are lost through the skin, but this is a minor function of the skin.

Secretion
Sebum is secreted by the sebaceous glands.

Vitamin D formation
The action of ultraviolet rays on the sterols in the epidermis results in the formation of vitamin D.

Storage
The skin acts as a storage depot for fat and water. The skin also acts as a reservoir for blood, which can be diverted to other organs as required.

Absorption
Absorption of certain particles through the skin does occur but it is limited to particles below a certain size. It is known that certain drugs and hormones and all essential oils will be absorbed through the skin into the bloodstream.

> **REMEMBER**
> Excretion removes waste products. Secreted substances have a function.

> **REMEMBER**
> The skin has eight functions.

Appendages of the skin

Skin contains the following structures:

1 sweat glands
2 nerves
3 sebaceous glands
4 blood vessels
5 lymphatic vessels
6 hair follicles
7 nails.

Sweat glands

- These glands consist of a single duct which leads from the body of the gland in the subcutaneous tissue and dermis to the surface of the epidermis. The duct is spirally coiled as it passes through the epidermis and opens through a minute opening called a sweat pore.
- Sweat glands excrete sweat, which is a waste product containing water, urea and salts.
- Sweat glands are found all over the body.
- Sweat glands are a type of exocrine glands, that is they excrete directly out of the tissues and not into the blood vessels.
- There are two types of sweat glands: eccrine glands and apocrine glands.

Eccrine glands

- These glands open directly onto the epidermis.
- These are the more numerous of the two types of glands.
- They excrete sweat which is mainly water, e.g. on the palms of the hand.
- These glands are under nervous control.

Apocrine glands

- These glands open into the hair follicle.
- These glands are restricted to certain parts of the body: the axilla (armpit) and the pubic regions.
- The sweat secreted is a milky odourless fluid which, if broken down by bacteria, can subsequently develop a characteristic odour, called body odour.

Normally sweat evaporates as soon as it is formed and is known as insensible sweat, but in hot and humid weather, and after excessive exercise, drops of water are seen on the skin. The main function of sweat is to control body temperature, by the surface evaporation of sweat.

Nerves

The skin supplies much of the body's sensory information and is provided with both sensory and sympathetic nerve fibres. Sympathetic nerve fibres are controlled by our subconscious and supply the blood vessels, the smooth muscles of the hair follicles and the secretory cells of the sweat glands (Figure 1.3).

Sensory fibres are widely distributed in the network of the skin and respond to:

- touch, through Meissner's corpuscles
- pressure, through Pacinian corpuscles

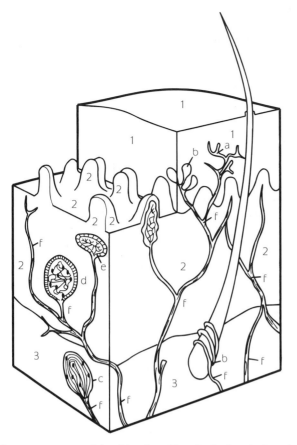

Figure 1.3 *Sensory receptors of the skin:* 1, *epidermis*; 2, *dermis*; 3, *subcutaneous tissue*: a, *pain nerve ending (sensitive to pain)*; b, *Meissner's corpuscle (sensitive to touch)*; c, *Pacinian corpuscle (sensitive to pressure)*; d, *Ruffini's end organ (sensitive to heat)*; e, *Krause's end bulb (sensitive to cold)*; f, *nerve fibre*

- pain, through pain corpuscles
- heat, through Ruffini's end organs
- cold, through Krause's end bulbs.

Sebaceous glands

- These glands start in the epidermis but lie in the level of the dermis.
- Most sebaceous glands open into a hair follicle via a duct. Each gland consists of a single duct opening from a cluster of alveoli or sacs, usually 2–5 but sometimes as many as 20.
- These glands secrete a substance called sebum, which is a fatty material. Sebum is formed by the cells of the gland accumulating drops of lipids (fats), which ultimately form sebum. At the same time the cell membrane breaks down to release the sebum.
- Sebaceous glands are found almost everywhere in the skin and are most abundant on the scalp, forehead, nose, chin and back. The glands are large on the nose and the face and often become enlarged because of the accumulation of pent-up secretion.
- The only places that do not have these glands are the plantar and palmar regions and the backs of the hands.
- Sebum acts as a natural lubricant to the hair and skin and protects the skin from the effects of moisture loss (desiccation), and bacterial action.

REMEMBER
The skin is made to be sensitive so you must be gentle when touching it.

REMEMBER
Sebaceous glands open up into hair follicles.

REMEMBER
Sebum and sweat form the acid mantle.

- The secretion of the gland does not appear to be under the control of the nerves, but is stimulated by hormonal activity, particularly androgens.
- During hormonal disturbances, these glands become overactive and often cause facial blemishes.
- Sebaceous glands are present at birth but remain small and inactive until puberty.
- Sebaceous glands are larger in men than in women.

Functions of sebum

1. It provides an emollient (softening) film to prevent evaporation of water from the horny layer cells.
2. It provides a barrier against chemical defatting.
3. It emulsifies various substances applied to the skin.
4. It aids vitamin D synthesis.
5. It prevents bacterial infection, by being mildly bactericidal.
6. It protects against fungal infections (after puberty).

Blood vessels

- The circulation of blood through the dermis nourishes the skin and plays an important role in the regulation of body temperature.
- The dermis contains an extensive network of blood capillaries arising from arteries in the subcutaneous layer.
- Each papilla of the dermis is supplied with a loop of capillaries which provides nourishment to the stratum germinativum.

Lymphatic vessels

- The dermis has a rich supply of lymphatic vessels, which carry waste and harmful substances out of the skin, so that the body can get rid of them.

Hair follicles

- Hairs are found on nearly every part of the body, except the plantar and palmar regions and the umbilicus.
- Hairs vary in length, thickness and colour in different parts of the body and in people of different races.
- The hair follicle grows out of the epidermal cells, but it extends into the dermis.
- Over most parts of the body the hairs are fine and downy, giving the appearance of hairlessness.
- During fetal life almost all of the skin of humans is covered with a fine hair called lanugo. This hair is mostly shed by birth and replaced by fine hairs called vellus hairs in the early months of postnatal life. These are retained in most regions, but are replaced by the hairs (terminal hairs) of the eyebrows and axillae and those on the face and chest of the male, which appear at puberty, their development and growth being under hormonal control.
- In furry mammals hair has the functions of temperature control and sensation of touch, and these functions also occur in humans.
- The lifespan of a single hair varies from about 4 months on the eyelashes and axilla to about 4 years on the scalp, after which it is shed and replaced by the new cells from the matrix of the hair.
- Arrector pili muscles are attached to each hair follicle, and when they contract they make the hair stand up on end, giving a goosepimple effect. This helps to retain heat when it is cold, i.e. a form of temperature control.

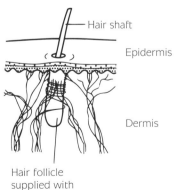

Hair shaft

Epidermis

Dermis

Hair follicle supplied with many blood capillaries

Figure 1.4 *A hair follicle*

1   List and explain the functions of the skin.
2   What type of gland is a sweat gland?
3   What are the two different types of sweat glands?
4   What are the different sensations that can be felt through the skin?
5   What is the function of sebaceous glands?
6   Where are sebaceous glands found?
7   What are the functions of sebum?

Nails

Nails are the hard translucent structures found at the end of the fingers and toes. Nails are a continuation of the stratum lucidum, and are made tough and resilient by the protein keratin they contain.

Cells of the skin (dermis)

Skin contains the following types of cells:

1   fibroblasts
2   mast cells
3   histiocytes
4   eosinophils
5   melanocytes.

Fibroblasts

These are cells in the dermis that may take up amino acids and convert them into polypeptide chains of collagen, which are then secreted into the dermis. Injury to the dermis stimulates fibroblast proliferation and collagen formation.

Mast cells

These cells vary in shape, and some are indistinguishable from fibroblasts. Their cytoplasm is filled with heparin, serotonin, adrenaline, noradrenaline, histamine and hyaluronic acid.

Under certain conditions mast cells become more numerous; wrinkled skin contains more mast cells than smooth skin. In skin cancer, mast cells are more abundant; they seem to form a barrier between the tumour and the normal tissue. Accumulations of mast cells occur in eczema, pemphigus and scleroderma.

When an antigen reacts with an antibody, mast cells release histamine, thus producing an allergic reaction.

Histiocytes

Histiocytes are cells that can ingest foreign particles, and so are macrophages.

Eosinophils

These cells are thought to be made in the bone marrow and are attracted to the specific tissue reaction sites of the allergic reaction. It has been suggested that eosinophils take up histamine, remove it from the site of reaction and carry it to other areas for detoxification (thus limiting the intensity of the allergic reaction).

Melanocytes

These are cells containing melanin, the pigment in the skin and hair.

Melanocytes are roughly triangular with numerous fine branching processes, which can transfer melanin to the surrounding cells. A melanocyte together with its surrounding group of cells is sometimes referred to as an 'epidermal melanin unit'.

The cells are sparingly distributed in the dermis; however they may be numerous in naevi, moles and other heavily pigmented areas. The majority of melanocytes in the skin are found in the basal layer of the epidermis.

The biological function of melanin is to protect the underlying tissues from ultraviolet light. Melanin is synthesised from tyrosine in melanosomes when stimulated by ultraviolet light.

Differences in skin colour are due to differences in packaging, distribution and degradation of the pigment. Black skin contains no more melanocytes than white skin, but the melanosome are larger and dispersed rather than being in clumps, and contain a different type of melanin.

Melanocytes in the basal layer of the epidermis

Melanocyte granules (melanosomes) gradually become more and more opaque as more melanin is laid down until no internal structures can be seen. At this point the melanosomes are essentially devoid of tyrosinase (the enzyme that speeds up the conversion of tyrosine to melanin). Melanosomes are then transported along the dendritic process and injected into the cytoplasm of the neighbouring basal layer cells. (They are sometimes engulfed or phagocytosed by these cells.)

The melanin granules cluster around the nucleus like a protective cap. The cells gradually migrate upwards towards the stratum corneum and the melanosomes either disintegrate or are eventually shed.

> **REMEMBER**
> The heat from diathermy treatment can alter the pigment in Asian and Negroid skin.

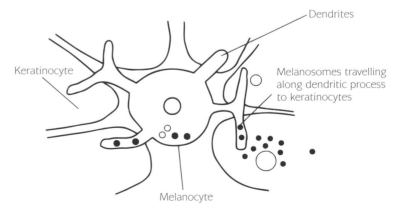

Dendrites

Keratinocyte

Melanosomes travelling along dendritic process to keratinocytes

Melanocyte

Figure 1.5 *Melanocyte in the basal layer of the epidermis*

Skin types

Skin types	Characteristics
Normal	Even, healthy colour over the face and neck. Smooth texture without blemishes. Facial lines relative to age.
Dry	Generally even colour although cheeks prone to redness. Skin texture usually slightly rough and uneven, pores small with little sebum produced. Prone to premature ageing.
Dehydrated	A temporary lack of moisture affecting any skin type. Texture rougher than normal and colour more pink.
Greasy/Oily	Although surface can be shiny from sebum, colour is dull. Pore size larger particularly on forehead, nose and chin. Less likely to wrinkle.
Combination	Combination of any skin types, mainly dry cheeks and oily centre panel.
Sensitive	Skin can be red and sore. Can develop irregular patches of dryness and irritation. Any skin type can be sensitive.
Acne vulgaris	Hormonal skin disease, papules, pustules, comedones and excess sebum present. May also be sore and inflamed.
Couperose	Red complexion with broken veins all over or in patches. Texture generally fine and maybe dry and sensitive.
Mature	Sebum production reduces with age thus drying out the skin. Feels fine and maybe wrinkled due to lack of collagen and elastin. Pigment becomes irregular with dark patches or 'age spots' developing.
Oedematous	Holds excess fluid giving puffy appearance. Seen on face and neck of clients with systemic illness.
Seborrhoeic	Extremely oily due to overactive sebaceous glands. Pore size large and sallow coloured.

Table 1.1 *Skin types and their characteristics*

Progress Check

1 Which parts of the body do not have hair on them?
2 What are the functions of the hair?
3 How long is the average life of a hair?
4 What is the muscle that makes the hair stand on end?
5 From what layer of the skin are nails made?
6 How does the allergic reaction occur?
7 What substance is melanin made from?

Skin diseases and disorders

We strongly recommend that electrologists purchase a copy of *A Colour Atlas of Dermatology* by G. M. Levene and C. D. Calnan, published by Wolfe, in order to familiarise themselves with the appearance of the conditions/diseases listed in this section.

A skin disease is any departure from the normal state of health of the skin.

Primary lesions
Macule
A flat spot or patch of a different colour from the surrounding skin.

Definitions	
Primary lesion	An initial alteration in the skin.
Secondary lesion	Deterioration of a primary lesion.
Tertiary lesion	A lesion, occurring only with serious diseases, after primary and secondary lesions.
Acute disease	A disease whose symptoms are of a more violent nature and are of short duration.
Chronic disease	A disease of long duration, usually mild and recurring.
Infection	A disease caused by pathogenic bacteria (see below), which gain access to the body after contact with contaminated people or objects.
Contagious	Communicable by contact.
Congenital	Present at birth.
Seasonal	Influenced by the weather.
Occupational disease	A disease due to constant contact with irritants at work.
Parasitic disease	A disease caused by a vegetable or animal parasite.
Pathogenic bacteria	Bacteria which cause disease.
Systemic disease	A disease due to under- or overactivity of an internal gland and affecting the whole body.
Allergy	Sensitivity to normally harmless substances.
Inflammation	Redness, pain, swelling, heat and possible itching.

Table 1.2 *Definitions of skin conditions and diseases*

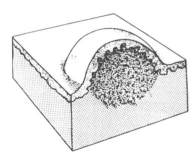

Figure 1.6 *Papule*

REMEMBER
Wheals can occur after electro-epilation treatments.

Ephilide
The correct name for a freckle.

Papule
A small elevated lump in the skin, containing no fluid but which may develop pus.

Tubercle (nodule)
A solid lump larger than a papule. It projects above the surface or lies within or under the skin. It varies in size from a pea to a walnut.

Tumour
The deepest and largest growing lump that occurs in the skin, varying in size.

Pustule
An elevation of the skin having an inflamed base, containing pus.

Wheal
A special type of papule which is usually an acute itchy, swollen lesion that lasts only a few hours (often associated with hives or the bite of an insect such as a mosquito).

Hives/urticaria
This is a nettle rash type of eruption producing red and white wheals which cause irritation on the surface of the skin. The condition is usually related to an allergic reaction or stress and may cause single wheals or a widespread reaction which will usually subside within a few hours.

Vesicle

A blister with clear fluid in it. Vesicles lie within or just below the epidermis.

Bulla

A large blister containing watery fluid.

Secondary lesions

Scale

An accumulation of epidermal flakes, dry or greasy (for example abnormal or excessive dandruff). Scales are found in the following conditions:

- psoriasis: silvery scales
- seborrhoeic dermatitis: yellow greasy scales
- eczema: fine shedding scales.

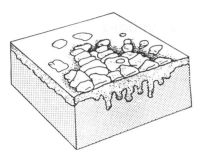

Figure 1.7 *Scale*

Crust (scab)

An accumulation of serum and pus and possibly epidermal material on the surface of the skin.

Excoriation

A skin sore or abrasion caused by scratching or scraping, for example after an injury, not necessarily the result of a skin disease.

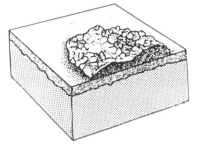

Figure 1.8 *Crust*

Fissure

A crack in the skin penetrating down into the dermis as in chapped hands or lips, caused by a skin condition or a harsh climate.

Ulcer

An open lesion of the skin or mucous membrane of the body accompanied by pus and the loss of skin depth.

Scar

Tissue that forms when an injury that has penetrated into the dermis is healing.

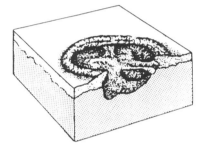

Figure 1.9 *Ulcer*

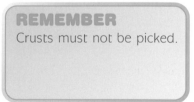

REMEMBER
Crusts must not be picked.

Stain

An abnormal discoloration that remains after the disappearance of moles, freckles or liver spots, also sometimes apparent after certain diseases.

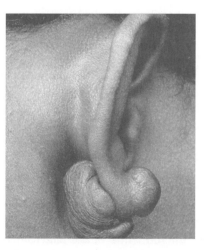

Figure 1.10 *Keloid*

Keloid scar

After a normal scar has formed as a result of an injury that has penetrated down into the dermis, additional tissue is produced from the dermis that results in overhealing, making the scar rise above the normal level of the skin. Black skin is prone to keloid scarring.

Progress Check

1 What are the differences between acute and chronic conditions?
2 What are the different causes of diseases?
3 What is a primary lesion? Name any three.
4 Give the simple names for the following terms:
   Crust
   Excoriation
   Fissure
   Stain.

Bacterial infections

Folliculitis

A bacterial infection of the hair follicle, leading to the production of a pustule and some inflammation in the follicle.

Impetigo

This is a highly contagious inflammatory bacterial infection. This condition is found especially in children. During the active stage fresh lesions appear and spread daily, usually on the face and limbs. The lesions are characterised by the oozing of serum, which coagulates into honey-coloured crusts that have a stuck-on appearance. Insanitary habits are usually to blame.

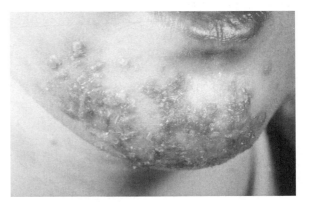

Figure 1.11 *Impetigo*

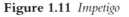

GOOD PRACTICE

Never work on anything contagious.

Boil (furuncle)

A boil is the result of inflammation of the hair follicle due to staphylococcal infection and denotes lowered resistance to infection.

It is a painful swelling with a central core of dead tissue which is eventually discharged. Boils may be a complication of acne in adolescents. The condition is painful even if it remains localised, but if the bacteria enter the bloodstream and cause blood poisoning it can be serious.

Fungal infections
Parasitic diseases of the skin (highly contagious)
Ringworm (tinea)
Ringworm is a contagious infection of the skin caused by a vegetable fungus. Ringworm starts as small reddened patches of vesicles which spread outwards and heal at the centre without scarring. Contact with infected articles, pets or people will spread the condition. The various types of ringworm are as follows.

Tinea pedis
Also known as athlete's foot or ringworm of the foot. The skin between the toes appears sodden and is easily knocked off to reveal deep splits/fissures and raw reddened areas. This is occasionally followed by vesicle formation and swelling of the foot and a characteristic unpleasant odour.

Tinea capitis
Ringworm of the scalp and hair is characterised by red papules at the follicle wall. The hair becomes brittle, tending to break off or fall from the enlarged follicle.

Tinea corporis
Ringworm of the body is characterised as flat, scaly, spreading ring-like lesions. Infection is by direct and indirect contact.

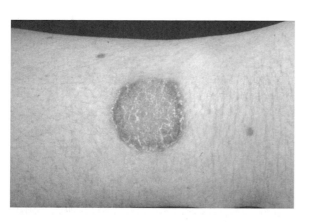

Figure 1.12 *Ringworm*

Tinea barbae
This is ringworm of the bearded area and neck.

Tinea manus
Ringworm of the hands.

Pityriasis versicolor (tinea versicolor)

This is a fungal infection of the epidermis that can be found all over the body, but is mainly seen on the trunk. The condition needs medication and is often caught from such places as sunbeds and sunchairs.

Viral infections (highly contagious)

Herpes simplex (cold sores)

This is a highly contagious recurring viral infection which results in vesicle formation around the mouth and nostrils. The attack begins as an itchy red patch, which is followed by swelling and vesicle formation. If scratched, the vesicles rupture and ooze serum, which rapidly crusts. Only in severe cases will the condition scar the skin. Sufferers who become ill or stressed or are exposed to excessive sun or wind will become prone to an attack of cold sores.

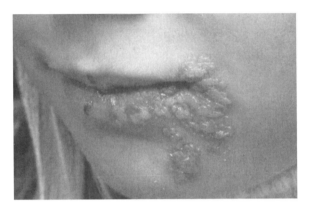

Figure 1.13 *Herpes simplex*

Herpes zoster

The virus causes shingles and is the same virus which causes chickenpox in children. It is thought to lie dormant in the body following a childhood infection with chickenpox. The onset is marked by itching and erythema and inflammation occurs along the pathway of a sensory nerve leading from the spine and is characterised by blisters and great pain. The nerves affected are usually those on the abdomen and chest of one side of the body. Sometimes the nerves on the face can be affected, which can cause serious damage to the eyesight.

Warts (verruca vulgaris)

This contagious viral infection results in the formation of firm papules with a rough surface varying in size. Warts are usually found on the hands but can spread to other areas of the face and body. Warts can develop individually or in clusters and can spontaneously disappear.

Verruca vulgaris (flat or common wart)
In this condition smooth pearly epidermal elevations are found, usually in groups, on the face and hands.

Verruca plantaris
This condition is characterised by warts on the soles of the feet (usually the ball of the foot). They become flattened by the pressure of the body. They may be single or multiple. They usually become painful at some

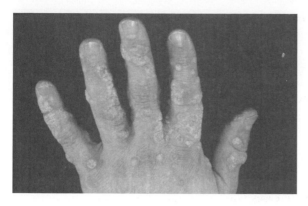

Figure 1.14 *Viral warts*

stage of development and they should be attended to as early as possible in order to avoid spreading the condition.

Insect infections
Pediculosis
A contagious condition caused by the infestation of lice (an insect).

Pediculosis capitis
An infestation of the scalp by lice. The lice lay their eggs, nits, near the base of the hair follicle. The nit which surrounds the hair then passes up and out of the follicle with the growing hair. The lice, once hatched, cause itching and secondary infections. They are transmitted through infected brushes, combs, hats and other personal articles.

Pediculosis corporis
An infestation of the body by lice. Intense itching is caused from the bite of the lice, which may bring about secondary lesions caused by scratching. Lice are transmitted by clothing. Boiling or dry cleaning will eliminate them.

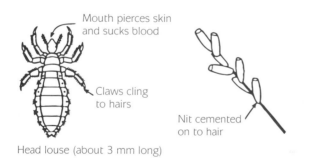

Figure 1.15 *Louse*

Scabies
This is a highly contagious skin disease caused by the infestation of itch mites. Mites burrow under the skin and lay eggs. These hatch and burrow further. It usually occurs on the hands and wrists, but can also affect the forearms, underarms, waist, inner thigh, buttocks and ankles, where papules, pustules, boils and ulcers can develop and produce an itchy sensation.

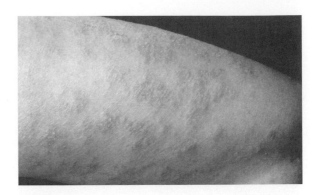

Figure 1.16 *Scabies*

Disorders of the sebaceous gland
Seborrhoea
This is caused by overactivity of the sebaceous gland, producing an excess secretion of sebum and so creating an abnormal oiliness on the surface of the skin. The main areas affected are the face, chest, scalp and back because of their high concentration of sebaceous glands. The cause of the imbalance is usually hormonal, and usually occurs during puberty. The characteristics of the condition are that the skin takes on a shiny appearance with a sallow colour and the pores appear enlarged, giving a coarse look to the skin. Seborrhoea is the basis of several other skin disorders, particularly acne vulgaris.

Sebaceous cyst (steatoma)
A sebaceous cyst or wen is a small retention of sebum under the skin that is usually blocked by an overgrowth of surface skin. The size of the cyst can vary from a pea to an egg, and the areas most affected are those where there are more sebaceous glands, i.e. face, chest, scalp and back, although they sometimes also occur on the underarm. The cysts may have an open or closed top and may need to be removed surgically.

Comedone (blackhead)
Occurring most frequently on the face, forehead and nose, comedones are worm-like masses of hardened sebum that form plugs in the hair follicle, creating a blockage at the mouth of the follicle. The exposed sebum at the mouth of the follicle turns black in time as a result of accumulation of dirt on the surface of the skin and oxidisation of sebum by the air. The follicle of the sebaceous gland may become inflamed, causing acne.

Milia (whiteheads)
These appear mostly on the cheekbones near the eye and are formed when sebum becomes trapped in a blind duct, with no surface opening. Milia appear as pearly white, round lumps under the skin or raised above depending on their size and are usually seen on people with dry complexions. The cause is unknown but may be due to diet or the use of skin products on the face which are too strong. Milia can disappear spontaneously after a period of regular massage or can be removed by piercing the surface of the skin and releasing the fatty material inside.

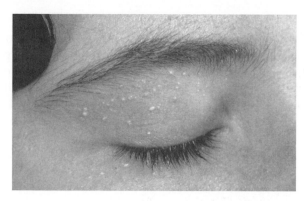

Figure 1.17 *Milia*

Seborrhoeic wart

This is a soft greasy warty lesion, usually pigmented and hyperkeratotic.
They are often found on the face and body of older people and may
occur singly or be very numerous.

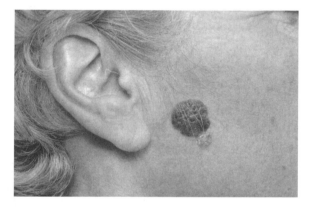

Figure 1.18 *Seborrhoeic wart*

Asteatosis

In this condition the sebaceous system is considered to have broken
down, as no sebum is secreted. The result is extremely dry skin, which is
susceptible to chapping, scaling and splitting.

Pigmentation disorders
Port wine stain (haemangioma)

A port wine stain consists of a large area of dilated capillaries, resulting in
a skin colour ranging from pink to purple, which presents a vivid
contrast to the surrounding skin. The stain is commonly found on the
face and often covers all of one side. As the skin texture is usually
normal, cosmetic camouflage is very successful. Port wine stains are
present at birth and persist throughout life.

Strawberry mark

This is a brightly pigmented area on the skin which is present at birth or
develops soon after. The mark usually disappears by about the fifth year
of life.

Chloasma

This pigmentation condition consists of harmless, light-brown patches of irregular size and shape. It is most frequently associated with pregnancy, involving the upper cheeks, nose and occasionally the forehead. The discoloration usually disappears spontaneously with the termination of the pregnancy, but if it persists, ordinary desquamation helps to remove it.

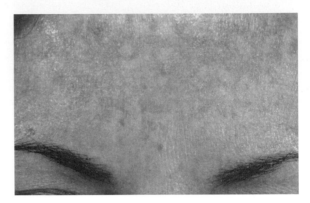

Figure 1.19 *Chloasma*

Leucoderma

This is an abnormal whiteness of the skin due to the absence of pigmentation occurring either in patches or over the entire surface. There are two types as follows.

Albinism

This is a congenital absence of pigment in the skin, hair and iris of the eyes. Albinos are extremely sensitive to light and they lack the ability to tan.

Vitiligo

There is complete loss of colour in the skin in well-defined areas of the body, face and limbs. It begins as small patches, which may converge to form fairly large areas. The skin around the patches sometimes appears hyperpigmented and the condition is most obvious on darker skinned individuals.

The basal cells are no longer able to produce melanin pigment to protect against ultraviolet light. Camouflage make-up can be used to disguise prominent areas on the face, neck and hands.

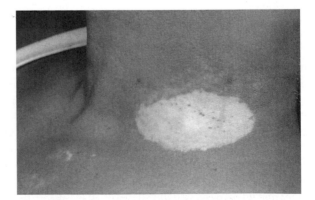

Figure 1.20 *Vitiligo*

Stains

These are abnormal patches of brown discoloration of irregular shape. They often appear after moles or chloasma have subsided, after certain diseases or in old age. They are macules.

Liver spots

These are brown patches commonly seen on the backs of the hands of elderly people. The patches are flat and smooth like large freckles.

Lentigine

These are brown patches like clumps of freckles, commonly seen on the face. Unlike freckles, the colour of lentigines is not affected by sunlight and they do not fade away in winter.

Ephelides

Ephelides or freckles are small brown patches on any area of the skin, more commonly on exposed areas. Freckles can become darker and larger when exposed to sunlight.

Naevi

This is a collective name for vascular and pigmented birthmarks. A coloured malformation of the skin results from a congenital alteration of pigment or dilation of superficial capillaries.

Papillomas (moles)

These are a form of pigmented naevi that are commonly found on the face and body. Moles vary in size and colour from pale tan to brown to bluish black. Deep terminal hairs often develop in them because they have a well-developed vascular supply.

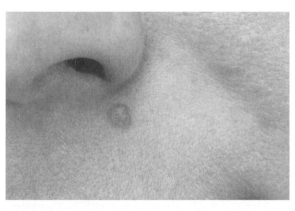

Figure 1.21 *Mole (cellular naevus)*

Spider naevi (telangiectasia angioma)

A spider naevus consists of a central dilated blood vessel with smaller capillaries radiating from it, like the legs of a spider. Spider naevi may be found in isolation of gathered together in clumps on such areas as the cheeks. They usually do not develop until adult life. Certain conditions can make spider naevi worse, for example extreme heat and cold, obesity, pregnancy or stress or pressure on the area.

Figure 1.22 *Spider naevus*

Telangiectasia (broken capillaries)

In this condition broken or dilated blood capillaries are visible on the surface of the skin. They are usually found on more exposed areas, such as the nose and cheeks. The skin appears to have small blood lines on it. These are usually red but become darker in colour as they worsen. Like spider naevi, broken capillaries are worsened by extremes of temperature, obesity, pregnancy and stress or pressure on the area.

Erythema

This is a superficial redness of the skin. It is a common occurrence after stimulation to the skin, as blood vessels become dilated. After all temporary hair removal and electro-epilation erythema will be present for a short time.

Disorders of the sweat glands

Prickly heat (milaria rubra)

This is an acute inflammatory condition causing itching of the skin and the production of small red vesicles, with inflammation of the sweat glands. This complaint may be caused by exposure to excessive heat or by closure of the sweat ducts by keratin plugs, particularly seen in the folds of the skin.

Bromhidrosis or osmidrosis

This is the condition of producing foul-smelling perspiration that is especially noticeable in the armpits or the feet and is caused by certain foods or drugs or occasionally by a rare disorder. The condition may be congenital, in which case the perspiration is the natural product of the apocrine sweat glands.

Anhidrosis

This is lack of perspiration, frequently caused by fever or underlying disease.

Hyperhidrosis

This is a condition causing excessive perspiration due to disease or a general disorder characterised by mental depression and exhaustion.

Skin cancers

Skin cancers vary in appearance, and it is important that we recognise these abnormalities. We suggest you use your college resource centre or the local library to look at photographs of the various skin cancers.

Malignant melanoma

This is the most serious type of skin cancer, which often spreads to internal organs with fatal results. A melanoma develops from moles or normal skin. It is usually blue/black, slate or black and arises from the cells which normally produce melanin. Melanomas lack hair and have a smooth shiny surface. Because moles which have been normal for years may suddenly become malignant, any mole of any colour with the following symptoms should receive immediate medical attention:

1   Increase in size.
2   Increase in depth of pigmentation or its extension into the surrounding skin.
3   Crust formation.

4   Bleeding.
5   Inflammatory ring of colour around the mole.
6   Any other symptom not seen or felt before.

Early diagnosis and treatment is essential.

Childhood exposure to sun is an important factor. The risk of malignant melanoma is increased in individuals who have been exposed to intense sun frequently but intermittently. This suggests that the increasing incidence of the condition may be especially related to increases in intermittent exposure. Studies have also shown that individuals who tend to burn easily, have difficulty in tanning, have light-coloured hair, skin and eyes, and who have increased numbers of benign pigmented naevi, have a greater risk of melanoma than darker skinned Caucasians.

Squamous cell carcinoma
This arises from the squamous epithelium of the skin, in light-exposed areas. It is more dangerous than basal cell cancer. It usually appears as an enlarged, red, scaly, rough dot about half an inch or larger in diameter and raised above the skin's surface. An irregular rough edge and a scab partly covering a portion of the growth are two observed characteristics. Most squamous cell cancers are caused by sun exposure and they therefore occur most often on the face, backs of hands or other sun-exposed areas. The treatment is surgical removal.

Basal cell carcinoma (rodent ulcer)
This is a type of cancerous tumour that appears on the face, generally fringing the lips, nostrils or eyelids, Rodent ulcers develop in the later stages of the condition. They spread slowly and if untreated can lead to mutilating destruction of the skin, muscle and bone. However, this type of cancer does not spread to other parts of the body via the bloodstream.

REMEMBER
It is not your job to diagnose skin diseases.

Non-contagious skin disorders
Rosacea
This is a common chronic disease of unknown cause characterised by diffuse facial erythema with inflamed papules and pustules (although scarring is not present). The skin appears tense and shiny and on close inspection often reveals telangiectasia.

Seborrhoea is not present in this condition and the skin looks shiny simply because of lymphoedema, which can be very marked, causing considerable swelling of the forehead and periorbital areas.

Rosacea is usually confined to the face, although it may spread onto bald scalps and rarely even onto the upper arms. It is usually middle-aged and elderly people who are affected. The condition is often exacerbated by exposure to sunshine or heat. Those affected sometimes complain of facial flushing, which may be brought on by emotion, alcohol or hot foods.

REMEMBER
Skin affected by rosacea will be sensitive to heat treatments.

Acne

This is an inflammatory skin disease of the pilosebaceous unit, affecting areas of the skin in which the sebaceous glands are very large and have tiny soft (vellus) hairs in their follicles.

Acne begins at puberty when the level of androgens in the body increases and causes changes in the pilosebaceous units. The sebaceous glands produce increased amounts of sebum as a result of testosterone stimulation, and acne forms deep in the follicle. Cell turnover and keratin formation in the lining of the follicle are altered, leading to the production of a thick, dense plug of sebum, keratin and cells deep within the follicle. Gradually this keratinous plug fills the lower part of the follicle, causing it to swell and forming a whitehead or closed comedone. As the process continues, sheets of cells form in the plug, like the layers of an onion, forcing the mouth of the follicle open. The surface layer of the plug becomes stained black by melanin, forming the open comedone or blackhead.

At puberty, bacteria begin to colonise the skin and the openings of follicles. These bacteria are more numerous in people with acne and are able to enter the follicles during comedone formation, causing the inflammation of acne.

Primary irritants of the initial inflammatory response are free fatty acids. These are formed from sebum under the influence of dihydrotestosterone, the level of which is increased about 20-fold in people with acne. The production of dihydrotestosterone is increased by the enzyme 5-α-reductase. Since production of the enzymes in the body is controlled by our genes, some people have a hereditary predisposition to acne.

Acne vulgaris

In this condition the skin appears greasy, with a dull sallow colour, and blackheads, papules, pustules and scars may be present. This condition is mostly found in adolescents, and may involve the entire face, chest and shoulder girdle, or just one of these areas. Seborrhoea is present and causes comedones of varying severity. Secondary infection of the comedone is sometimes present because of infection with the bacteria *Staphylococcus*, with inflammation and pustules forming around the blackhead. The infection may spread to involve other sebaceous glands, and a deep-seated pustular condition becomes established.

GOOD PRACTICE

- Handle active acne skin as little as possible to avoid spreading infection.
- The use of antiseptic before treatment on the skin is essential.

Eczema

It is difficult for the electrologist to differentiate between eczema, dermatitis and psoriasis. Advise clients to seek help for these conditions from their GP and do not carry out electro-epilation until the area is clear and skin healing is complete.

Eczema is a non-infectious inflammatory skin disorder which starts as redness and blisters. The skin is very itchy, and scratching results in the oozing of serum followed by the formation of crusts along with further itching and burning progressing to dry scaly patches with continued vesicle formation and weeping. Eczema is commonly found on the thin skin inside joints.

The different types of eczema are described below.

Atopic eczema
This familial condition is seen in infancy and childhood and is also linked with asthma, hay fever and migraine. Patches of eczema break out on the face, forearms and backs of legs. In most cases the child grows out of the condition at about puberty, but it will persist in some.

Allergic eczema
This is usually caused by a food allergy and can be controlled.

Occupational eczema
This may be caused by skin irritants, typically mineral oil, detergents, degreasing agents, soap and some cosmetics.

Dermatitis
This is a non-infectious inflammatory skin disorder that may result from infection or an allergy. The condition may be acute, with swelling, redness and the formation of vesicles, or chronic, persisting for a long time and resulting in a thickened skin with a leathery appearance.

The different types of dermatitis are described below.

Contact dermatitis
This arises from touching substances to which the person is sensitive.

Exfoliative dermatitis
In this condition there is widespread scaling and itching of the skin, sometimes occurring as a reaction to certain drugs.

Occupational or industrial dermatitis
This is caused by exposure to certain chemicals or other substances in the workplace.

Sensation dermatitis
This is caused by an allergic reaction to sunlight.

Traumatic dermatitis
In traumatic dermatitis there is inflammation due to injury.

Varicose dermatisis
This usually occurs on the lower legs as a result of the smaller veins becoming varicosed.

Psoriasis
Psoriasis is a non-contagious condition that can affect the whole face and body to varying degrees. The cause of the condition is unknown but is thought to be linked to emotion and hereditary factors. In affected individuals the severity of the condition varies throughout life.

The lesions of psoriasis start as full red papules the size of pinheads and develop into bright red patches with flaky silvery white scales overlying the surface. The lesions are typically found on areas of thicker skin, such as the knees and elbows.

Skin tags

This is a common fibrous skin condition most frequently found on the neck and face. The tags may be single or multiple and are composed of loose fibrous tissue. Their colour is usually that of normal skin, but they can be hyperpigmented, making them more obvious.

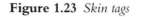

Figure 1.23 *Skin tags*

Corns

Corns are areas of thickened dense skin on pressure areas such as the toes.

Ageing skin

Many factors contribute to the ageing process of the skin. The principal one is damage from ultraviolet rays. This is now generally recognised as the main cause of premature ageing to the skin as well as the cause of skin cancers.

The effects of ageing include:

- dry skin, sebum secretion reduced
- thinning skin
- loose skin and wrinkles
- irregular pigmentation.

Allergic reaction

An allergy is sensitivity to normally harmless substances. The allergen or antigen stimulates the body causing the mast cells to release histamine. The typical changes due to the allergy include:

- rash or red blotches
- stinging or itching
- hot and inflamed sensation.

Progress Check

1. What are the main symptoms of impetigo?
2. What are the different types of fungal infection?
3. How would you recognise a wart?
4. What is the correct name for body lice?
5. Compare milia and comedones.
6. Compare port wine stains with strawberry marks.

Skin diseases and disorders which should be referred to a GP

Disease/ disorder	Cause	Appearance	Treatment
Impetigo	Staphylococcal infection	Oozing lesions forming honey-coloured crusts	Highly infectious. Refer to GP for antibiotic treatment
Ringworm	Fungal infection	Red patches which spread outwards and heal from the centre	Infectious. Refer to GP
Herpes simplex (cold sore)	Viral infection permanently dormant in the skin of infected people erupting when the sufferer is ill, under stress or exposed to ultraviolet light	Itchy red patch oozing and forming crusts	Highly infectious. Proprietary topical cream available or refer to GP
Viral wart	Viral infection	Papules of varying size. May be single or in clusters, rough or smooth	Highly infectious. Refer to GP, who may remove the wart or leave it in the hope that the body will develop an immunity
Scabies	Mite burrows into skin, where it lays eggs	Itchy excoriated papules which spread over the body and limbs	Highly contagious. Refer to GP
Sebaceous cyst	Small retention of sebum blocked by overgrowth of surface skin	Small hard nodule	Harmless but can be removed by GP
Seborrhoeic wart	Overpigmented hyper-keratotic growth appearing in middle to old age	Warty lesions found on face and body, singly or numerous	Very common, benign tumours. Can be removed by GP or advanced electrologist with written GP approval
Naevus (mole)	Malformation of the skin resulting from alteration of pigment or dilation of superficial capillaries	Vary from unpigmented to brown to deepest black, also varying in size. Often develop deep terminal hairs	Usually harmless. Can be removed surgically or by short-wave diathermy or laser. GP's permission required for hair removal
Malignant melanoma	Change in development of moles or normal skin	Possible rapid change in size, colour, bleeding, ulceration, inflamed surrounding skin	Seek advice from GP urgently. Usually excised for histological examination
Squamous cell carcinoma	Overexposure to UV light, most frequent in the elderly	Enlarged, irregular, red, raised ulcerated lesion	Refer to GP for surgical removal
Basal cell carcinoma	Most common form of skin cancer due to over-exposure to ultraviolet light	Translucent, nodular, raised edge, to shiny lesion, possibly ulcerated	Refer to GP for removal
Eczema	Allergy	Non-infectious inflamed skin. Patches are itchy, dry or oozing	Refer to GP or complementary therapist

Table 1.3 *Skin diseases and disorders which should be referred to a GP*

Dermatitis	Allergy	Non-infectious inflamed skin. There may be swollen, red or thickened skin	Refer to GP or complementary therapist
Psoriasis	Non-contagious condition linked to emotional or hereditary factors	Tiny red patches developing to bright-red larger patches with white scales	Refer to GP or complementary therapist

It is often quite difficult to differentiate between eczema, dermatitis and psoriasis

Table 1.3 *continued*

Progress Check

1 What are the different types of vitiligo?
2 What causes an erythema?
3 Name all the different types of skin cancer and describe each.
4 What are the main characteristics of rosacea and what makes it worse?
5 What causes acne?
6 What are the different types of eczema and what causes each?
7 What are the different types of dermatitis and what causes each?
8 What does psoriasis look like?
9 Where are skin tags usually found?
10 What does the term skin disease mean?

ACTIVITIES

1 Do you know anyone with any of these skin conditions? If so, talk to them about their symptoms, treatment, etc. It is important that your learn to recognise skin conditions/diseases.
2 Go to your college resource centre or local library to look at books showing photographs of skin diseases/disorders.

Key Terms

You will need to know what these words and phrases mean. Go back through the chapter or check the glossary to find out.

- Allergy
- Capillary meshes
- Collagen
- Congenital
- Contagious
- Corium
- Dermis
- Elastin
- Epidermis
- Excretion
- Infectious
- Keratin
- Lesion
- Malignant
- Melanin
- Mitosis
- Parasite
- Pathogenic
- Sensation
- Subcutaneous layer
- Tumour

1   Link the layers of the epidermis with the best description of their function.

Stratum germinativum   Consists of translucent cells which light can pass through.

Stratum corneum   These cells have bridges running between them called desmosomes.

Stratum spinosum   Keratin is produced in this layer.

Stratum lucidum   Contains scale-like cells which are continually being shed.

Stratum granulosum   This is the layer responsible for the growth of the epidermis.

2   Tick all the following statements that are correct about the papillary layer of the dermis.

a)   This is the deeper of the two layers of the dermis.
b)   Papillae are cone-shaped projections pointing up from the dermis into the epidermis.
c)   This is a thin layer containing branching collagen fibre bundles.
d)   This layer contains some of the skin's pigment, melanin.
e)   The papillary layer contains more collagen and elastin than the reticular layer.

3   The correct body temperature is?

a)   34°C.
b)   38°C.
c)   37°C.
d)   32°C.

4   Indicate whether the following statement is true or false.

Sweat glands are endocrine glands.

True   False
☐   ☐

5   Fill in the blanks from the list of words beneath. You will not be able to use all the words.

The main function of sweat is to control _____ by _____.

blood temperature
body temperature
skin temperature
the evaporation of sweat
the production of sweat

6 Tick the places where sebaceous glands are most abundant.

Palms of the hands ☐

Scalp ☐

Forehead ☐

Cheeks ☐

Nose ☐

Chin ☐

Abdomen ☐

Chest ☐

7 Indicate whether the following statement is true or false.

Sebaceous glands are larger in men than in women.

True   False

☐   ☐

8 Link the following terms with the correct description.

Terminal hair   Is found on the body in fetal life.
Lanugo hair   Develops in postnatal life.
Vellus hair   Is found in regions such as the scalp and eyebrows.

9 Tick which of the following are appendages of the skin.

Nails ☐

Keratin ☐

Melanin ☐

Collagen ☐

Blood vessels ☐

Sweat glands ☐

Sebaceous glands ☐

10 Which of these cells produce the allergic reaction in the skin?

a) Fibroblasts.
b) Mast cells.
c) Histiocytes.
d) Eosinophils.

11 Which is the enzyme that speeds up the production of melanin?

a) Melanase.
b) Tyrosine.
c) Tyrosinase.

12 Indicate whether the following statement is true or false.

Black skin contains more melanocytes than white skin.

True   False

☐   ☐

HAIR

After studying this chapter you will be able to:
- list the different types of hair
- describe the structure of the hair and follicle
- understand the functions of the hair and follicle parts
- name and understand the stages of the hair growth cycle.

Hair types

Hairs are dead structures made up of the strong protein, keratin, found situated in tube-like indentations called hair follicles. There are three different types of hairs:

- lanugo hairs
- vellus hairs
- terminal hairs.

Lanugo hairs

These hairs are only found on the unborn child. They are shed soon after or before birth. Lanugo hairs are very soft and lack pigmentation. They grow from the sebaceous gland and do not become terminal hairs unless stimulated by topical or systemic conditions. If the hair is stimulated, it may grow down, first becoming an accelerated lanugo hair, i.e. longer than its neighbours but with no bulb, then a shallow terminal hair. This change may take from a few months to a few years.

Lanugo hairs are shed and replaced more slowly than terminal hairs.

Vellus hairs

These are soft fine hairs, sometimes called down, covering most areas of the body except:

- palms of hands
- soles of feet
- lips
- genital areas.

> **REMEMBER**
> Vellus hair growth is normal.

Vellus hairs replace lanugo hairs and are classed as primary hairs.

Terminal hairs

These replace lanugo or vellus hairs and are deep-rooted, well-developed, coarse, pigmented hairs found:

- on the scalp
- under the arms
- in the pubic region
- on some other parts.

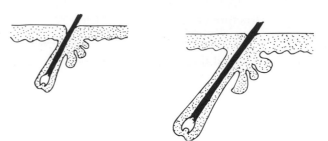

Lanugo

Accelerated lanugo

Shallow terminal

Deep terminal

Figure 2.1 *Stages of transition from lanugo to terminal*

A terminal hair has three layers:

- inner medulla
- cortex
- outer cuticle.

Structure of hairs

The medulla
This is the central part of the hair. It is composed of large loosely connected cells containing keratin. The medulla is sometimes not continuous within the same hair, which creates air spaces that determine the sheen and colour tones of the hair.

The cortex
This is the layer of the hair outside the medulla. It is composed of elongated cells containing keratin that are cemented together. Melanin, the colour pigment, is found in this layer. If melanin is absent then the hair appears white or grey.

The cuticle
This is a single layer of overlapping or imbricated cells with the free margins directed upwards towards the tip of the hair. These cells interlock with the cells of the cuticle of the inner root sheath. The function of the cuticle is to anchor the hair in the follicle, and it also provides elasticity to the hair. The outside of the cuticle is surrounded by an insoluble lipid and carbohydrate layer which is thought to protect the hair from chemical and physical agents.

Hair follicle
The hair follicle is a pore in the skin that opens at the epidermis and extends downwards into the dermis and in some cases into the

subcutaneous tissue. Each hair follicle usually contains one hair, and the depth of the hair follicle is determined by the stage of the hair growth cycle of the hair it contains.

Anagen hairs, which are in the first stage of the growing phase of the hair growth cycle, have the deepest follicle. As the hair progresses through the catagen and telogen phases the hair follicle progressively moves towards the surface.

It is only the lower transient part of the hair follicle that can change in length, by the lower parts of the follicle disintegrating as the hair moves up and out. The upper part of the follicle is classed as permanent as it never disintegrates and disappears. This part of the hair follicle will be present even if the hair has fallen out.

The hair follicle can be considered as continuous with the surface of the skin, as the epidermis forms the outer root sheath of the follicle or the inner wall of the follicle.

The lower part of the follicle is called the bulb because it is wider than the upper part. Within the bulb region is the hair matrix, where the new hair cells and the new inner root sheath cells are made.

An indentation at the bottom of the bulb contains the blood supply (dermal papilla) to the follicle. The blood provides the hair with the nourishment it needs to grow.

The sebaceous gland opens into the top third of the hair follicle. This gland produces the oily substance sebum, which empties into the pilosebaceous unit to lubricate the hair and the skin's surface.

The arrector pili muscle joins the bottom of the hair follicle to the bottom of the epidermis. This muscle, when it contracts, does just as its name says: it causes the hair to become erect. This is controlled by the subconscious and occurs when it is cold, to keep in heat, or when we are frightened.

Figure 2.2 *Outer root sheath continuous with the surface of the skin*

Figure 2.3

Figure 2.4

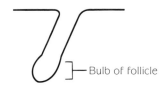

Figure 2.5

Figure 2.6

Figure 2.7

The apocrine sweat gland can be found opening up into the hair follicle in the underarm and groin region. Apocrine sweat glands become active at puberty.

Note that the hair follicle is set at an angle to the surface of the skin. Hairs on different parts of the body are set at slightly different angles.

Figure 2.8 *Complete hair follicle. Note that the hair follicle lies at an angle to the skin and so therefore does the hair shaft*

Structure of the hair follicle

The hair follicle surrounds the hair and comprises the following layers:

1 the inner root sheath:
   cuticle of inner root sheath
   Huxley's layer
   Henle's layer
2 the outer root sheath
3 the vitreous membrane
4 connective tissue.

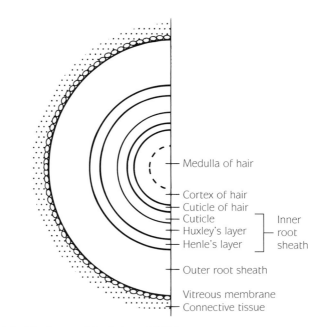

Figure 2.9 *The layers of the hair and follicle*

Cuticle of the inner root sheath

The cells of this layer point downwards, so interlocking with the cuticle of the hair.

Inner root sheath

Huxley's layer is the second layer of the inner root sheath and is the thickest of all the three layers.

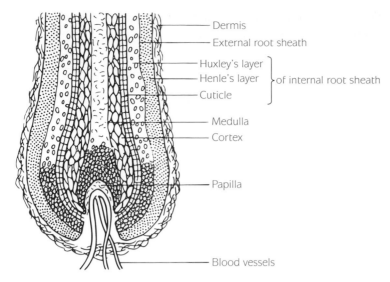

Figure 2.10 *The hair structure*

Henley's layer is the third layer of the inner root sheath.

This inner root sheath only grows up as far as the sebaceous gland. The inner root sheath is not continuous with the rest of the skin; instead it becomes attached to the hair.

Outer root sheath
This layer surrounds the inner root sheath, and is continuous with the germinative layer of the epidermis, making the follicle an indentation of the epidermis. The thickness of the outer root sheath varies, which makes the hair off-centre within the follicle. This layer contains large amounts of water-soluble starch (glycogen) and appears to be spongiest around the centre of the follicle.

The outer root sheath is the permanent source of the 'hair germ cells', which are responsible for the production of new hair. New hair cells are produced by mitosis, the process of cell division, at the base of the follicle by the dermal papilla.

Vitreous membrane (outer root sheath)
This layer separates the outer root sheath from the connective tissue. The membrane consists of two layers.

- Outer layer: surrounds the entire follicle and is continuous with the basement membrane of the epidermis.
- Inner layer: found in the lower half of the follicle.

Connective tissue
The connective tissue sheath is a continuation of the papillary layer of the dermis and includes the dermal papilla (blood supply). The layer surrounds the follicle and sebaceous gland, and supplies blood and nerves to the hair. There are two layers of connective tissue, both consisting of collagen and elastin fibres.

Dermal papilla
This is the area of the follicle that contains the nerve endings and the blood supply that provides nourishment for the entire follicle structure.

> **REMEMBER**
> It is the blood that feeds the hair and makes it grow. During epilation we attempt to cauterise the blood supply.

The blood supply also carries hormones from the endocrine glands, which can affect the growth of the hair.

⏱ **Progress Check**

1   What are the main differences between the three types of hair?
2   What part of the hair contains melanin?
3   What is the function of the cuticle of the hair?
4   How do the cuticle of the hair and the cuticle of the inner root sheath fit together?
5   What are the three parts of the inner root sheath?

The different shapes of hairs and follicles

> **REMEMBER**
> Temporary methods of hair removal may distort the follicles.

Club hairs
These hairs have a clubbed end and are usually in the catagen stage of hair growth. Their shape is due to the bulb having disintegrated.

Corkscrew hair/follicles
The pilosebaceous section of the hair follicle has been damaged and the whole follicle is distorted.

Embedded hairs
This hair does not come through the skin as it should. This may be the result of constantly wearing tight-fitting clothes or the surface of the skin may grow over the follicle and block off the hair.

The condition is manifested by a small bump on the skin. Scratching at the skin causes the hair to be released.

Figure 2.11 *Corkscrew (a truly distorted follicle)*

> **REMEMBER**
> Embedded hairs do not look like infected ingrowing hairs.

Ingrowing hairs
Ingrowing hairs are hairs that continue to grow just beneath the surface of the skin and often become infected. An ingrowing hair should be freed from the skin so that it can rise above the surface. If the hair is not infected it can be treated with electro-epilation. If it is infected then the hair should be cut just to the surface of the skin until the infection has cleared.

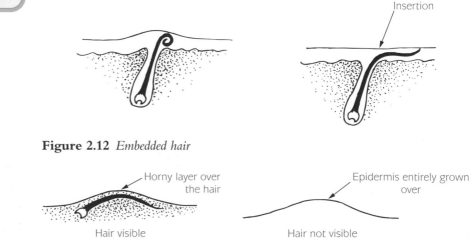

Insertion

Figure 2.12 *Embedded hair*

Horny layer over the hair

Epidermis entirely grown over

Hair visible

Hair not visible

Figure 2.13 *Entrapped/ingrown hairs*

Lanugo comedones (bundlehairs)

A lanugo comedone is a bundle of very fine lanugo hairs in sebum. This structure can be lifted from the skin with tweezers without causing damage.

Lanugo comedones are more common on oily skins and are usually considered a skin problem rather than a hair problem.

Figure 2.14 *Lanugo comedones*

Pili multigemini

In this condition two or more hairs emerge from the same hair follicle. This is caused by a follicle having more than one papilla. Each of the hairs is complete with its own individual inner and outer root sheath.

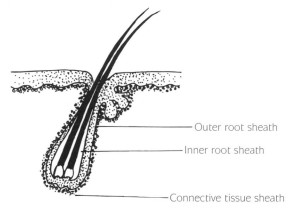

Outer root sheath

Inner root sheath

Connective tissue sheath

Figure 2.15 *Pili multigemini*

Regrowth hairs

These are hairs that grow through the skin after treatment by electro-epilation, showing that the follicle has been only partially destroyed.

Regrowth hairs can be much finer in texture, paler in colour, shallower in the skin and slower to regrow than untreated hairs.

Tombstones

Sometimes when a telogen hair is removed by electro-epilation it is found that the follicle also contains a new anagen hair that has not grown out of the skin. As a result of the movement of the skin cells, the anagen hair progresses towards the surface. These so-called tombstone hairs are thicker and darker than normal hairs and easily lift out of the skin without pulling or electro-epilation.

Trapped hair protruding

Trapped anagen hair

Figure 2.16 *Tombstones*

Virgin hairs

These are superfluous hairs that have never been worked on.

The stages of the hair growth cycle

The hair growth cycle, as it names suggests, is a cycle of events that is repeated as long as nourishment is available. The cycle consists of three stages:

- anagen, the growing phase (A = active)
- catagen, the changing phase (C = change)
- telogen, the resting phase (T = tired).

After telogen the process of hair growth returns to anagen again.

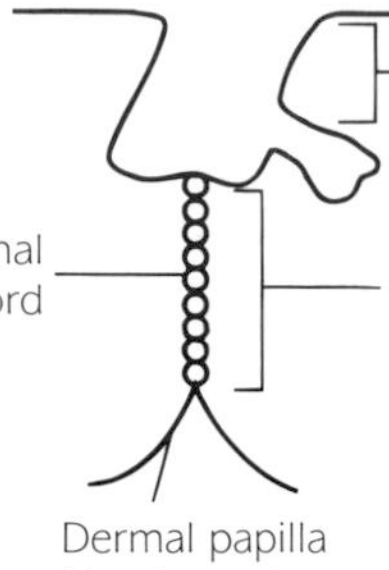

Anagen

1   After telogen, the previous phase, only the permanent part of the hair follicle remains, attached to the dermal papilla by a chain of cells known as the dermal cord. To form a new anagen hair, a hair germ cell passes from the base of the permanent follicle down the dermal cord to the dermal papilla.

2   When the hair germ cell reaches the dermal papilla it begins to reproduce by the process of mitosis, a form of cell division. The cells receive their nourishment from the dermal papilla.

3   The area where the cells reproduce is known as the matrix and is found within the bulb of the hair follicle.

4   As more cells are produced they are pushed upwards and they differentiate to form the different parts of the hair and follicle, e.g. medulla, cortex, cuticle of the hair, the three layers of inner root sheath.

5   As the cells move up further they reach the area known as the zone of keratinisation. This is where the hard protein keratin is laid down to strengthen the hair.

6   As more cells are produced the new hair forms a cone and pushes its way through the dermis, re-establishing the transient part of the hair follicle.

7   When the hair reaches the level of sebaceous gland it pushes up through the dermis into the permanent part of the follicle and then up and out the top of the skin. Once it emerges through the skin and becomes visible it is known as the hair shaft.

8   In general, hairs remain in the anagen stage for about 2–3 weeks. However, terminal hairs on the head can be in anagen for about 2 years.

Catagen

This is the second stage of the hair growth cycle. It occurs when the hair is already fully grown and mitotic activity in the matrix has stopped. The hair now passes up the hair follicle, so moving away from the dermal papilla, its previous source of nourishment. At this stage the hair has to receive its nourishment from the surrounding cells of the hair follicle.

As the hair moves up the follicle, the part of the follicle that was left behind below the hair degenerates and disappears. As this part of the follicle is capable of disappearing and being reformed it is called transient or temporary. The transient part of the follicle never disappears totally; instead it forms the dermal cord, which is a chain-like structure that allows the maintenance of contact with the dermal papilla (see Figure 2.17).

Figure 2.17 *Dermal cord*

Labels: Permanent part of the follicle; Dermal cord; Transient part of follicle; Dermal papilla blood supply

REMEMBER

When treating a hair in advanced anagen electro-epilation will be most successful as the current is nearer the blood supply.

Telogen

This is the third and final stage of the hair growth cycle, also known as the rest phase. The length of time the hair spends in this stage varies between individuals and also according to the type of hair.

The hair is no longer receiving any nourishment and the inner root sheath dries out and shrivels up. The hair continues to move up the follicle until finally it drops out.

It is sometimes possible for a new anagen hair to have started forming at the very base of the follicle around the dermal papilla before the old telogen hair has fallen out. In this case the new developing hair often pushes the old hair out of the follicle.

REMEMBER
Electro-epilation will be less effective on a hair in the catagen or telogen stages of the hair growth cycle.

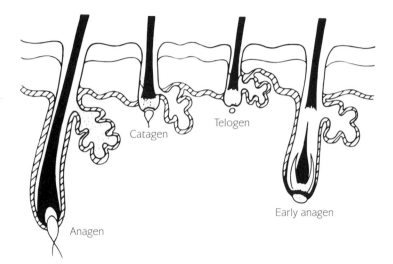

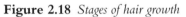

Figure 2.18 *Stages of hair growth*

Progress Check

1   What causes new hairs to be formed?
2   What is the dermal papilla?
3   Briefly explain what happens in anagen.
4   What changes occur to the hair in the catagen stage?
5   Why does a telogen hair not require any blood?

Relating the hair growth cycle to epilation

Anagen

This is the first stage of the cycle, the growth phase. This hair is fully attached to its blood supply and it has a large bulbous root. If a hair is removed at this stage of the cycle then it will take longer to regrow because the root of the hair has to be totally reformed again. The average time taken for this hair to grow back is around 6 weeks.

Catagen

This is the second stage of the cycle, the change phase. In the first part of this stage the hair is fully attached to the blood supply, but towards the end the hair breaks away and separates; at this point the hair is no longer receiving nourishment from the blood. A hair removed at this stage of the growth cycle will regrow sooner than an anagen hair. The average time taken for this hair to grow back is around 4–6 weeks.

Telogen

This is the third and final stage of the cycle, the rest phase. Not only is the hair not connected to the blood supply, it will also have moved quite a long way up the hair follicle and be ready to fall out. Sometimes another hair will have started to form at the base of the follicle even before the first hair has fallen out. So if a hair is removed at this stage it may not take long before another hair grows through.

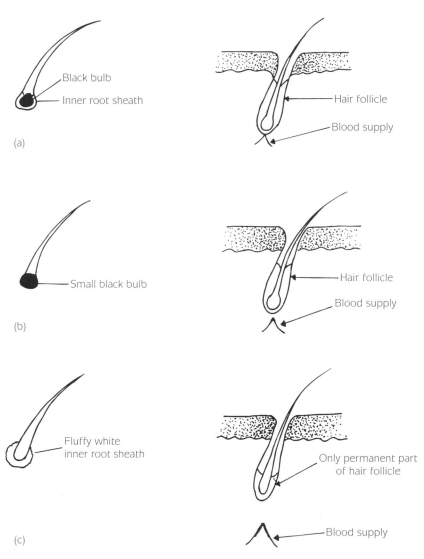

Figure 2.19 *Simplified diagram to show the difference in the inner root sheath in the three stages of hair growth: (a) anagen (b) catagen (c) telogen*

Complete the chart below to compare the different types of hair:

	Name of hair	Location of hair	Description of hair
1			
2			
3			

Progress Check

1 Which part of the hair contains the colour?
2 What is it that makes hairs shine?
3 Why do hairs contain keratin?
4 What is the function of the cuticle?
5 What is a hair follicle?
6 Where are hair follicles found?
7 What is the transient part of the hair follicle and where is it?
8 If a hair is pulled out, does the follicle come out with it?
9 Where does the hair grow from?
10 What starts the hair growth?
11 What does the hair need to grow?
12 What is the growth stage of a hair's life cycle called?

Key Terms

You will need to know what these words and phrases mean. Go back through the chapter or check the glossary to find out.

- Anagen
- Catagen
- Cortex
- Cuticle
- Inner root sheath
- Lanugo hair
- Medulla
- Outer root sheath
- Telogen
- Terminal hair
- Vellus hair
- Vitreous membrane

3

After studying this chapter you will be able to:

- name all the endocrine glands and the hormones they produce
- understand the effects of hormones
- describe the effects of hormone imbalances
- recognise all the terms relating to the endocrine system
- understand the links between the whole system.

The endocrine system

The endocrine system is a series of endocrine glands throughout the body. Endocrine glands are glands that secrete hormones.

The function of the endocrine system is to control the slower processes and reactions in the body as growth and development, digestion, excretion and sexual activity. (The quicker reactions are controlled by the nervous system.)

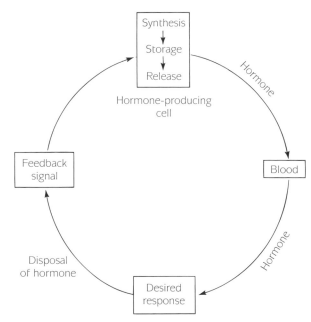

Figure 3.1 *Physiology of the endocrine system*

Endocrine glands

An endocrine gland has no duct leading from it linking it to another part of the body, so it is often called a ductless gland. These glands produce hormones and release these hormones directly into the bloodstream to be carried around the body.

The pituitary gland controls the secretions of many of the other endocrine glands and is often called the master gland.

Hormones

A hormone is a chemical messenger made by an endocrine gland. Hormones are proteins. They are secreted into the blood and carried in the blood to their target organ, i.e. the organ on which they have their effect.

Hormones help regulate internal growth and development and contribute to the reproductive processes.

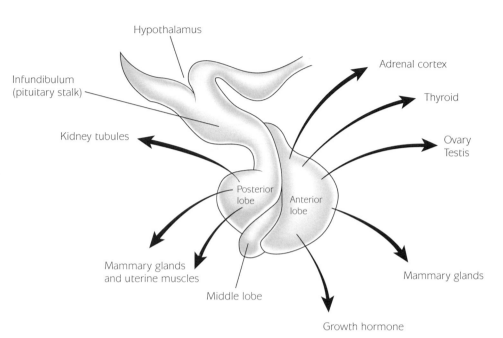

Figure 3.2 *Target tissues of hormones released by the pituitary gland*

We know when to produce hormones because the hypothalamus, part of the brain, can detect when the level of any particular hormone in the body is lower than it should be. The hypothalamus, by secreting another hormone, stimulates the pituitary gland to cause the production of the necessary hormone.

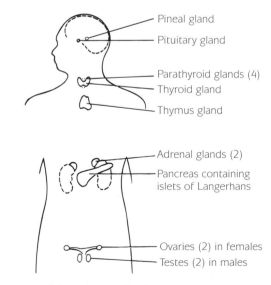

Figure 3.3 *Location of the endocrine glands*

When the hormone reaches its correct level in the bloodstream, it causes the hypothalamus to stop secreting the stimulating hormone. This process is called negative feedback. The hypothalamus then releases an inhibitory hormone that acts on the pituitary, which causes production of the hormone to be stopped.

Each hormone is recognised only by its target organ, which means that the action of hormones is specific, i.e. they cause only one particular effect.

The pituitary gland (master gland)

The pituitary is situated at the base of the brain.

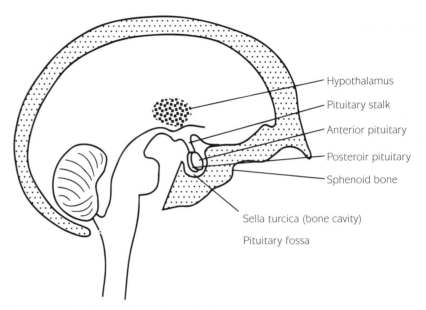

Figure 3.4 *Location of the pituitary gland*

Structure of the pituitary (hypophysis)

This gland is divided into three lobes:

1   the anterior lobe, at the front (adenohypophysis)
2   the middle lobe
3   the posterior lobe, at the back (neurohypophysis).

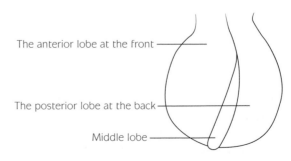

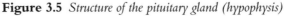

Figure 3.5 *Structure of the pituitary gland (hypophysis)*

Anterior lobe (adenohypophysis)
This part of the gland is stimulated to produce or stop producing hormones by releasing or inhibitory factors secreted by the hypothalamus.

Middle lobe
This part of the pituitary produces melanin-stimulating hormone. This hormone denotes the colour the skin is able to tan to.

Posterior lobe (neurohypophysis)
This part of the gland is stimulated by nervous control from the hypothalamus. An impulse will be transmitted via a nerve from the hypothalamus to the posterior lobe.

Hormones produced by the anterior pituitary gland

Somatotrophin (growth hormone)
This hormone promotes growth and repair of tissues by stimulating protein synthesis. Exercise, anxiety, sleep and hypoglycaemia (low blood sugar level) all affect the amount of growth hormone produced.

Thyrotrophin (thyroid-stimulating hormone)
This hormone stimulates growth and activity of the thyroid gland, which secretes the hormones thyroxine and triiodothyronine.

> **REMEMBER**
> We need iodine in the diet to be able to make the thyroid hormones.

Adrenocorticotrophin (ACTH)
This hormone stimulates the adrenal cortex to produce:

- glucocorticoids
- mineralocorticoids
- sex hormones.

Secretion of these hormones is affected by the brain, the level of sugar and cortisol in the blood, exercise and stress.

Gonadotrophins (follicle-stimulating hormone, luteinising hormone)
Female
In women follicle-stimulating hormone (FSH) stimulates the development and ripening of ovarian follicles. During their development ovarian follicles produce oestrogen. Oestrogen causes the endometrium (the lining of the uterus or womb) to become thicker in preparation for the implantation of a fertilised ovum. When the oestrogen level in the blood reaches a certain point, FSH secretion is inhibited.

Luteinising hormone (LH) promotes final maturation of the ovarian follicle and stimulates ovulation (discharge of mature ovum). The main function of LH is to promote the formation of the corpus luteum, the progesterone-secreting body. As the level of progesterone in the blood increases the production of LH is inhibited.

Male
In men FSH stimulates the epithelial tissues of the seminiferous tubules in the testes to produce spermatozoa.

LH stimulates the interstitial cells of the testes to secrete testosterone.

REMEMBER
The function of the mammary glands is to produce milk after childbirth.

Lactinogenic hormone (prolactin)

This hormone stimulates production of milk by the mammary glands and maintains the existence of the corpus luteum in pregnancy.

Hormones produced by the posterior lobe of the pituitary gland

Antidiuretic hormone (ADH) (vasopressin)

This hormone increases the permeability of the collecting tubules in the kidneys, causing more water to be reabsorbed into the body and less water to be lost in urine.

The amount of ADH released depends on the osmotic pressure of the blood, which is detected by the hypothalamus.

Oxytocin

This hormone causes contraction of the uterus in childbirth.

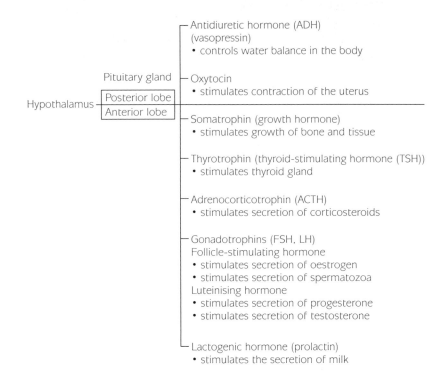

Figure 3.6 *Hormones produced by the pituitary gland*

Progress Check

1   What is an endocrine gland?
2   What is the function of endocrine glands?
3   Name all the endocrine glands.
4   What part of the brain controls the endocrine system?
5   What is the function of the pituitary gland?

Disorders of the anterior pituitary gland

Effects of excess growth hormone – hypersecretion

◆   excessive growth of bones
◆   enlargement of internal organs
◆   excessive growth of connective tissue

- enlargement of the heart and a rise in blood pressure
- reduced glucose tolerance and a predisposition to diabetes mellitus.

Gigantism   Normal stature   Dwarfism

Figure 3.7 *An illustration to compare the effects of different quantities of growth hormone on the body*

Gigantism
Gigantism is the result of excess growth hormone production before ossification is complete. The effects are evident mainly in the bones of the limbs.

(a)   (b)

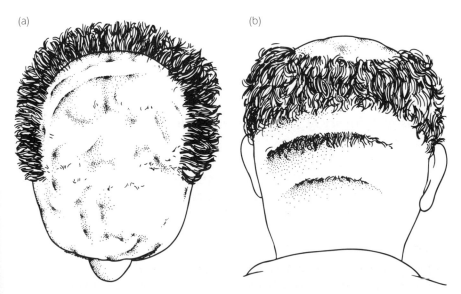

Figure 3.8 *Acromegaly. Note marked thickening of skin on* (a) *scalp and* (b) *posterior of head*

Acromegaly

Acromegaly is the result of excess growth hormone production after ossification is complete. The bones become abnormally thick, the facial features are noticeably coarse with overproduction of facial hair and the hands and feet are excessively large.

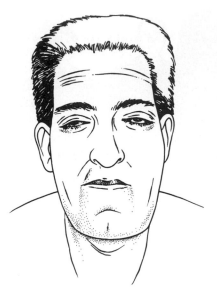

Figure 3.9 *Acromegaly. Note large head, exaggerated forward projection of jaw and projection of frontal bone*

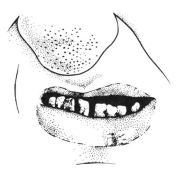

Figure 3.10 *Acromegaly. Note enlarged skin pores and separation of lower teeth*

Effects of deficiency of growth hormone – hyposecretion

Lorain–Lévi syndrome

This syndrome is caused by severe deficiency of growth hormone and possibly other hormones in childhood. Puberty is delayed and there may be episodes of hypoglycaemia. Affected individuals are of small stature but well proportioned, with mental development not affected.

Fröhlich's syndrome

This syndrome is caused by a deficiency of growth hormone, follicle-stimulating hormone and luteinising hormone. Affected individuals are obese with diminished growth, a lack of sexual development and retarded mental development.

Disorders of the posterior pituitary gland
Diabetes insipidus
This is a relatively rare condition caused by a lack of ADH, resulting in deficient water reabsorption from the collecting duct in the kidney. This causes dehydration and extreme thirst (polydipsia), and those affected often produce more than 10 litres of urine per day. The condition is unlikely to be serious unless substantial amounts of fluid cannot be taken into the body.

Simmond's disease (Sheehan's syndrome)
This syndrome is caused by total underproduction of the pituitary hormones, although the posterior pituitary is usually unharmed. This condition occurs mostly in women following a difficult labour, especially if there has been haemorrhage and a substantial fall in blood pressure. The pituitary gland becomes necrosed (dead). The immediate effect may be failure of lactation and later deficient stimulation of the target glands. The outcome of this condition depends on the extent of pituitary necrosis and hormone deficiency.

The pineal gland
The pineal gland regulates the pituitary gland and releases serotonin and melatonin. The pineal responds to daylight stimulation through the eye.

The thyroid gland
The thyroid gland is found in the neck in front of the larynx (voice box) and the trachea (windpipe) at the level of the fifth, sixth and seventh cervical vertebrae and the first thoracic vertebra. The thyroid has two lobes, one on each side of the trachea, and they are joined in the centre by a narrow piece of tissue called the isthmus.

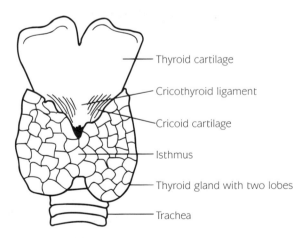

Thyroid cartilage

Cricothyroid ligament

Cricoid cartilage

Isthmus

Thyroid gland with two lobes

Trachea

Figure 3.11 *Position of the thyroid gland*

The thyroid gland is made up of two types of cells.

- Follicular cells make up most of the bulk of the gland.
- Parafollicular cells are found in the small spaces between the follicles.

The follicular cells make the hormones triiodothyronine and thyroxine and the parafollicular cells make the hormone calcitonin.

Hormones produced by the thyroid

- Thyroxine (T4) controls the general metabolism and growth and differentiation of tissues.
- Triiodothyronine (T3) is thought by some to be the tissue-active thyroid hormone.

Iodine is needed for production of both of these hormones.

- Calcitonin reduces the blood level of calcium by inhibiting its reabsorption from the bones.

Disorders of thyroid hormones

Hypersecretion

Graves' disease (thyrotoxicosis)
In people with this condition there is an abnormally large number of cells in the thyroid gland (hyperplasia), resulting in production of excess T3 and T4. Symptoms include weight loss, sleep disturbance, heat intolerance and exophthalmos (protruding eyeballs) due to excess fat and tissue deposits behind the eyeball.

The condition is thought to be due to autoimmunity to thyroid tissue and thyroid hormones. As a result of negative feedback, the abnormally high blood levels of T3 and T4 depress the secretion of the thyroid-releasing factor from the hypothalamus and of thyroid-stimulating hormone (TSH) from the anterior pituitary.

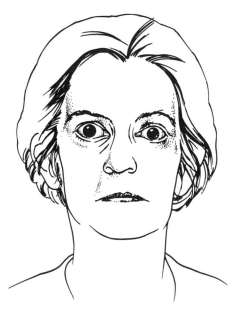

Figure 3.12 *Graves' disease, caused by hypersecretion by the thyroid gland*

Toxic nodular goitre
An increase in the size of the thyroid (hypertrophy) also results in excess production of T3 and T4, giving rise to the effects of a raised metabolic rate as described above for Graves' disease. It appears to be larger than toxic goitre because of the nodules found within the goitre.

Hyposecretion

Cretinism

Lack of T3 and T4 results in retarded physical and mental development in children, because these hormones are essential just before and after birth for development of the brain and bones. Affected individuals are dwarves with severe mental deficiency, slow heart rate, failure to develop sexually, coarse facial features and a pot belly.

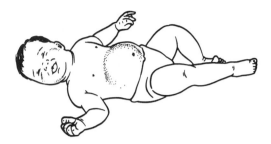

Figure 3.13 *Cretinism*

Myxoedema

Myxoedema is due to lack of T3 and T4 after normal mental health and physical development is complete, resulting in an abnormally low metabolic rate and a lack of response by the body to demand for increased energy. The signs and symptoms include yellowish pallor, oedema (swelling) of the face, large tongue and sluggishness.

Figure 3.14 *Myxoedema, a condition produced by hyposecretion of the thyroid gland during the adult years. Note the oedema around the eyes and facial puffiness*

The causes include autoimmune thyroiditis, severe prolonged iodine deficiency or a deficiency of thyroid releasing factor (TRF) and/or thyroid-stimulating hormone (TSH).

Toxic goitre

In this condition there is a lack of T3 and T4 in spite of excess TRF and TSH. The cells of the gland increase in number (hyperplasia) and size

Figure 3.15 *Nodular goitre caused by hypersecretion of the thyroid gland*

(hypertrophy), and an enlarged gland may cause pressure damage to tissues in the region. Sometimes the extra thyroid tissue is able to maintain normal hormone levels; if not myxoedema develops.

The causes include persistent iodine deficiency, genetic abnormality and/or chemicals that interfere with hormone synthesis.

Autoimmune thyroiditis
In this condition, the body does not recognise T3 and T4, thyroglobulin and the thyroid gland cells as 'self', treating them as 'foreign' antigens, and so produces antibodies against them. The antibodies attack the antigens, preventing the synthesis of and destroying the hormones, causing myxoedema.

The thyroid gland becomes swollen due to an accumulation of lymphocytes and plasma cells.

Variants of this disease include Hashimoto's disease, primary myxoedema and facial thyroiditis. The causes are not known.

> **REMEMBER**
> You need a letter of permission from the GP to treat a patient with a systemic illness.

Parathyroid glands

There are four small parathyroid glands, two embedded in the posterior surface of each lobe of the thyroid gland.

Structure of the parathyroid
Each parathyroid is composed of cells surrounded by a connective tissue capsule.

Hormone produced by the parathyroid glands
The parathyroid glands secrete parathormone (PTH), the production of which is regulated by the amount of ionised calcium in the blood.

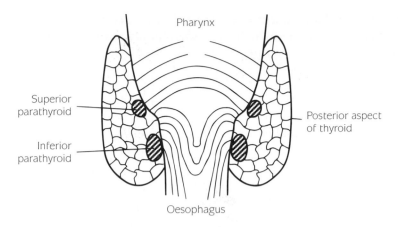

Figure 3.16 *Position of the parathyroid glands*

Parathormone increases the amount of calcium in the blood, and thus opposes the action of calcitonin from the thyroid gland.

Disorders of the parathyroid glands
Hypersecretion
Hyperparathyroidism

Excess parathormone secretion is usually due to benign tumours of the gland. The condition causes reabsorption of calcium from the bones, raising the blood calcium level. The effects include formation of kidney stones, pyelonephritis (inflammation of the kidney), kidney (renal) failure and calcification of soft tissues.

Hyposecretions
Hypoparathyroidism

Lack of parathormone causes abnormally low blood calcium levels. This condition reduces absorption of calcium from the small intestine and reabsorption from the bones and kidney filtrate.

Figure 3.17 *Hypoparathyroidism. For a severe case see Figure 3.18*

A low level of blood calcium causes:

- increased skeletal muscle tone and in severe cases tetany
- development of cataracts in the eyes
- behavioural disturbances and in extreme cases dementia.

The causes include damage to or removal of the gland, ionising radiation used to treat hyperparathyroidism, autoimmunity to the parathyroid glands or congenital abnormality of the glands.

Tetany
Tetany is caused by a low level of ionised calcium in the blood. The condition causes very strong painful contractions of the skeletal muscle, resulting in characteristic bending inwards of the hands, forearms and feet. There may also be laryngeal spasm and convulsions.

Figure 3.18 *Tetany*

This condition is associated with hypoparathyroidism, defective absorption of calcium or lack of calcium, excess excretion of calcium in the urine, chronic renal failure and alkalosis (the pH of the blood is higher than normal).

The thymus gland

The thymus gland produces one of the types of white blood cells, the T lymphocytes. T lymphocytes defend the health of the body.

The adrenal glands

The adrenals or suprarenals are positioned one on top of each kidney.

Structure of the adrenals
There are two parts, which differ anatomically and physiologically. The outer part of the gland is the adrenal cortex and is essential to life; the inner part of the gland is the adrenal medulla and is not essential to life. The glands are enclosed within the renal fascia.

Hormones produced by the adrenal glands
From the adrenal cortex
- Glucocorticoids. These are steroid hormones which control the metabolism of carbohydrates, proteins and fats, e.g. cortisol.
- Mineralocorticoids. These are steroid hormones which regulate electrolyte levels by causing sodium reabsorption in the renal tubules, e.g. aldosterone.

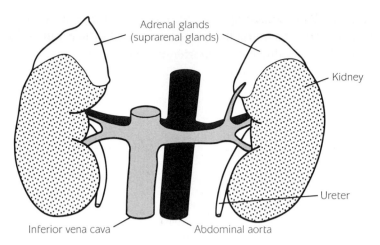

Figure 3.19 *Position of the adrenal glands*

- Androgens (sex hormones). These are steroid hormones, e.g. testosterone, which produce the male secondary characteristics. They are believed to be of little significance compared with those produced by the gonads.

From the adrenal medulla
- Adrenaline prepares the body for 'fight or flight' by acting on the sympathetic nervous system, to increase its effects.
- Noradrenaline decreases the cardiac heart rate and cardiac output. It also raises the blood pressure by causing vasoconstriction.

Disorders of the adrenal glands
Hypersecretion of cortex hormones
Cushing's syndrome
The symptoms and signs of Cushing's syndrome resulting from excess glucocorticoids and androgens include:

- virilism (excessive hair growth on the face, chest and pubic area)
- amenorrhoea (cessation of normal periods)
- gradual atrophy (wasting away) of the breasts
- development of a moon face or very bloated face and a buffalo hump/fatty hump on the back of the neck
- increased body fat not affecting the limbs
- backache and abdominal pain.

This syndrome can be caused by excessive cell development or by tumours of the adrenal cortex or the pituitary gland.

Excessive aldosterone affects the function of the kidney, causing:

- excessive sodium, sodium chloride, chloride and water reabsorption, resulting in hypertension (high blood pressure)
- excessive excretion of potassium, resulting in hyperkalaemia (too much potassium in the blood), which leads to cardiac arrhythmia (abnormal heart rhythm), alkalosis, muscle weakness and syncope (fainting).

Primary aldosteronism (Conn's syndrome)
In this condition, which usually affects one gland but may affect both, there is excessive production of aldosterone due to a tumour or hyperplasia of the adrenal cortex.

Secondary aldosteronism
In this case excess aldosterone is produced by normal glands because of high levels of blood renin, resulting from a new level of sodium chloride in the blood carried to the kidneys.

Hyposecretion of cortex hormones

Hyposecretion of glucocorticoids
A lack of cortisol causes diminished gluconeogenesis (glucose formation from fats and proteins), low blood glucose, muscle weakness and pallor.

Primary disease is due to deficient production of cortisol by the adrenal cortex. Secondary disease is due to deficiency of adrenocorticotrophin production by the pituitary gland. In primary deficiency there is also hyposecretion of aldosterone, but in secondary disease the aldosterone level is normal.

Hyposecretion of mineralocorticoids
When there is a lack of aldosterone the kidneys fail to regulate sodium, potassium and water excretion leading to:

- blood sodium deficiency and potassium excess
- dehydration and low blood volume, causing low blood pressure.

Addison's disease
This is due to a lack of all the adrenal cortex hormones, the most common causes being autoimmunity to cortical cells and metastatic (secondary) tumours and infections. The most important effects include muscle weakness and wasting, gastrointestinal disturbances, increased pigmentation of the skin, menstrual disturbances, electrolyte imbalances and chronic dehydration.

The adrenal glands have a considerable amount of reserve tissue and Addison's disease is not usually severely debilitating unless more than 90% of the cortical tissue is destroyed.

Hypersecretion of medulla hormones

Hormone-secreting tumours are the major cause of hypersecretion of adrenaline and noraderenaline. The effects of hypersecretion of these hormones include:

- hypertension (high blood pressure) often associated with arteriosclerosis and cerebral haemorrhage
- raised blood glucose and glycosuria (glucose in urine)
- excessive sweating and alternate flushing and blanching
- raised metabolic rate.

Phaeochromocytoma
This is a benign tumour occurring in one or both of the glands causing secretion of the hormones to be increased continuously or intermittently. This condition is usually triggered by injury in the region of the tumour.

> **REMEMBER**
> Gluconeogenesis occurs when the body has to use its supplies of protein and fat for energy.

Neuroblastoma

This is a malignant tumour occurring in infants and young children under 15. Those tumours that develop early tend to be highly malignant, but spontaneous regression may occur. Haemorrhagic necrosis (death of the part of the body due to an absence of blood supply) and calcification may destroy the gland. This type of tumour spreads rapidly to the thoracic lymph nodes and the liver and bones.

Stress

When the body is not coping well it secretes higher levels of adrenaline for prolonged periods of time. The effects of the 'fight and flight' reaction are sustained leading to the condition known as stress. The symptoms of stress are very varied but do become worse with time adversely affecting many of the body's functions.

The islets of Langerhans

These are found in clusters, irregularly distributed throughout the substance of the pancreas.

Structure of the islets of Langerhans

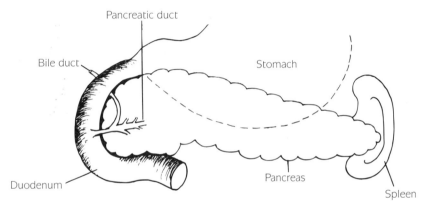

Figure 3.20 *Location of the pancreas*

There are three types of cells in the islets:

- alpha cells
- beta cells
- delta cells.

Hormones made by the islets

- Alpha cells produce glucagon (which converts glycogen to glucose in the liver).
- Beta cells produce insulin (which converts glucose to glycogen in the liver).
- Delta cells produce somatostatin (which inhibits the action of somatotrophin – growth hormone).

Disorders of the islets of Langerhans

Hyposecretion (diabetes mellitus)

Hyposecretion of insulin causes disordered sugar and starch metabolism. In diabetes mellitus sugar is not taken up and used by the cells of the

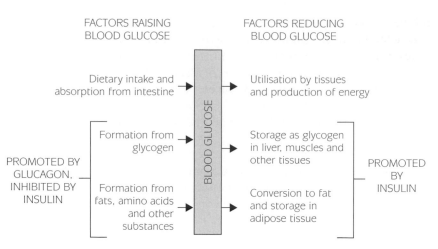

FACTORS RAISING
BLOOD GLUCOSE

FACTORS REDUCING
BLOOD GLUCOSE

BLOOD GLUCOSE

Dietary intake and
absorption from intestine

Utilisation by tissues
and production of energy

Formation from
glycogen

Storage as glycogen
in liver, muscles and
other tissues

PROMOTED BY
GLUCAGON,
INHIBITED BY
INSULIN

PROMOTED
BY
INSULIN

Formation from
fats, amino acids
and other
substances

Conversion to fat
and storage in
adipose tissue

Figure 3.21 *The regulation of blood glucose levels*

body, but instead accumulates in the blood and is excreted by the kidneys, hence the large quantities of sugar found in the urine of diabetics.

There are two types of diabetes mellitus. The most common type is non-insulin-dependent diabetes mellitus (NIDDM), sometimes called type 2 or maturity-onset diabetes. In this type, the pancreas produces some insulin but not enough to cope with the amount of glucose in the blood. This condition is often caused by obesity and excessive food intake, and can be treated by diet alone or by drugs that lower the blood sugar level (oral hypoglycaemics).

In insulin-dependent diabetes mellitus (IDDM), also called type 1 or juvenile diabetes, there is a total or almost total failure of the pancreas and sufferers need daily insulin injections for the rest of their lives in order to keep blood glucose levels stable.

There are many causes of diabetes mellitus. Genetic factors are known to play a part, and diabetes can follow the removal or destruction by disease of the pancreas. Several diseases of the endocrine glands can also cause diabetes, e.g. acromegaly and thyrotoxicosis, and people taking steroid hormones, e.g. corticosteroids, ACTH, or some diuretic drugs may develop diabetes as a side-effect. The effects of diabetes include a raised level of glucose in the blood, the production of vast quantities of urine that contains glucose, weight loss and acidosis (blood pH lower than normal).

Reproductive organs

Male
The male gonads are the testes. They are suspended in the scrotum by the spermatic cords.

Structure of the testes
Each testis contains 200–300 tubules composed of germinal epithelium cells; between the tubules there are groups of interstitial cells. At the upper pole of the testes the tubules combine to form a single tortuous

tubule, the epididymis, which leaves the scrotum as the deferent duct (vas deferens) in the spermatic cord. Blood and lymph vessels pass to the testes in the spermatic cord.

The testes are surrounded by the three layers of tissue:

- the tunica vaginalis, the outer covering, a downgrowth of the pelvic peritoneum
- the tunica albuginea, the fibrous middle covering
- the tunica vasculosa, the inner covering made from a network of capillaries supported by delicate connective tissue.

Hormones made by the testes
Testosterone is made by the interstitial cells between the tubules.

Male in puberty
Puberty in the male begins between the ages of 10 and 14. Secretion of pituitary hormones leads to the increase in the production of testosterone, causing the following changes:

- growth of muscle and bone and increase in height and weight
- enlargement of the larynx and deepening of the voice (it breaks)
- growth of hair on the face, axillae, chest, abdomen and pubis
- maturation of the seminiferous tubules and production of spermatozoa.

In the male, fertility and sexual ability tend to decline gradually with ageing. There is no period comparable to the menopause in the female.

Female
The female gonads are the ovaries. They are located in a shallow fossa (hollow) on the lateral walls of the pelvis. Each is attached to the upper part of the uterus by the ligament of the ovary and to the back by a broad band of tissue, the mesovarium.

Structure of the ovaries
The ovaries are composed of two parts.

- The medulla lies in the centre and consists of fibrous tissue, blood vessels and nerves.
- The cortex surrounds the medulla. It has a framework of connective tissue, or stroma, covered by germinal epithelium. It contains ovarian follicles, each of which contains an ovum.

Hormones made by the ovaries
- oestrogen, from the follicle lining cells in the ovary
- progesterone, from the corpus luteum.

How do the female reproductive organs work?
Before puberty the ovaries are inactive but the stroma already contains immature (primordial) follicles. During childbearing years one ovarian follicle matures, ruptures and releases its ovum into the peritoneal cavity during each menstrual cycle. FSH (from the anterior pituitary) stimulate maturation of the follicle, causing the cells of the follicle lining to produce oestrogen. After ovulation, when the egg leaves the follicle, the follicle develops into the corpus luteum (yellow body), under the

influence of LH (from the anterior pituitary). The corpus luteum produces progesterone.

If the ovum is fertilised it embeds in the uterus wall, where it grows and develops and produces chorionic gonadotrophin hormone, which stimulates the corpus luteum to continue secreting progesterone for the first 3 months of pregnancy. If the ovum is not fertilised the corpus luteum degenerates, menstruation occurs and the next cycle begins.

Sometimes more than one follicle matures at one time, releasing two or more ova in the same cycle. When this happens and the ova are fertilised the result is a multiple pregnancy.

Female in puberty
Puberty in the female begins between the ages of 10 and 14. The internal reproductive organs reach maturity and the following changes take place.

- The uterus, uterine tubes and ovaries reach maturity.
- The menstrual cycle and ovulation begin.
- The breasts develop and enlarge.
- Pubic and axillary hair begins to grow.
- There is an increase in the rate of growth of the pelvis, which becomes wider.
- There is increased fat deposition in the subcutaneous tissue.

Menstrual cycle
This is a series of events occurring on average every 26–30 days during woman's childbearing life. The hypothalamus secretes releasing factors stimulating the anterior pituitary to release:

- FSH, which promotes maturation of the ovarian follicles and secretion of oestrogen, leading to ovulation
- LH, which stimulates development of the corpus luteum and secretion of progesterone.

The stages of the menstrual cycle are:

- the proliferative phase, lasting 10 days
- the secretory phase, lasting 14 days
- the menstrual phase, lasting 4 days on average.

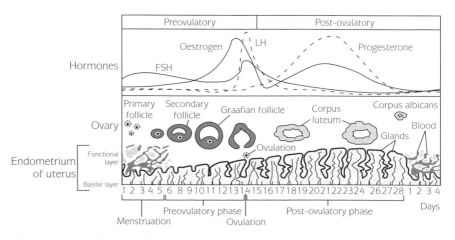

Figure 3.22 *Changes in hormone levels during a woman's monthly cycle and the corresponding changes in the thickness of the endometrium*

Disorders of the ovaries

Polycystic ovary syndrome (Stein–Leventhal syndrome)
Ovarian cysts may be associated with hormonal changes and ovulation, in which case they may come and go without treatment (though they may be painful at the time). Larger cysts may cause symptoms of internal pressure and need to be removed.

Cancer of the ovary
This is rare and occurs mainly in older women. Symptoms include masculinisation, hirsutism, amenorrhoea and occasionally obesity and retarded breast development.

Menopause

The menopause usually begins between the ages of 45 and 50. Failure to form ovarian follicles and ova results in the cessation of periods (menopause). There is a dramatic fall in the blood level of oestrogen but the level of gonadotrophins (see pituitary) and androgens increases.

Symptoms
During the menopausal period, women may experience some or all of the following symptoms:

- hot flushes
- night sweats
- vaginal dryness due to vaginal tissue becoming thin and secreting less moisture; as a result sexual intercourse may be difficult
- vaginal shrinkage and loss of elasticity
- poor memory
- poor concentration
- tearfulness
- anxiety
- loss of interest in sex
- bones become thinner – osteoporosis (decrease in bone density, increase in brittleness)
- increased risk of coronary artery disease and stroke
- hypertrichosis, especially on the sides of the chin and upper lip.

Treatment

The symptoms of the menopause can be relieved by hormone replacement therapy, although not in women who have been treated for breast cancer, or by beta blockers.

Progress Check

1. List the hormones each endocrine gland produces.
2. What is meant by the terms hypersecretion and hyposecretion?
3. How does the body know when to stop producing hormones?
4. Which endocrine disorders cause changes in the hair growth pattern?
5. List all the disorders of the endocrine system and state whether they are due to hypo- or hypersecretion and of which hormone.
6. What is autoimmunity?
7. How are hormones carried around the body and how do they know where to work?
8. Explain the menstrual cycle.

Key Terms

You will need to know what these words and phrases mean. Go back through the chapter or check the glossary to find out.

- Antibody
- Antigen
- Atrophy
- Disease
- Disorder
- Endocrine gland
- Endocrine system
- Exocrine gland
- Gonads
- Hormone
- Hypersecretion
- Hyposecretion
- Master gland
- Menopause
- Menstruation
- Syndrome

1 Write in the name of the hormones which cause the following effects then, in the table below, show whether they are secreted by the anterior or posterior pituitary.

💧 Stimulates secretion of corticosteroids:

_____

💧 Stimulates contraction of the uterus:

_____

💧 Stimulate the gonads:

_____

💧 Stimulates adrenal glands:

_____

💧 Stimulates secretion of milk:

_____

💧 Controls water balance in the body:

_____

Anterior pituitary	Posterior pituitary

2 What is another name for the pituitary gland and why?

_____

3 Fill in the gaps.
Hypersecretion of growth hormone causes:

a) Excessive growth of _____.

b) _____ of connective tissue.

c) _____ of internal organs.

d) _____ of the heart and a _____ in blood pressure.

e) _____ glucose tolerance and a predisposition to diabetes mellitus.

4 Compare the two endocrine disorders:

Gigantism	Acromegaly

5 Which form of hyposecretion of growth hormone gives an individual of small stature but well proportioned, with mental development not affected?

_____

6 What hormone is responsible for diabetes insipidus?

_____

7 What mineral is needed for normal functioning of the thyroid gland?

_____

8 Name the two parts of the adrenal gland.

_____

9 Link the following types of cells in the islets of Langerhans to the hormones they produce, by drawing a line to link them up.

Alpha cells	Insulin
Beta cells	Somatostatin
Delta cells	Glucagon

10 For each of the following disorders, name the hormone responsible and say whether it is hyper- or hyposecreted.

Disorder	Hormone	Hyper/hypo
Addison's disease		
Aldosteronism		
Autoimmune thyroiditis		
Cushing's syndrome		
Diabetes mellitus		
Graves' disease		
Hyperparathyroidism		
Hypoparathyroidism		
Myxoedema		
Simmond's disease		
Tetany		
Toxic goitre		

11 In the table below, compare the changes in the male and female in puberty.

Male	Female

12 In the table below, compare the changes that occur in the mammary glands.

Puberty	Pregnancy	Menopause

13 What is the function of the mammary glands?

_____

CAUSES OF UNWANTED HAIR

4

After studying this chapter you will be able to:

- explain the term electro-epilation
- describe and understand the different causes of superfluous hair
- give examples of the causes of superfluous hair
- recognise the different types of hair.

Electro-epilation is the permanent removal of superfluous or unwanted hair. There are three types of permanent electro-epilation:

- short-wave diathermy (SWD), which uses a high-frequency alternating current (see p. 161)
- galvanic, which uses a direct current (see p.182)
- blend, a combination of galvanic and diathermy (see p. 191)

People who will benefit from treatment include:

- those with hypertrichosis, i.e. excessive hair growth
- women with hirsutism: excess hair growth in the male hair pattern, i.e. on the face, neck, chest, abdomen
- male-to-female transsexuals with unwanted face and body hair
- those who, for cosmetic reasons, require removal of hair from the eyebrows, underarms, bikini area or face.

Causes of superfluous hair

- Congenital, i.e. present since birth: some people are born with a normal excess of face and body hair in the pattern that is inherited.
- Topical: stimulation or friction to an area of skin may cause excess hair growth.
- Systemic: both normal and abnormal hormonal changes may stimulate hair growth.

Examples of causes of superfluous hair

- Females with low levels of the female hormones oestrogen and progesterone and higher levels of the male hormones androgens can develop superfluous hair. In the most severe cases the hair growth will take on the very definite male pattern.
- People of different races have different amounts of body hair. For example Northern Europeans, i.e. those from Britain and Scandinavia, have less hair than people from the Southern Mediterranean countries or India. Negroes have relatively little hair, while people of Mongolian and Oriental race have the least body hair.
- Stress causes secretion of hormones from the adrenal cortex. If stress continues for a long period of time excess androgen

stimulates superfluous hair growth. Again the hair growth can conform to the male pattern.

- At puberty gonadotrophins and the sex hormones begin to be released. The onset of puberty can cause a hormonal imbalance, and if the level of androgens produced by the adrenal cortex or ovaries is too high this can stimulate the production of superfluous hair. This problem usually corrects itself in time if the individual is otherwise healthy.
- During pregnancy many hormonal changes and often temporary imbalances occur. The androgen level can be raised, resulting in the superfluous hair growth. This condition will often correct itself after the birth when the androgen level returns to normal. Any remaining superfluous hairs may need to be removed by electro-epilation.
- At the menopause the ovaries begin to degenerate as their reproductive function is no longer required. As a result there is a reduction in the levels of oestrogen, progesterone and androgens produced by the ovaries. However, the adrenal cortex continues to produce androgens and the relatively high level of androgens can lead to the production of superfluous hair in the male growth pattern.
- Certain drugs can lead to the production of superfluous hair in patients. These include dilantin, cyclosporine, danazol, anabolic steroids, minoxidil, diazoxide, tamoxifen and high doses of cortisone over long period of time.
- Illness and disease: polycystic ovaries and idiopathic hirutism (of known cause) account for 90% of cases or hirsutism; ovarian/adrenal tumours account for 1%.

Normal congenital hair growth patterns
This includes the hair we are born with.

Hair	Region of body	Function
Cilia	Eyelashes	Shade To prevent dust, dirt, etc. entering the eyes
Supercilia	Eyebrows	Shade To prevent dust, dirt, etc. entering the eyes
Vibrissae	Nostrils	Filtration of incoming air
Capilli	Scalp	Protection against ultraviolet light Maintenance of body temperature
Hirci	Body hair	To retain body heat and protect against friction

Table 4.1 *Normal congenital hair growth*

Abnormal congenital hair patterns
Hypertrichosis that is present at birth is a very rare genetic condition requiring many years' treatment.

Topical hair growth

This is hair growth in response to any potential threat to the epidermis caused by rubbing or other types of irritation. Stimulation of the blood supply to the skin in the immediate area causes the hair to grow deeper and coarser as a protective mechanism. Moles and birthmarks are frequently a cause of excessive hair growth because of the unusual development of capillaries near the surface of the skin.

Normal systemic causes of hair growth

Androgens are the only hormones capable of stimulating target follicles to produce hair. Androgen levels are usually higher in men than in women. However, at certain times of a woman's life, e.g. at puberty, menopause and during pregnancy, the level of androgens is increased, causing disturbance of the normal hair growth pattern. Changes in the hair growth pattern during a period of hormone imbalance vary between individuals.

Puberty

At puberty the gonads and adrenal cortex secrete large amounts of steroid hormones, causing the development of the normal male and female hair patterns.

Pregnancy

During pregnancy excess androgen production can cause hairs to develop on the upper lip, chin and the sides of the face. After birth, when the endocrine balance is restored, these hairs usually disappear.

Menopause

Menopause marks the end of a woman's reproductive life. It is a gradual process occurring over a number of years. Reduction in the levels of oestrogen and progesterone allows the effects of adrenal androgens to dominate.

Abnormal systemic causes of hair growth

Hormonal imbalances may be hereditary or due to endocrine gland defects, acquired disease or infection, tumours or a deficiency of the diet. The conditions known to disturb the normal hair growth patterns are listed below, but for further information refer to Chapter 3.

Cushing's syndrome

In this condition there is hypersecretion of the adrenal cortex hormones, including androgens, resulting in hirsutism.

Adrenogenital syndrome (adrenal hyperplasia, congenital)

Congenital adrenogenital syndrome is present from birth and results from a genetic defect that causes overproduction of androgens by the adrenal cortex. Production of glucocorticoids and mineralocorticoids is reduced, resulting in the body being unable to retain salt and water, causing dehydration, weight loss, low blood pressure and hypoglycaemia.

The adrenal glands are enlarged as a result of pituitary stimulation in an effort to increase output of glucocorticoids and mineralocorticoids.

Androgens accumulate in the fetus. In girls this results in virilisation of the genital tract: enlargement of the clitoris and some degree of fusion of the outerlips of the vulva makes the female sex organs look like the male organs. In affected males an enlarged penis is present at birth or develops thereafter. In males puberty may occur prematurely; in females menstruation is delayed and there may be hirsutism and possibly infertility.

Archard–Thiers syndrome

This is a very rare condition found in some women who suffer from diabetes. The adrenal glands and ovaries produce too much androgen and some of the symptoms of Cushing's syndrome are present.

Polycystic ovary syndrome

This syndrome is characterised by irregular periods or absent periods, infertility, hirsutism and obesity. Hirsutism and obesity are thought to affect only 50% of sufferers.

Anorexia nervosa

Anorexia nervosa is a psychological disorder. Affected individuals have a drastically reduced food intake and may exercise to excess, resulting in weight loss, fatigue and weakness. Sufferers periodically undertake binge eating, followed by induced vomiting or use of laxatives to promote weight loss. Lanugo hair (baby hair) develops on the body, while there is thinning of hair on the head.

Acromegaly

In this condition, which is due to the hypersecretion of growth hormone after growth is complete, certain parts of the body begin to develop for a second time. The resultant effects include large hands and feet, coarse facial features and changes in the levels of androgens secreted. Excess androgens stimulate excessive hair growth in the male hair growth pattern, i.e. on the face and chest and in the pubic region.

Treatment of patients

The majority of your clients will have a small amount of unwanted hair on the upper lip, chin or chest. However, as your reputation as a good electrologist grows you will be required to treat much greater problems and possibly clients referred by their GP or the local hospital endocrinology department. All unwanted hair can be successfully removed, but the speed at which hair responds depends on the cause.

Clients must be patient and understand from the beginning that permanent removal does take time. They will look to you to encourage them to persist with treatment knowing that completion of treatment will completely change their life.

Progress Check

1 What is the main difference between hypertrichosis and superfluous hair growth?
2 What are the two main factors that increase hair growth?
3 What are the causes of superfluous hair growth?
4 Which races are considered to be the hairiest?
5 What does the term hirsute mean?
6 Which areas of the body should have no hairs at all?

7 Why do moles and birthmarks often have strong hairs on them?

8 The wearing of a plaster of Paris cast will cause excess hair to grow in the area. Is this permanent?

9 Why can tweezing cause hairs to become stronger?

10 Why does diabetes prove a problem in electro-epilation treatments?

11 Do the ovaries produce androgens?

12 What are the gonads?

13 What is the main hormone change in the menopause?

14 Which endocrine disorders result in hypertrichosis?

15 How does stress affect hair growth?

Key Terms

You will need to know what these words and phrases mean. Go back through the chapter or check the glossary to find out.

- Congenital
- Gonads
- Hereditary
- Hirsutism
- Hypertrichosis
- Menopause
- Pregnancy
- Puberty
- Superfluous hair
- Systemic
- Topical

1   Link one of the following causes of superfluous hair with each description.

Topical   A condition that has been with the person since birth
Congenital   Caused by changes in the endocrine system.
Systemic   Excess hair growth caused by anorexia nervosa
Excess hair growth due to friction or stimulation in the area

2   In the following examples of superfluous hair insert the missing words. (Words can be used more than once and you might not use them all.)

Stress makes hair growth _____ due to the _____ glands being very active.

Cortisone and some contraceptive _____ can make hair growth _____.

_____ races have least hair growth. In _____ the female hormones are _____ due to the degeneration of the ovaries.

heavier   menopause
increased   Oriental
Asian   lighter
pregnancy   adrenal
pills   reduced

3   Say which of the following statements are true. (Put a tick by the true statements.)

In puberty the gonads, adrenal cortex and islets of Langerhans secrete large amounts of steroid hormones.   ☐

In pregnancy the production of excess androgens can cause hairs to appear.   ☐

In menopause the production of all hormones decreases.   ☐

4   Which of the following words describes the overproduction of hair?

a)   Hypertrichosis.
b)   Hypotrichosis.

OTHER SYSTEMS OF THE BODY

5

After studying this chapter you will be able to understand:

- cells and tissues
- the skeletal system
- the muscular system
- the heart and circulation
- the lymphatic system
- the respiratory system
- the excretory system
- the digestive system and nutrition
- the nervous system
- the reproductive system
- the mammary glands.

Cells and tissues

After studying this section you will be able to:

- describe the structure of a cell
- draw a simplified diagram of a cell
- understand how a cell functions.

A cell is the smallest basic unit of life. The human body is made up of a great number of cells, performing many different functions.

Contents of a cell
Nucleus
The nucleus acts like the brain of the cell. It is essential for cell reproduction. Nearly all cells have a nucleus, except for mature red blood cells, in which its loss limits the activity and lifespan of the cell. The nucleus contains one or more nucleoli, chromosomes (in humans 23 pairs) and threads of chromatin.

Nucleoli
Seen as dark dots in the nucleus, nucleoli contain RNA (ribose nucleic acid), which is needed for cell reproduction.

Nuclear membrane
This membrane is double layered, with the layers joining at intervals to form pores. The presence of pores makes the membrane semipermeable, allowing molecules smaller than the size of the pores to pass through it.

Centrosome
This is a dense region of cytoplasm that is always found near the nucleus. It consists of two central fibres called centrioles, surrounded by nine peripheral fibres. Like the nucleoli, the centrosome is important for the cell division; it contains DNA (deoxyribose nucleic acid). Without the centrosome cell replacement is impossible.

Cytoplasm

This is a semitransparent fluid inside the cell membrane but outside the nuclear membrane. Cytoplasm consists of up to 90% water with inorganic substances and sugars. Many chemical reactions occur in this part of the cell.

Vacuole

This is a small fluid-filled sac. It contains enzymes that destroy harmful substances. Once destroyed the vacuole transports the substances out of the cell.

Cell/plasma membrane

This is a semipermeable membrane that surrounds the entire cell. It allows molecules smaller than the size of the pores to pass through it.

Mitochondria

This is the powerhouse of the cell. It provides all the energy needed.

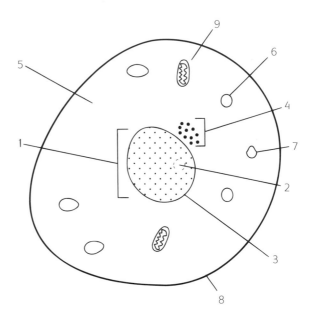

Figure 5.1 1, *nucleus*; 2, *nucleolus*; 3, *nuclear membrane*; 4, *centrosome*; 5, *cytoplasm*; 6, *vacuole*; 7, *lysosome*; 8, *cell/plasma membrane*; 9, *mitochondrion*

Cell division

Cells reproduce/divide by mitosis. This is the process of cell/nuclear division, in which one parent cell divides to form two identical daughter cells.

Only nerve cells are not replaced, so they are called permanent cells.

The process involves a series of changes involving duplication of the centrioles and chromosomes so that each of the two new cells contains a nucleus with 23 pairs of chromosomes.

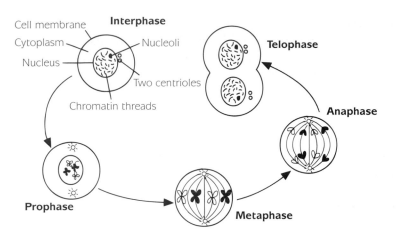

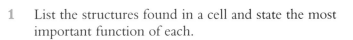

Figure 5.2 *Simplified diagram to illustrate the changes occurring in a cell during each stage of mitosis*

Progress Check

1 List the structures found in a cell and state the most important function of each.
2 What is mitosis?
3 Which parts of a cell are required for mitosis?
4 What is the main difference between a cell membrane and a nuclear membrane?
5 What does semipermeable mean?
6 Draw and label a diagram of a cell.

Key Terms

You will need to know what these words mean. Go back through the section or check the glossary to find out.

● Cell
● Mitosis
● Nucleus

Test your knowledge of cells and tissues on page p. 107.

Skeletal system

After studying this section you will be able to:

● describe the structure of the skeleton
● understand the functions of the skeleton.

Skeletal system

The skeleton is made up of 206 bones which provide the bony framework for the body, supporting the soft tissues, protecting sensitive parts such as the brain and spinal cord and giving the point of attachment for muscles, thus allowing movement at the joints.

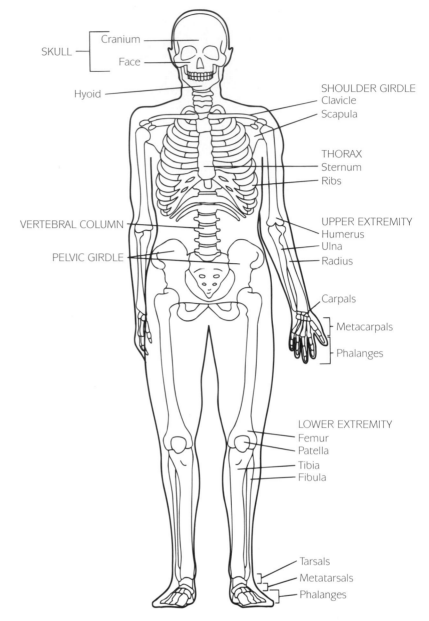

Figure 5.3 *The bones of the skeleton (anterior view)*

The study of the skeleton
Osteology is the study of anatomy dealing with the skeleton and bones, and the bony structure of animals.

The different parts of the skeleton
The bones of the skeleton can be divided into two parts, the axial skeleton and the appendicular skeleton.

The axial skeleton
This forms the central line of the body, i.e. the cranium, vertebral column and thoracic cage. Movement can occur in this part of the skeleton, but it is not freely moveable.

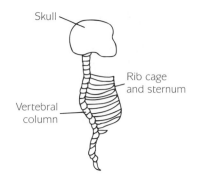

Figure 5.4 *The axial part of the skeleton*

The appendicular skeleton

This is made up of the bones of the shoulder, arm and hand, pelvis, leg and foot. These parts of the skeleton are freely moveable like pendulums.

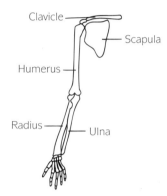

Figure 5.5 *The appendicular part of the skeleton (arm)*

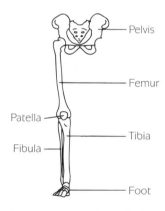

Figure 5.6 *The appendicular part of the skeleton (leg)*

Functions of the skeleton

- It provides the framework of the body to give support, as all the other tissues apart from bone and cartilage are soft.
- It gives attachment to muscles and bones.
- It permits movement of the body as a whole and parts of the body, by forming joints that are moved by muscles.
- It forms the boundaries of the cranial, thoracic and pelvic cavities, protecting the organs they contain.

- The bones of the skeleton contain red bone marrow in which red blood cells develop.
- It provides a reservoir for calcium.

Bone
Bone is made from approximately 50% water and 50% solids.

Of the 50% solids, 30% is organic matrix (ground substance and collagen fibres) and 70% is bone salts (calcium and phosphorous salts).

Progress Check

1 What is osteology?
2 Compare the axial and the appendicular skeleton.
3 As briefly as possible list the functions of the skeleton.
4 Explain the composition of bone.

Key Terms

You will need to know what these words mean. Go back through the section or check the glossary to find out.

- Bone
- Muscle
- Skeletal system

Test your knowledge of the skeletal system on p. 108.

Muscular system

After studying this section you will be able to:

- describe the difference types of muscle tissue
- understand the structure and function of muscle.

Muscular system
This is the system concerned with movement. The contraction of muscles results in movement of the bones to which they are attached. Muscle is fibrous tissue made of 75% water and 25% solid, of which 20% is the protein myosin.

Types of muscle
There are three types of muscle tissue.

1 Voluntary, skeletal or striated muscle. These three names are used to describe the same type of muscle.
2 Involuntary, smooth or visceral muscle.
3 Cardiac muscle.

Skeletal muscle
Skeletal muscle moves the skeleton. Under a microscope this type of muscle looks striped (striated), because it has light and dark bands.

Contraction of skeletal muscle is under the control of our will, i.e. voluntary. A stimulus from the brain or spinal cord causes the muscle to move promptly on demand, obeying the 'all or nothing' law. Skeletal muscles are said to be in a state of tone when a few muscle fibres are stimulated and held in a state of partial contraction.

Without glucose and oxygen the muscle becomes fatigued if overworked, causing a build-up of lactic acid and the symptoms of cramp.

The fibres of this type of muscle are arranged in bundles bound by connective tissue called fasciae. At the muscle ends the fascia of each muscle bundle join together to form tendons or aponeuroses, which attach the muscle to bone or tissue.

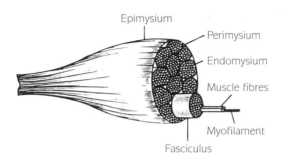

Figure 5.7 *Gross structure of skeletal muscle*

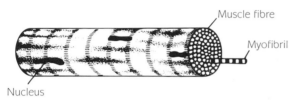

Figure 5.8 *Microscopic structure of skeletal muscle*

Involuntary muscle
This type of muscle is not controlled by the will of the individual. It is smooth in appearance and is found in the walls of internal organs and blood vessels. This type of muscle contracts more slowly and evenly than skeletal muscle and does not show fatigue, it is normally controlled by involuntary nerves of the autonomic nervous system, which is the subconscious part.

Cardiac muscle
Cardiac muscle is found only in the heart, and it is not controlled by the will of the individual. Cardiac muscle contracts rhythmically even without the nervous stimulation that all other types of muscle tissue need. A specialised area of heart tissue (the sinoatrial node) controls the beating of the heart muscle. Under normal circumstances cardiac muscle does not tire because the muscle fibres do not all contract together, but instead work alternately. The only time this muscle will tire is if the rate of heart beat is drastically increased for a long period of time with no rest.

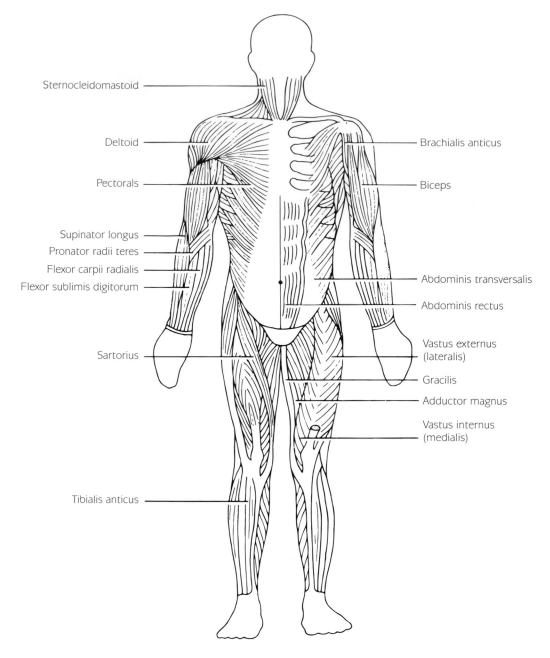

Figure 5.9 *The major skeletal muscles (anterior view)*

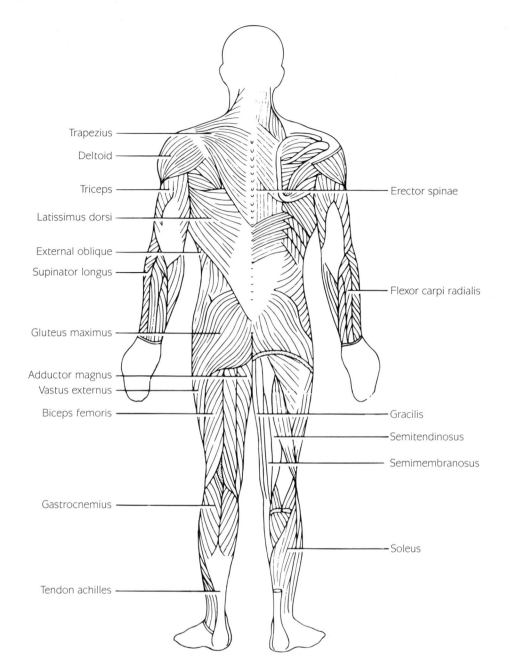

Trapezius

Deltoid

Triceps

Latissimus dorsi

External oblique

Supinator longus

Gluteus maximus

Adductor magnus

Vastus externus

Biceps femoris

Gastrocnemius

Tendon achilles

Erector spinae

Flexor carpi radialis

Gracilis

Semitendinosus

Semimembranosus

Soleus

Figure 5.10 *The major skeletal muscles (posterior view)*

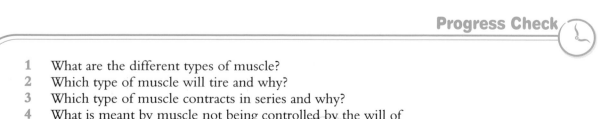

1   What are the different types of muscle?
2   Which type of muscle will tire and why?
3   Which type of muscle contracts in series and why?
4   What is meant by muscle not being controlled by the will of the individual?

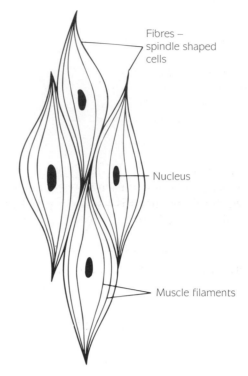

Fibres –
spindle shaped
cells

Nucleus

Muscle filaments

Figure 5.11 *Involuntary muscle fibres.*

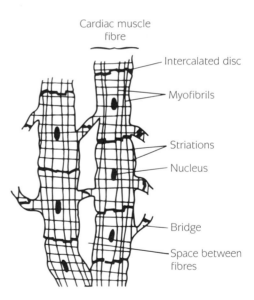

Cardiac muscle
fibre

Intercalated disc

Myofibrils

Striations

Nucleus

Bridge

Space between
fibres

Figure 5.12 *Cardiac muscle fibre*

Key Terms

You will need to know what these words and phrases mean. Go back through the section or check the glossary to find out.

- Cardiac muscle
- Involuntary muscle
- Muscular system
- Voluntary muscle

Test your knowledge of the muscular system on p. 109.

Heart and circulation

After studying this section you will be able to:

- describe the location of the heart
- describe the structure of the heart
- understand the function of the heart
- explain the structure of blood
- list the functions of blood.

Heart and circulation

The heart is a cone-shaped hollow muscular organ about the size of a clenched fist. Anatomically the heart is a single organ, but physiologically the right and left halves of the heart act as two separate organs.

The heart is situated behind and slightly to the left of the sternum (breastbone), positioned between the thoracic cage and the lungs and above the diaphragm.

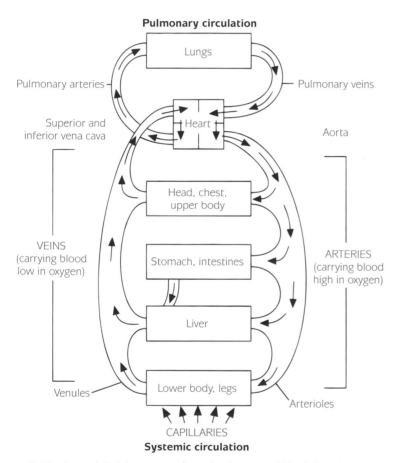

Figure 5.13 *A simplified diagram to show the direction of blood flow through the heart and around the body*

Structure of the heart

The heart is composed of cardiac muscle and is divided into four hollow chambers, two on each side. The upper chambers are thin-walled receiving chambers (atria) and the lower are thicker walled pumping chambers (ventricles). The right half of the heart is divided from the left half by a muscular wall, the septum. The upper chambers are separated from the lower chambers by valves, which can open to allow blood to flow from the upper chamber to the lower chamber but not back again.

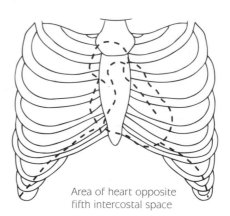

Area of heart opposite
fifth intercostal space

Figure 5.14 *Position of the heart in the thorax*

The heart is composed of three layers:

- ◆ Endocardium. This lines the heart cavities on the inside and is continuous with the blood vessels.
- ◆ Myocardium. This is the middle thick layer of cardiac muscle making up the bulk of the heart. It is supplied with blood from the coronary arteries and drained by the coronary veins and coronary sinus.
- ◆ Pericardium. This is the outer covering of connective tissue and serous epithelium, forming a double-layered serous membrane with pericardial serous fluid between the two layers, to prevent friction in movement.

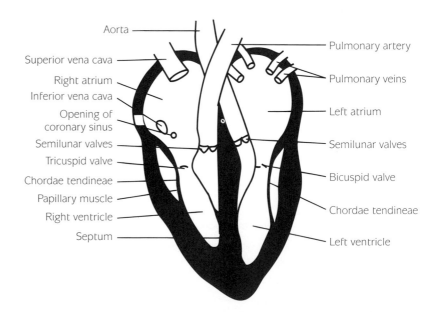

Figure 5.15 *A simplified diagram of the structure of the heart and major blood vessels*

Function of the heart

The heart maintains a constant circulation of blood throughout the body through a series of events known as the cardiac cycle.

Blood

Blood is a fluid connective tissue, forming the chief transport system of the body, carrying substances towards and away from different regions of the body. We have between 5 and 6 litres of blood in our body.

> **REMEMBER**
> Blood is the main circulatory system.

Structure of the blood

Fluid part

The fluid part of the blood, called plasma, constitutes 55% of blood. It is made up of:

- water (90–93%)
- blood proteins
- inorganic salts
- enzymes
- hormones
- vitamins
- food: amino acids, fats, fatty acids and glucose
- waste, chiefly urea and some uric acid
- gases: oxygen, nitrogen and carbon dioxide.

Solid part

The solid part of blood (45%) is composed of the following types of cells/corpuscles:

- red blood cells (erythrocytes)
- white blood cells (leucocytes)
- platelets (thrombocytes).

Functions of the blood

- To carry oxygen to the tissues via the haemoglobin in the red blood cells.
- To carry fresh nutrients around the body.
- To remove waste products (carbon dioxide, urea and water) from the tissues and take them to the specific organ for excretion.
- To carry hormones around the body.
- To defend the body against invasion.
- To carry lymphocytes around the body for the immune system.
- To carry antibodies to the site of infection.

Specific functions of the blood cells

Erythrocyte structure

Erythrocytes are shaped like biconcave discs. They have no nucleus. Erythrocytes are made in the red bone marrow.

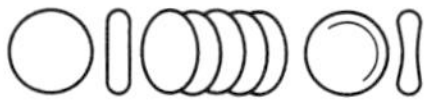

Figure 5.16 *Red blood cells (erythrocytes)*

Erythrocyte function

Erythrocytes transport oxygen and carbon dioxide around the body. These cells contain haemoglobin, which binds to oxygen, improving the efficiency of its transport from the lungs to the tissues by a factor of 70. Haemoglobin releases oxygen when there are cells with a low concentration of oxygen nearby. It then binds to the waste gas carbon dioxide, carrying it to the lungs to be excreted.

Leucocytes

There are several different kinds of leucocytes.

> **REMEMBER**
> The overall function of the leucocytes is to protect the body.

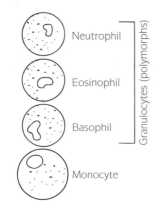

Figure 5.17 *The different types of white blood cells (leucocytes)*

Figure 5.18 *Platelets/thrombocytes*

Granulocyte structure
The majority (65–75%) of leucocytes are called granulocytes. Granulocytes, of which there are also several types, are so called because they contain many granules in their cytoplasm. They also have a large lobulated nucleus, the number of lobules increasing with age. Granulocytes are formed in the red bone marrow.

Granulocyte function
The function of granulocytes are phagocytosis and production of lysozyme, which destroys some bacteria and damaged tissue cells.

Monocyte structure
Monocytes are formed in lymph and constitute 2–4% of leucocytes. Monocytes are larger than other white blood cells and have a large round nucleus with a few granules in the cytoplasm.

Monocyte function
Monocytes are phagocytic cells.

Lymphocyte structure
Lymphocytes make up 20–25% of leucocytes. They have round nuclei and clear cytoplasm.

Lymphocyte function
Lymphocytes defend against antigens by producing antibodies.

Thrombocyte structure
Thrombocytes are minute rounded discs formed from bone fragments. They have clear cytoplasm and no nucleus.

Thrombocyte function
Thrombocytes or platelets play an important role in blood clotting. Platelets accumulate at the site of damage of a blood vessel, forming a temporary plug and releasing substances that cause the blood vessel to constrict, thus preventing blood loss. The formation of a permanent clot, made of the protein fibrin, involves a complicated series of reactions and requires vitamin K and calcium.

Progress Check

1   Explain what atria and ventricles are.
2   What is the role of the septum?
3   What is the function of the valves in the heart?
4   What is the main function of the heart?
5   What are the three layers surrounding the heart called?
6   Briefly explain the structure of blood.
7   List the different types of blood cells and their functions.
8   Briefly list the functions of blood.

Key Terms

You will need to know what these words mean. Go back through the section or check the glossary to find out.

◆ Circulation
◆ Erythrocyte
◆ Heart

◆ Leucocyte
◆ Thrombocyte

Test your knowledge of the heart and circulation on p. 110.

Lymphatic system

After studying this section you will be able to:

- describe how lymph is formed
- explain the function of the lymphatic system and how it works
- describe the structure of a lymph node
- list the main lymph nodes in the body

The lymphatic system consists of lymph nodes linked by lymph vessels that carry the fluid lymph around the body. It also includes other lymphatic tissue and the spleen and thymus gland. This system collects fluid and waste from the tissues and returns it to the blood after it has been purified in the numerous lymph nodes.

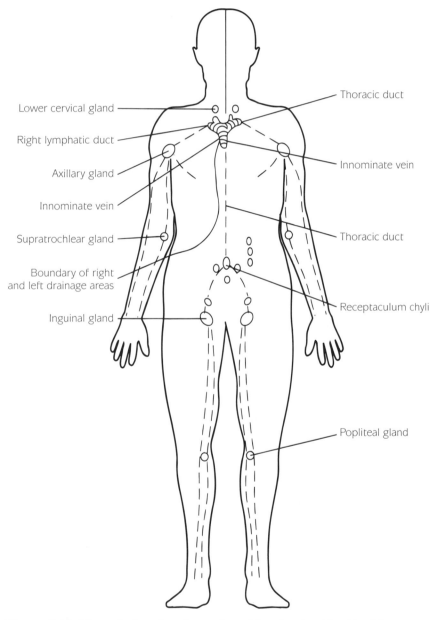

Figure 5.19 *The major lymph nodes are ducts. Note that the right side of the lymphatic system covers only the right side of the head, the right arm and the right side of the thorax. The left side of the lymphatic system covers the left side of the head, the left arm, the left side of the thorax, the abdomen and both legs*

Lymph

This is the fluid that circulates in this system. It is similar to blood plasma but contains less protein, less food material and more waste material. It contains no erythrocytes but plenty of lymphocytes.

How is lymph made?

Some of the plasma in the blood escapes by diffusion and filtration from the blood capillaries into the tissues. This fluid bathes the tissues and is at this stage known as tissue fluid. Tissue fluid is then collected by the lymphatic system. When the fluid is in the lymph vessel it is known as lymph.

Function of lymph

Lymph flows away from the tissues to the nearest lymph node, where all the waste or harmful substances it contains are filtered out. If the lymph is not totally filtered in one node then it can be carried to the next successive node, where more filtration will occur. This process will continue until the lymph is clear. Finally, at the end of its life, lymph returns back into the blood.

◆ Plasma moves from the capillaries into the tissues, forming tissue fluid.

◆ Some of the tissue fluid moves back into the blood; the rest enters the lymphatic system, forming lymph.

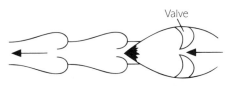

Figure 5.20 *Cross-section of a lymph vessel to show the presence of valves*

Lymph nodes

These structures are found in groups along the lymph drainage system. Each node has a fibrous coat that undulates and dips inwards into the node. The node contains reticular (net-like) fibres with spaces called sinuses and masses of lymphoid tissue.

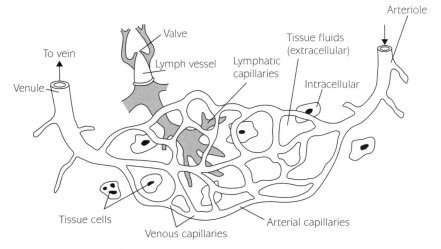

Figure 5.21 *An illustration to show how all blood vessels unite. Lymph vessels are blind ended and are buried between capillary networks to absorb waste products*

Lymph enters the lymph nodes via many afferent lymphatic vessels and leaves by fewer efferent lymphatic vessels after passing through the reticular sinuses.

Each node contains phagocytic cells which are able to remove particulate matter and germs from the lymph. The node also contains cells which produce lymphocytes (a type of white blood cell). These cells can remain in the node or can be shed into the lymph stream. Lymphocytes produce antibodies to fight invading antigens, such as bacteria. When the lymph node is actively producing these cells it may become inflamed, swollen and painful.

Lymph vessels
These start as blind-ending capillaries in between the tissues. The vessel wall is the same as a blood vessel wall, but more permeable. As the lymph is not under any pressure the lymph vessels have more valves to prevent backflow.

> **REMEMBER**
> All blood vessels unite at some point. Lymph vessels do not and thus have blind ends.

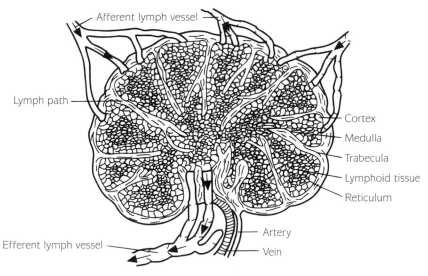

Figure 5.22 *Cross-section of a lymph node*

Where are the lymph nodes?
As well as the nodes shown in Figure 5.22, lymphoid tissue can also be found in the following places: tonsils, adenoids, parts of the intestine and nodules in the spleen. The thymus also contributes to lymphocyte production up until the age of about 13.

Lymph return into the blood
After the lymph has passed through the lymphatic system it is collected into the main lymph vessels or ducts. Lymph from the right side of the head and thorax and the right arm drains into the right lymphatic duct. Lymph from the rest of the body drains into the thoracic duct. These vessels open into the right and left subclavian veins respectively, in the neck.

Lacteals
These are small lymphatic capillaries which drain lymph from the small intestine. Fat absorbed from the small intestine passes into the lacteals, giving the lymph a milky appearance. Because of the fat it contains, the

lymph entering the thoracic duct is called chyle. Eventually the fat is returned to the blood.

Progress Check

1   What is lymph and where is it found?
2   What does lymph do?
3   How do lymph nodes purify lymph?
4   List the names of the main lymph nodes in the body and the two main ducts.
5   How is lymph finally returned to the blood?

Key Terms

You will need to know what these words and phrases mean. Go back through the section or check the glossary to find out.

◆   Lymph
◆   Lymph node
◆   Lymphatic system

Test your knowledge of the lymphatic system on p. 111.

Respiratory system

After studying this section you will be able to:

◆   understand the structure of the respiratory system
◆   explain how the respiratory system functions and why.

REMEMBER
Respiration is to do with the movement and use of gases.

The respiratory system consists of the bronchial tree and the lungs. The first part of the bronchial tree, the windpipe or trachea, subdivides into the right and left bronchi (entering the right and left lungs respectively). The bronchi further subdivide into smaller bronchioles, then terminal bronchioles, respiratory bronchioles, alveolar ducts and finally terminal end sacs or alveoli in the lungs.

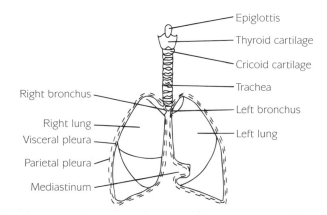

Figure 5.23 *A simplified diagram of the structure of the lungs*

Position of the lungs

The lungs are in the thorax (chest) region, surrounded by a serous membrane called the pleura. The parietal pleura is on the outside and the visceral pleura lies next to the lungs. In between the two membranes is the pleural cavity, which contains a little pleural fluid to prevent friction between the two layers when the lungs move.

Function of the lungs

Breathing is the function of the lungs. Although we can have control over our breathing, it is usually a reflex action, speeding up or slowing down depending on the body activity and the level of carbon dioxide in the blood.

How is breathing carried out?

Breathing in (inspiration)

Stimulation from the phrenic nerve causes contraction of the diaphragm. This increases the depth of the thorax. Stimulation from the intercostal nerve causes contraction of the intercostal muscles (between the ribs), increasing the diameter of the thorax.

As the volume of the thorax increases, the pressure decreases and becomes less than atmospheric. This pressure difference causes air to be sucked into the body.

Breathing out (expiration)

Expiration is caused by elastic recoil when the diaphragm and intercostal muscles relax, as a result of stimulation from the vagus nerve.

As the volume in the thoracic region decreases, the pressure increases, which forces air out of the lungs.

There is then a pause before the cycle begins again.

Muscles of respiration in quiet breathing

Quiet breathing is normal breathing. The muscles involved are the diaphragm and the intercostal muscles.

Muscles of respiration in forced breathing

Forced breathing occurs during exertion or when someone is taking deep breaths deliberately. It requires contraction of the abdominal, pectoral and sternocleidomastoid muscles.

Respiration

This is the process of taking oxygen into the body and removing carbon dioxide and water. Oxygen is required for the process of oxidation, which liberates energy from food. Carbon dioxide and water are the waste products of oxidation. Respiration involves breathing and the transport of gases around the body in the blood.

External respiration occurs in the lungs. Internal respiration occurs in the cells and tissues of the body.

External respiration

This is the means by which oxygen is obtained from the environment and carbon dioxide is excreted into the environment. It can also be called gaseous exchange.

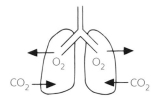

Figure 5.24 *Direction of movement of gases between the lungs and the body*

Figure 5.25 *Alveoli of lungs surrounded by a capillary network*

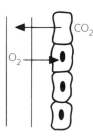

Figure 5.26 *Direction of movement of gases between the cells of the body and the blood*

Internal respiration

Internal respiration is a series of chemical processes occurring in every living cell to release energy needed for the body's activities. It requires oxygen. It can also be called tissue respiration.

The process of external respiration

1   When we inhale, air enters the lungs. One of the gases that air contains is oxygen, the gas our body needs to survive.
2   When the oxygen reaches the alveoli of the lungs it dissolves in the moisture of the membrane and, because of the concentration gradient between the lungs and the blood, the oxygen diffuses into the blood. At the same time, and for the same reason, carbon dioxide diffuses out of the blood into the lungs to be exhaled.
3   When the oxygen enters the blood some is carried round the body in the red bloods cells and some dissolves in the plasma of the blood.
4   Oxygen is taken round the body in the blood to areas where it is needed.

The process of internal or tissue respiration

Glucose from food, and oxygen, diffuse into the tissues from the blood. In the tissues glucose is broken down in the presence of oxygen. The waste product carbon dioxide is formed, and water, heat and energy are also released.

Control of respiration

Respiration is partly under the control of the brain and nerves and partly under chemical control. When the level of carbon dioxide in the blood increases, this is detected by structures called chemoreceptors in the blood vessels. As a result, the chemoreceptors cause the rate of breathing to be increased, so increasing the rate at which carbon dioxide is expelled from the body.

Progress Check

1   What is the thorax region?
2   What are the different parts of the bronchial tree?
3   What are the terms for breathing in and breathing out?
4   What is the diaphragm?
5   Where are the intercostal muscles?
6   What are the main differences between internal and external respiration?
7   How is respiration controlled?

Key Terms

You will need to know what these words and phrases mean. Go back through the section or check the glossary to find out.

♦   Carbon dioxide
♦   Diaphragm
♦   Lungs
♦   Oxygen
♦   Respiratory system

Test your knowledge of the respiratory system on p. 112.

Excretory system

After studying this section you will be able to:

- explain what excretion is
- describe the excretory organs and the products they excrete
- list the functions of the kidneys
- understand the way urine production is controlled.

Because the kidneys balance the water and metabolic waste materials not lost in other ways, they, with their ducts, are called the excretory system.

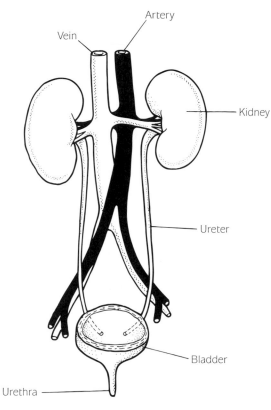

Figure 5.27 *Excretory system*

The excretory system consists of:

- two kidneys
- two ureters
- the urinary bladder
- the urethra.

What is excretion?

Excretion is the process of removal of waste and harmful substances from the body.

Table 5.1 shows the substances we excrete.

Location of the kidneys

The kidneys lie against the back wall of the abdomen behind the liver and stomach, covered by the peritoneum and embedded in fat.

> **REMEMBER**
> The kidneys are not protected by the skeleton.

Excretory products	Organs excreted from				
	Kidney	Skin	Liver	Lungs	Alimentary canal
Urea	*	*			
Salt	*	*			*
Water	*	*			*
Residues of food					*
Heat		*		*	
Carbon dioxide				*	
Bile pigments			*		

Table 5.1 *Substances we excrete*

The function of the kidneys

The general function is to purify the blood of harmful substances by:

- excretion of metabolic waste, especially urea, in the form of urine
- osmoregulation, i.e. regulation of the composition of body fluids
- elimination of excess salts, maintaining ionic balance
- maintenance of acid–alkali balance
- secretion. The cells of the juxtaglomerular filtrate produce two hormones, renin and erythropoietin. Renin is involved in the regulation of blood pressure. Erythropoietin controls the production of erythrocytes by red bone marrow.

The bladder

The bladder is a very elastic, extensible sac.

Location of the bladder

The bladder lies in front of the pelvis and the ureters curve around the lower part of the abdomen to meet it.

The function of the bladder

The function of the bladder is to act as a temporary store for urine. The bladder can hold up to a pint of urine, but it is usually emptied when just under half full.

Location of the urethra

The urethra of the female is short (4 cm), and opens in front of the vagina. The urethra of the male is joined by the reproductive ducts and is elongated to open at the tip of the penis (approximately 20 cm).

Urine

Urine is the waste product from the kidneys, containing:

- water (96%)
- salts (2%)
- nitrogenous waste, chiefly in the form of urea (2%).

Variations in the composition of urine reflect the ability of the kidneys to regulate the water and salt content of the body fluids.

Homeostasis

Homeostasis is the maintenance of a constant internal environment within the cells of the body. For cells to function effectively, the following variables must be maintained within a narrow range:

1   pH
2   temperature
3   osmotic pressure (balance between fluid and particles)
4   carbon dioxide levels in the blood.
5   ionic and chemical composition
6   waste products
7   glucose level.

Control of the water balance of the body

The water balance of the body is controlled by changing the permeability of the collecting duct in the nephron. This regulates the amount of water reabsorbed into the body. Antidiuretic hormone (vasopressin), produced by the posterior lobe of the pituitary gland, can increase the permeability of the collecting duct.

Antidiuretic hormone (ADH)

When ADH is released the urine becomes more concentrated because the hormone opens the pores in the collecting duct, allowing water to be reabsorbed into the body. When ADH is absent the urine is dilute because the pores of the collecting duct have not been opened so that no water can be reabsorbed: all the water passing through the kidney is excreted in the urine.

Our brain detects how much water there is in our bodies and will release ADH if there is not enough. The amount of ADH released depends on the amount of water that needs to be reabsorbed.

Diuretics increase the volume of urine produced by reducing the quantity of water that is reabsorbed, thus reducing the amount of water in the body.

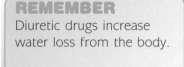

REMEMBER
Diuretic drugs increase water loss from the body.

Progress Check

1   What is excretion?
2   List all the products excreted from the body.
3   What are the functions of the kidneys?
4   What is the composition of urine?
5   What is homeostasis?
6   What is antidiuretic hormone and what does it do?
7   Where does antidiuretic hormone come from?
8   What does the term diuretic mean?

Key Terms

You will need to know what these words and phrases mean. Go back through the section or check the glossary to find out.

◆   Antidiuretic hormone
◆   Bladder
◆   Excretory system
◆   Kidneys

Test your knowledge of the excretory system on p. 113.

Digestive system and nutrition

After studying this section you will be able to:

- understand the structure of the digestive system
- list the elements of a healthy diet.

The digestive system is concerned with nutrition, which includes ingestion, digestion, absorption, assimilation and egestion.

Digestion

Digestion is the process by which food is broken down. There are two types:

- mechanical digestion (chewing)
- chemical digestion (hydrolysis by enzymes).

Structure of the alimentary canal

Digestion takes place in the alimentary canal, consisting of:

- buccal cavity (mouth): ingestion, mastication and digestion of carbohydrate
- pharynx: swallowing
- oesophagus, links pharynx to stomach
- stomach: digestion of protein; mixing up all food; temporary reservoir for food
- small intestine (duodenum, jejunum, ileum): completion of digestion
- large intestine (caecum, appendix, colon and rectum): water absorption
- rectum: formation and storage of faeces
- anus: egestion and control of egestion.

The salivary glands, pancreas and liver are organs associated with the digestive system.

Peritoneum

The peritoneum is the largest serous membrane of the body. It consists of a closed sac within the abdominal cavity. The outer layer is called the parietal layer and the inner layer is called the visceral layer and in between them is serous fluid. These are protective layers that allow movement of the digestive organs without the build-up of heat.

Sphincter

A sphincter is a circular band of muscle that controls the opening and closing of an organ. Contraction of the sphincter closes the organ and relaxation opens it. In the digestive system sphincters are found at the entrance and exit of the stomach and in the anus.

The functions of the stomach

The stomach has several functions:

- to store food temporarily
- to churn up food
- to release acid, aiding digestion and neutralising alkali from the mouth
- to digest protein
- to absorb alcohol.

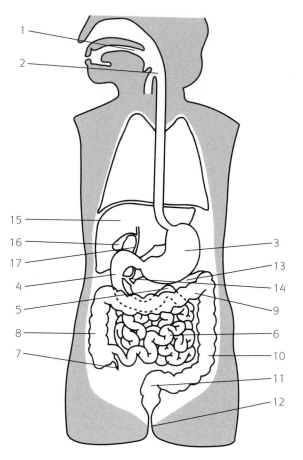

Figure 5.28 *Digestive system*: 1, *pharynx*; 2, *oesophagus*; 3, *stomach*; 4, *duodenum*; 5, *jejunum*; 6, *ileum*; 7, *appendix*; 8, *ascending colon*; 9, *transverse colon*; 10, *descending colon*; 11, *rectum*; 12, *anus*; 13, *pancreas*; 14, *pancreatic duct*; 15, *liver*; 16, *gall bladder*; 17, *bile duct*

Nutrition

Nutrition concerns the digestion of food and how the food is used by the body for metabolism, e.g. growth, maintenance and repair.

Components of a balanced diet

A balanced diet contains all of the following elements:

- carbohydrate
- protein
- fat
- vitamins
- minerals
- roughage
- water.

> **REMEMBER**
> These seven essential nutrients need to be taken in the correct quantities.

Carbohydrate

Carbohydrates are foods made from carbon, hydrogen and oxygen. Examples include sugars, starches and cellulose and related material.

Carbohydrates provide:

- energy and heat
- roughage.

Protein

Proteins are made of carbon, hydrogen, oxygen, nitrogen, sulphur and phosphorus.

The functions of protein are:

- growth and repair of the body
- synthesis of hormones, enzymes, plasma proteins and antibodies
- provision of energy if there is not enough carbohydrate or fat in the body.

Fat

Fat is also made of carbon, hydrogen and oxygen. Fat is required for:

- storage of energy in the body
- production of energy and fat
- correct function of some organs in the body, e.g. kidneys and eyes
- transport of fat-soluble vitamins (i.e. vitamins A, D, E, K)
- formation of part of the nerve sheath and sebum in the sebaceous gland
- formation of cholesterol and steroid hormones.

Vitamins

Vitamins are chemical compounds that are essential for health. Certain chemical reactions in the body cannot take place without them.

Minerals

Mineral salts are inorganic compounds necessary for all bodily processes. Each mineral has many functions.

Roughage

Roughage is the indigestible part of the diet. It is required to:

- give bulk to the diet and help satisfy the appetite, mainly because of the cellulose it contains
- stimulate peristalsis, the movement of food through the intestine
- stimulate bowel movements, helping to prevent some gastrointestinal disorders.

REMEMBER
A lot of people lack roughage in their diet.

Water

Water is made up of hydrogen and oxygen. It is needed to:

- provide a moist environment for the body (about two-thirds of the body weight is water)
- dilute and moisten food
- assist in the control of body temperature
- form blood and tissue fluid
- dilute waste products and poisonous substances in the body
- contribute to the formation of urine and faeces.

We can survive only a few days without water.

Foods containing the components of a balanced diet
Carbohydrates

Carbohydrates are found in cane or beet sugar, milk, bread, potatoes, cereals, fruit and animal blood.

Protein

Proteins can be divided into two classes, found in the following foods.

- Complete proteins: meat, fish, milk, eggs, soya beans.
- Incomplete proteins: margarine and vegetable oils.

Fat

Fats can be divided into animal and vegetable fats.

- Animal fat: milk, cheese, butter, eggs, meat and oily fish.
- Vegetable fat: margarine and vegetable oils.

Vitamins

There are many vitamins and they are found in the following foods.

- Vitamin A: cream, eggs, fish oil, milk, cheese, butter, green vegetables, fruit, carrots.
- Vitamin D: eggs, fish oil, cheese, butter.
- Vitamin E: milk, butter, peanuts, lettuce, wheatgerm, whole cereal.
- Vitamin K: fish, liver, leafy green vegetables, fruit.
- Vitamin B1: nuts, yeast, egg yolk, liver, legumes, meat, germ of cereal.
- Vitamin B2: leafy green vegetables, yeast, milk, liver, eggs, kidney, cheese, roe.
- Folic acid: liver, kidney, leafy green vegetables, yeast.
- Nicotinic acid: liver, cheese, yeast, cereal, eggs, fish, peanuts.
- Vitamin B_6: egg yolk, peas, beans, soya beans, yeast, meat, liver.
- Vitamin B_{12}: liver, meat, eggs, fermented liqueurs.
- Pantothenic acid: egg yolk, liver, tomatoes.
- Vitamin C: blackcurrants, oranges, grapefruit, lemons, rosehips, green vegetables.

Minerals

The following foods are good sources of the most common minerals.

- Calcium: milk, cheese, eggs, green vegetables, some fish.
- Phosphorus: cheese, oatmeal, liver, kidney.
- Sodium: most foods, fish, meat, eggs, milk, table salt.
- Potassium: widely in all foods.
- Iron: liver, kidney, beef, egg yolk, wholemeal bread, green vegetables.
- Iodine: salt water fish, table salt.

Progress Check

1 Draw and label the digestive system.
2 List the seven elements of a healthy diet and say where each can be obtained.
3 Explain the reasons the seven elements are required.
4 Define the following terms:
   Mastication
   Sphincter
   Enzyme
   Peristalsis

Test your knowledge of the digestive system and nutrition on p. 114.

Nervous system

After studying this section you will be able to:

- list the parts of the central and peripheral system
- describe the different types of peripheral nerves and what they do
- understand the effects of the subconscious or involuntary nervous system.

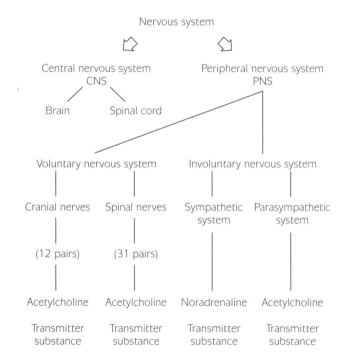

Figure 5.29 *Nervous system*

The nervous system is the body's control centre, rapidly conducting messages around the body. The nervous system deals with all the quick reactions and changes in the body.

The nervous system consists of:

- central nervous system (CNS), which consists of the brain and spinal cord
- peripheral nervous system (PNS), which consists of the nerves and nerve endings and includes voluntary and involuntary systems.

Function of the nervous system

The function of the nervous system is the rapid conduction of messages from the body to the CNS via sensory nerves and from the CNS to the body (PNS) via motor nerves.

Properties of nervous tissue

Nervous tissue has the following properties:

- irritability – the ability to sense things
- conductivity – the ability to carry impulses around the body.

Brain and spinal cord

The brain and spinal cord are one continuous structure. The brain is situated in and protected by the cranium, and the spinal cord is situated in and protected by the vertebral column.

The peripheral nervous system

This is made up of all the nerves around the body, outside of the brain and spinal cord.

Sensory (afferent) nerve

This is a type of nerve cell, or neuron, that carries a sensory impulse from different regions of the body to the brain and spinal cord to be interpreted.

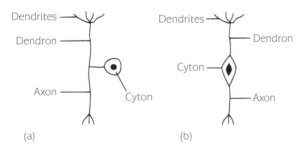

Figure 5.30 (a) *A unipolar sensory nerve* (b) *A bipolar sensory nerve*

Motor (efferent) nerve

This is a type of nerve cell, or neuron, that carries a motor impulse from the brain or spinal cord to regions of the body, to bring about some change.

Motor point

This is the point where a motor nerve enters a muscle.

Involuntary or autonomic nervous system

This part of the nervous system controls involuntary functions. The autonomic nervous system operates below the level of consciousness, and the functions it controls often act to protect or defend the body.

The involuntary nervous system is made up of:

1 the sympathetic nervous system
2 the parasympathetic nervous system.

Functions of the sympathetic and parasympathetic systems

The sympathetic and parasympathetic systems have opposing effects.

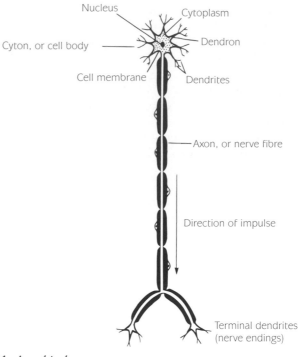

Figure 5.31 *A multipolar motor nerve*

System	Sympathetic stimulation	Parasympathetic stimulation
Cardiovascular	1 Increases the rate and force of the heart beat 2 Increases the blood supply to heart muscle 3 Dilates blood vessels 4 Increases the volume of circulating blood 5 Raises blood pressure 6 Slows down digestion, raising the volume of available blood	Has the opposite effect of sympathetic stimulation in each case
Respiratory	Dilates bronchi allowing more oxygen into lung, and more carbon dioxide out	Constricts bronchi
Digestive	1 Liver converts more glycogen to glucose making more available energy 2 Stimulates the release of adrenaline and noradrenaline to sustain sympathetic stimulation effects 3 Contracts the stomach and small intestine and delays digestion 4 Inhibits micturition and defecation as a result of contraction of the urethral and anal sphincters 5 Relaxes the bladder wall	1 Increases the production of insulin and pancreatic juice in the pancreas 2 Increases digestive absorption and movement of food 3 Relaxes urethral and anal sphincters 4 Contracts the bladder wall and anal muscles, causing micturation and defecation
Eye	1 Dilates pupil 2 Opens eyes wider	1 Constricts pupil 2 Eyes close a little
Skin	1 Increases sweat and heat loss 2 Contracts arrector pili (causing 'goose bumps') 3 Constricts surface blood vessels, reducing heat loss	There is no parasympathetic supply to the skin
Genitalia	Causes generalised vasoconstriction	Vasodilation, erection of penis

Table 5.2 *Functions of the sympathetic and parasympathetic systems*

1   What are the differences between afferent and efferent nerves?
2   What are the parts of the central nervous system?
3   What areas of the body are affected by the involuntary nervous system?
4   What is the main difference between the sympathetic and parasympathetic parts of the involuntary nervous system?

Key Terms

You will need to know what these words and phrases mean. Go back through the section or check the glossary to find out.

◆   Central nervous system
◆   Involuntary
◆   Nerve
◆   Nervous system
◆   Peripheral nervous system
◆   Voluntary

Test your knowledge of the nervous system on p. 115.

Reproductive system

After studying this section you will be able to:

◆   describe the male and female reproductive organs
◆   understand the process of fertilisation.

The reproductive system is the system that enables us to have children.

Structure of the reproductive system
Male
The male reproductive system consists of two testes, associated glands and a system of ducts which eventually open on the tip of the penis.

The testes (gonads) develop in the abdomen. Just before birth they descend into the groin in the scrotum. Each testicle is an ovoid body containing many seminiferous tubules bound into lobules by connective tissue. Between the lobules lie interstitial cells. The walls of the tubules produce spermatozoa and the interstitial cells produce testerosterone, which is responsible for secondary sexual characteristics.

Female
The female reproductive system consists of two ovaries, the fallopian tubes and the uterus (womb).

The ovaries are two small ovoid structures, one on either side of the uterus. They are suspended from the ovarian ligament at the point at which the fallopian tubes are joined to the uterus. The ovary has an inner medulla of loose connective tissue containing cells which are thought to be the same as the interstitial cells of the testes and an outer cortex of stroma containing ovarian follicles which produce the ova or eggs. The tunica albuginea is the outer layer of the ovaries. It is covered by a simple layer of cuboidal epithelium called germinal epithelium.

The ovaries produce androgens.

Process of sexual reproduction

Reproduction involves the following stages.

1   Sexual excitement of the male results in erection of the penis.
2   Ejaculation in the male releases semen, consisting of sperm suspended in mucus and a milky fluid from the prostate gland. (It is the prostatic fluid that stimulates the sperm to swim.) Most of the ejaculated fluid comes from the seminal vesicle.
3   When sexual excitement reaches a peak in the female, peristalsis occurs in the reproductive tract, which may help to carry the sperm into the fallopian tubes. In this way the sperm are propelled efficiently to areas where the ova are found.
4   Fertilisation usually takes place in the upper regions of the fallopian tubes, involving the entry of a sperm nucleus into the secondary oocyte.
5   The oocyte is usually surrounded by many small cells called the corona radiata.
6   As a spermatozoon reaches the oocyte, the acrosomal cap of the spermatozoon dissolves, secreting the enzyme hyaluronidase. This enzyme disperses the corona radiata.
7   The spermatozoon adheres to the surface of the oocyte by antigen-antibody reaction.
8   When the acrosomal filament contacts the cytoplasm of the oocyte, the oocyte extends around it, engulfing the sperm head in the fertilisation cone, changing the oocyte to an ovum.
9   A fertilisation membrane now forms around the ovum (zona pellucida), preventing the entry of further sperm.
10 A female pronucleus now forms around the ovum and the sperm head swells to form another pronucleus; the two pronuclei merge.
11 Virtually as soon as this happens, spindles form (cleavage spindles), along which the chromosomes arrange themselves.

REMEMBER
Meiosis is a much more complex form of cell division than mitosis.

The process is called meiosis. This is a special form of cell division that reduces the number of chromosomes in each case from 46 to 23, thus ensuring that when an ovum and spermatozoon fuse the cell so formed (and thus all future cells of the embryo) contains the correct number of chromosomes.

The urethra, a common genitourinary duct, runs through the penis. When unaroused the penis is short. Sexual stimulation causes the arteries in the penis to become distended with blood and the erectile tissue to stiffen. Erection enables the semen to be injected into the vagina of the female during copulation.

1 What are the names of the male and female reproduction organs?
2 Where are the ovarian follicles in a woman?
3 Where are the spermatozoa made in the male?
4 Where are the eggs made in the female?
5 Briefly state the main stages in the process of fertilisation.

Key Terms

You will need to know what these words and phrases mean. Go back through the section or check the glossary to find out.

♦ Gonads
♦ Reproductive system

Test your knowledge of the reproduction system on p. 116.

Mammary glands

After studying this section you will be able to:

♦ describe the structure of the mammary glands
♦ understand the function of the mammary glands
♦ understand how the mammary glands change and why.

Structure of the mammary glands

The mammary glands consist of three types of tissue:

♦ glandular tissue (alveoli)
♦ fibrous tissue
♦ fatty tissue.

Function of the mammary glands

These glands are active only during pregnancy and after the birth of the baby, when they produce milk.

The childbearing role

In the early stages of pregnancy the breasts enlarge slightly and the areola around the nipple darkens. This colour fades a little after childbirth. The actual structure of the breasts starts to change under the influence of the increased amounts of oestrogen and progesterone secreted from the placenta. The amount of adipose tissue in the breasts increases, the blood circulation increases and the breasts appear full and heavy.

The breast feeding role

It is not known if breast feeding causes the breasts to change in shape. The greatest difference in breast structure and appearance occurs during pregnancy as a result of hormonal stimulation over which we have no control.

> **REMEMBER**
> During pregnancy and after childbirth the hormone balance is very different from normal.

The flow of milk after birth is initiated by suckling. In the absence of suckling the flow of milk soon ceases, but the breasts may be distended with milk for some time, causing discomfort.

On termination of natural lactation, the breast resumes its resting condition, any remaining milk is absorbed and the alveoli shrink. The adipose tissue may reduce or be used up by the body for its needs. The connective tissue and collagen fibres change, so giving the breast a soft deflated appearance. The suspensory ligaments may become less supportive causing the breasts to droop.

Menopause

The role of the breast as a mammary gland is now finished. The breast decreases in size and the ducts degenerate and almost completely disappear. The breast attachment to the chest wall may become narrow and the actual breast may hang down below the level of attachment. Not all women have a droopy bust after the menopause, but firmness requires regular exercise.

Progress Check

1 What different types of tissue are mammary glands made of?
2 When do the mammary glands first become active?
3 What stimulates the activity of the mammary glands?
4 How do the mammary glands change after breast feeding?
5 Why do the mammary glands change in the menopause?

Key Terms

You will need to know what these words and phrases mean. Go back through the section or check the glossary to find out.

♦ Lactation
♦ Mammary glands

Test your knowledge of the mammary glands on p. 117.

1   Link the part of the cell with the correct description.

Nucleus   The basic unit of life.
Centrosome   Acts like the brain of the cell, essential for cell
             reproduction.
Cell   A region of dense cytoplasm always found near to
             the nucleus.

2   On average how much water does cytoplasm contain?

a) 75%
b) 50%
c) 90%
d) 99%

3   Put numbers by the following stages of mitosis to show the order
    in which they occur.

____ Interphase
____ Metaphase
____ Prophase
____ Telophase
____ Anaphase

4   How many pairs of chromosomes are in a healthy cell?

a) 32.
b) 23.
c) 46.
d) 64.

5   Choose the correct definition of mitosis:

a) Cell division producing three identical cells.
b) Cell/nuclear division producing two similar daughter cells.
c) Cell/nuclear division producing two identical daughter cells.

On the skeletal system

1   Tick to show whether the following statement is true or false.

The tibia is the main shin bone.

True   False
☐   ☐

2   Which of the following sentences is the correct definition of the axial skeleton and which of the appendicular skeleton?

a) The appendicular skeleton forms the centre of the body, i.e. vertebrae and ribs.
b) The legs and the pelvis form the appendicular skeleton.
c) The appendicular skeleton forms the central line of the body and is not freely moveable.
d) The appendicular skeleton comprises the bones of the shoulder, arm and hand, pelvis, leg and foot and allows free and easy movement.
d) The axial skeleton forms the central line of the body, cranium, vertebral column and thoracic cage, and is not freely moveable.

3   What is the correct composition of bone?

a) 45% water and 55% solids (30% organic matrix, 70% bone salts).
b) 40% water and 60% solids (70% organic matrix, 30% bone salts).
c) 50% water and 50% solids (30% organic matrix, 70% bone salts).

1   Group together the terms which refer to the same type of muscle.

Voluntary
Cardiac
Visceral
Striated
Smooth
Involuntary
Skeletal

2   Indicate whether the following statements are true or false.

a)   Skeletal muscles are under the control of our will.

True   False
☐   ☐

b)   The contraction of involuntary muscle is slower than skeletal muscle.

True   False
☐   ☐

c)   Cardiac muscle is controlled by the will of the individual.

True   False
☐   ☐

3   Which type of muscle suffers from cramp?

a)   Striated.
b)   Smooth.
c)   Involuntary.
d)   Visceral.
e)   Cardiac.

4   Which is the main protein in muscle?

a)   Myosin.
b)   Mosyn.
c)   Melanin.

On the heart and circulation

1 Link the linings of the heart with the correct definition.

Myocardium	The inner layer of the heart continuous with the blood vessels.
Pericardium	The middle thick layer of cardiac muscle.
Endocardium	The outer covering forming a double-layered serous membrane.

2 Fill in the gaps by selecting one word or phrase from each column below.

The heart is a _____ muscular organ about the size of _____ .

oval	a tennis ball
round	a clenched fist
cone-shaped	the palm of your hand
diamond-shaped	a golf ball
heart-shaped	a football

3 Link the following blood cells' names with the function they perform.

white blood cells	thrombocytes	carry oxygen
platelets	red blood cells	protect the body
erythrocytes	leucocytes	cause blood clotting

4 What is haemoglobin required for?

a) Making blood red.
b) Making oxygen.
c) Protection.
d) Transporting oxygen.

1 Which of the following structures are part of the lymphatic system?

Lymph nodes ☐

Blood vessels ☐

Spleen ☐

Liver ☐

Thyroid ☐

2 What happens to the lymph fluid at the end of its cycle?

a) It is excreted by the body.
b) It is destroyed by the body.
c) It is put back into the blood.
d) It goes around the cycle again.

3 Indicate whether the following statement is true or false.

Lymph fluid contains lymphocytes but no erythrocytes.

True ☐   False ☐

4 Which of the following functions take place in a lymph node?

a) Phagocytosis.
b) Production of erythrocytes and lymphocytes.
c) Production of lymphocytes and antibodies.
d) Filtering of lymph.
e) Production of lymph.

5 On which side of the body are the main lymphatic ducts?

Thoracic duct

Right ☐   Left ☐

Lymphatic duct

Right ☐   Left ☐

On the respiratory
system

1   Put the following parts of the respiratory tract into the order in
    which they occur.

    _____ Alveoli
    _____ Trachea
    _____ Bronchus
    _____ Bronchioles

2   Which type of membrane is the pleura around the lungs?

    a) Mucous.
    b) Serous.
    c) Synovial.

3   Put the following statements into the correct group.

    Inspiration   Expiration

    Caused by elastic recoil of the diaphragm.
    Due to stimulation from the vagus nerve.
    Due to stimulation from the phrenic and intercostal nerves.
    Increased volume inside thorax and decreased pressure.
    Negative pressure sucks air into the body.

4   Which gas do we excrete from the lungs?

    a) Nitrogen.
    b) Hydrogen.
    c) Carbon.
    d) Carbon dioxide.
    e) Carbon oxide.

5   Fill in the gaps with the words below (you will not need to use all
    the words).

    Control of respiration is part _____ and part
    _____.

    Muscular
    Nervous
    Heat
    pH
    Chemical

1 Which of the following is the correct definition of excretion?

   a) The removal of harmful substances from the body.
   b) The removal of harmful substances from the blood.
   c) The removal of waste and harmful substances from the organs.
   d) The removal of waste and harmful substances from the body.

2 Fill the table in with ticks or stars to indicate which products are excreted from which organs.

Excretory product	Organs excreted from				
	Kidneys	Skin	Liver	Lungs	Alimentary canal
Urea					
Salt					
Water					
Residues of food					
Heat					
Carbon dioxide					
Bile pigments					

3 Choose the most typical composition of urine.

   a) 95% water, 3% nitrogenous waste, 2% salts.
   b) 96% water, 3% nitrogenous waste, 1% salts.
   c) 96% water, 2% nitrogenous waste, 2% salts.

4 Indicate whether the following statement is true or false.

Homeostasis is the maintenance of a constant external environment for the cells of the body.

True   False
☐   ☐

5 Which of the following is an effect of antidiuretic hormone?

   a) The production of concentrated urine.
   b) The production of dilute urine.
   c) The stoppage of the production of urine.

On the digestive system and nutrition

1   Indicate the order in which the following stages occur.

_____ Assimilation
_____ Ingestion
_____ Egestion
_____ Absorption
_____ Digestion

2   Which of the following statements correctly describe the peritoneum?

a)   The largest serous membrane.
b)   A serous membrane.
c)   The largest synovial membrane.
d)   A mucous membrane.

a)   Surrounds the thorax and abdominal cavity.
b)   Surrounds the abdominal cavity.
c)   Consists of a closed sac within the abdominal cavity.

a)   Allows free and easy movement of the digestive organs.
b)   Protects the digestive organs.
c)   Allows movement of the digestive organs without the build-up of heat.

3   Which of the following is not a function of the stomach?

a)   To digest proteins.
b)   To digest carbohydrates.
c)   Temporary store of food.
d)   To neutralise hormones.
e)   To neutralise alkali from the mouth.

4   How many elements are needed in a balanced diet?

a)   5.
b)   6.
c)   7.
d)   8.

5   Link the following nutrients with their function.

Carbohydrate   Provides energy and heat.
Protein   Stores energy in the body.
Fat   Used for growth and repair.

1   What are the properties of nervous tissue?

   a) Irritability and transport.
   b) Calmness and conductivity.
   c) Calmness and transport.
   d) Irritability and conductivity.

2   Circle the correct word.

The nervous system deals with quick / slow reactions and changes
in the body.

3   Indicate whether the following statement is true or false.

We have full control over every part of the nervous system.

True   False

☐   ☐

4   Which regions are affected by the autonomic nervous system?

   a) Respiratory, eyes, skin, genitalia, reproduction.
   b) Digestive, genitalia, eyes, cardiovascular, brain, skin.
   c) Cardiovascular, respiratory, digestive, eyes, skin, genitalia.

5   Tick the parts that make up the autonomic nervous system.

Sympathetic   ☐

Unsympathetic   ☐

Paraunsympathetic ☐

Parasympathetic   ☐

On the reproductive system

1 Indicate whether the following statement is true or false.

The testes develop in the abdomen and descend into the scrotum just before birth.

True   False

☐   ☐

2 Where is the female ovum or egg made?

a) In the womb.
b) In the uterus.
c) In the fallopian tube.
d) In the ovary.

3 Which of the following stimulates the sperm to swim?

a) The warmth inside the vagina.
b) The drop in temperature inside the vagina.
c) The fluid from the testes.
d) The fluid from the prostate gland.
e) The fluid from the seminal vesicle.

4 Fill in the gap.

The ovum reproduces by the process of _____.

5 Which system controls the reproductive process?

a) The nervous system.
b) The endocrine system.

1   Of which types of tissues are the mammary glands composed?

a)   Glandular ☐

b)   Muscular ☐

c)   Fatty ☐

d)   Fibrous ☐

e)   Endocrine ☐

2   What initiates the flow of milk in the mammary glands after birth?

a)   Hormonal release.
b)   Nervous stimulation.
c)   The baby suckling.

3   Indicate whether the following statement is true or false.

It is not known whether breast feeding changes the shape of the
mammary glands.

True   False
☐   ☐

4   Which of the following points are true?

                                                              True False

The mammary glands become inactive at menopause.   ☐   ☐

The mammary glands always shrink at menopause.   ☐   ☐

The mammary glands change shape at menopause.   ☐   ☐

5   When do the mammary glands become active?

a)   At puberty.
b)   At pregnancy.

Part II

Equipment

ELECTRICAL CURRENTS

6

After studying this chapter you will be able to:

◆ describe the structure of an atom
◆ understand the different types of electrical current
◆ describe the different reactions caused by electrical currents
◆ recognise a range of electrical terms and be able to define them.

There are two types of electrical currents:

◆ alternating current (a.c.)
◆ direct current (d.c.)

Alternating current

This type of current constantly changes direction; it moves from negative to positive and back to negative and so on. Each current movement from neutral into negative, then into positive, then back to neutral, is called an oscillation or a cycle. For this reason an alternating current may also be called an oscillating current.

The number of times an alternating current moves from negative to positive per second is called the frequency. The unit of frequency is the hertz (hz), e.g. 500 cycles/second is 500 Hz. The frequency of an alternating current can be changed from a low frequency to a high frequency by increasing the number of oscillations per second.

Alternating current, as a result of the friction caused by the oscillations, can produce heat. Short-wave diathermy epilation treatments use a high-frequency alternating current to cause the production of heat.

The heat builds up in the hair follicle like a tear drop around the lower part of the needle and follicle. The area covered by the current is called the high-frequency field.

Heat will cauterise anything with which it comes into contact, thus destroying it.

Direct current

This current never changes direction; it continuously flows from negative to positive. Direct current requires positive and negative electrodes between which the current flows to complete the circuit. The positive electrode is called the anode. The negative electrode is called the cathode.

All the time the current is flowing it causes chemical changes at the electrodes.

When an electrolyte is present the anode ⊕ will attract anything negative ⊖ towards itself as they are opposite. The negative ion is called the

> **REMEMBER**
> Alternating current is the type of electricity at the power points in buildings.

> **REMEMBER**
> Diathermy electro-epilation works using a high-frequency alternating current.

anion. The cathode $\ominus$ will attract anything positive towards itself as they are opposite. The positive ion is called the cation.

In galvanic treatment the chemical change around the anode is the production of acid and the chemical change around the cathode is the production of alkali.

Galvanic electrolysis uses the production of chemicals to destroy the hair follicle.

The negative electrode, the cathode, is the needle and the client then holds as a saturator the positive pole. Because of the salt water in the body the galvanic current flows through the body, causing the chemical changes at the two electrodes.

Salt water is water containing sodium chloride (NaCl), i.e. salt. Na is the chemical symbol for sodium and Cl is the chemical symbol for chlorine. In salt, sodium is present as a cation (i.e. Na^+) and chlorine is present as an anion, chloride (Cl^-).

Water is composed of two molecules of hydrogen and one of oxygen; its chemical formula is H_2O.

When acted upon by a galvanic current, salt water is split into an acid at the anode and an alkali at the cathode. NaCl and H_2O are split into separate atoms (Na, Cl, H, H and O). They rejoin as HCl (hydrochloric acid) at the anode and NaOH (sodium hydroxide) at the cathode. Sodium hydroxide (NaOH) builds up around the needle in the follicle and has very destructive effects.

Blend

When carrying out a blend electro-epilation treatment, a.c. and d.c. are used, combining heat and chemicals.

Electrical safety precautions to be followed

● Buy well-made apparatus which complies with the British Standard of safety.
● Make sure that all equipment is earthed.
● Ensure that the equipment is correctly wired to the plug.
● Place the machine/epilator on a solid stable trolley.
● Position the trolley near the operator: continuous movement could result in loose wiring.
● Do not leave leads trailing on the floor or dangling over trolley edge to prevent the machine being accidentally pulled over.
● Regularly clean and maintain equipment to ensure maximum working efficiency and client safety.
● Have equipment checked annually by an electrician; this is now a legal and insurance requirement.

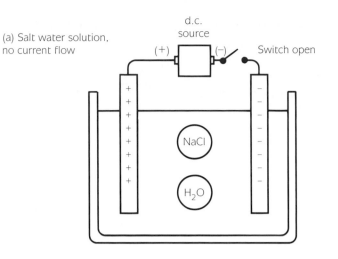

(a) Salt water solution, no current flow

(b) Solution ionises with passage of direct current

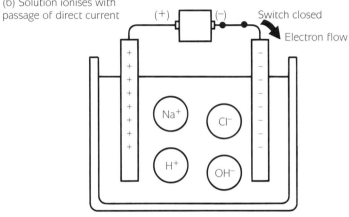

(c) At the cathode $H^+ + H^+ \rightarrow H_2$(gas) and $Na^+ + OH^- \rightarrow$ NaOH(lye)

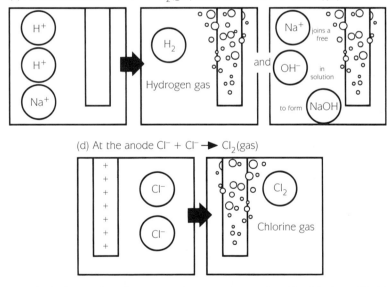

(d) At the anode $Cl^- + Cl^- \rightarrow Cl_2$(gas)

Figure 6.1 *Galvanic electrolysis in a salt water solution (model of the hair follicle)*

Basic electricity: useful terms

Alternating current	An oscillating current changing direction of flow from ⊖ to ⊕ constantly
Amperage	The strength of an electric current measured in amperes (amps)
Anode	Positive electrode
Atom	The smallest quantity of an element which can take part in a chemical reaction
Battery	A power pack capable of producing d.c.
Cathode	Negative electrode
Circuit breaker	A safety device that will break to prevent the flow of current when too much is flowing. A circuit breaker, unlike a fuse, can be reset when the overload has been removed from the circuit
Conductor	Material that will allow the easy flow of electrical current through it, e.g. metal
Direct current	An uninterrupted current that only flows from ⊖ to ⊕
Fuse	A safety device found in a plug to prevent too much current flowing through a circuit and overloading it
Insulator	Material that will prevent the flow of an electrical current through it, e.g. rubber
Mains current	This is the supply of electricity from the sockets in buildings. (This is a.c.)
Molecule	The simplest unit of a chemical compound that can exist, consisting of two or more atoms held together by chemical bonds
Ohm	The unit of electrical resistance
Ohm's law	The law that states that voltage (V) across a circuit is proportional to the resistance (R) of the circuit and the current (I) flowing through it: $V = IR$
Rectifier	An appliance within a circuit which changes a.c. to d.c.
Rheostat	A variable resistor
Transformer	A device to change a.c. voltages from (input) one voltage to (output) a higher or lower voltage
Volt	The unit of electromotive force
Watt	The unit of electrical strength

Table 6.1 *Useful terms*

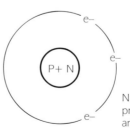

Nucleus of atom contains
protons (positively charged)
and neutrons (neutral)

Orbit contains negative
electrons constantly moving
around the nucleus

Figure 6.2 *Structure of an atom*

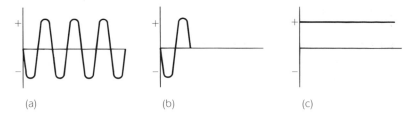

(a)   (b)   (c)

Figure 6.3 (a) *alternating current* (b) *an oscillation or cycle or alternating current* (c *direct current*

Progress Check

1 Draw and label a diagram to show a direct current.
2 Describe with an illustration what an oscillation is.
3 When heat is released from the needle during a diathermy treatment what pattern does it make?
4 Explain what chemical reaction takes place with the galvanic current.
5 Define the term 'fuse'.
6 How often must electrical appliances in the salon be checked?
7 State the direction a direct current flows in?
8 What does the term 'cauterise' mean?
9 What current is used in a blend treatment?
10 What is Ohm's law?

Key Terms

You will need to know what these words and phrases mean. Go back through the chapter or check the glossary to find out.

- Alternating current
- Anode
- Atom
- Cathode
- Cycle
- Direct current
- Electricity
- Electrode
- Electron
- Frequency
- Neutron
- Oscillation
- Proton

1   Link the type of electrical current with the reaction it causes.

a.c.   Heat
d.c.   Chemical

2   Which of the following statements is true?

		True	False
a)	In electricity negative always attracts positive.	☐	☐
b)	In electricity the cathode attracts alkali chemicals.	☐	☐
c)	In electricity the anode is positive.	☐	☐
d)	In electricity insulators pass a current on.	☐	☐

3   Link the word with the correct definition

Watt   The electromotive force.
Atom   An appliance that changes a.c. to d.c.
Rheostat   A variable resistor.
Rectifier   The unit of electrical strength.

4   Which type of currents are used in short-wave diathermy treatments?

a)   High-frequency alternating current.
b)   Low-frequency alternating current.
c)   Medium-frequency alternating current.

5   Which pole is used in galvanic electrolysis to insert into the hair follicle?

a)   Negative – cathode.
b)   Positive – anode.
c)   Negative – anode.
d)   Positive – cathode.

After studying this chapter you will be able to:

- recognise all equipment necessary to carry out electro-epilation
- understand the different types of epilators available
- choose equipment for the different modalities
- pick out equipment features and benefits.

Certain fundamental equipment is required for electro-epilation. The list is not long, but this equipment is essential for comfortable, safe and effective treatment of the client.

Equipment needed for epilation

- treatment couch
- trolley
- stool
- magnifying lamp
- epilation machine
- forceps
- sterilising facility
- sharps box
- waste bin
- mirror

Treatment couch

This can be either portable or static.

A portable couch is essential for electrologists offering a home visiting service as they can be folded down, put in the car and carried to clients' homes. For salon practices a portable couch is also useful for very busy periods and for open days, promotional events, taking to talks, demonstrations, etc.

GOOD PRACTICE

Consider your treatment room carefully before buying a couch.

Portable couches have an adjustable back rest, and some are available with a 'breathing hole' for massage. This type of couch is designed to be light and portable and is therefore not as substantial as its static counterpart.

The static couch is robust and comes in a variety of forms. The standard type is known as a plinth; it is generally not multipositional but the top third does lift up to form a back rest. This couch design is based upon the classic massage couch as used by doctors, physiotherapists and beauty therapists.

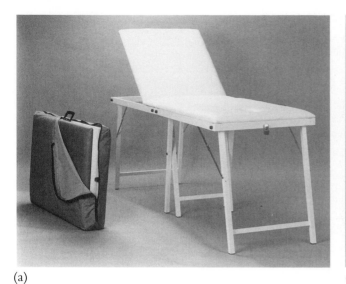

(a)

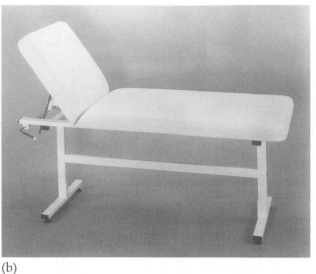

(b)

Figure 7.1 (a) *Portable couch* (b) *Static couch*

The most expensive type of couch is the electric or hydraulic couch, which is multipositional, can be adjusted to different heights (ideal for less able-bodied clients), and has superb upholstery and a high level of comfort. This type of couch is usually purchased by experienced practitioners who have an existing clientele and therefore the income to pay the extra cost.

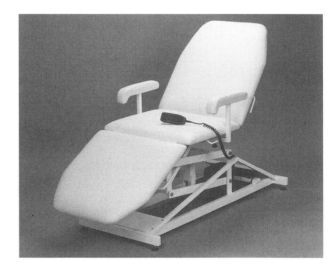

Figure 7.2 *Electric couch*

Trolley

The size of your treatment room will dictate the size of your trolley. It would be unwise to have enormous trolley in a small cubicle or a tiny one in a large room. There are some basic guidelines that should be observed. A trolley must be able to hold all essential equipment in an easy-to-use and accessible layout. Choose a trolley that has a side panel with (1) a socket to house the magnifying lamp and (2) electric sockets to plug in machines. This looks neater and avoids having many wires trailing on the floor that you or your clients might fall over.

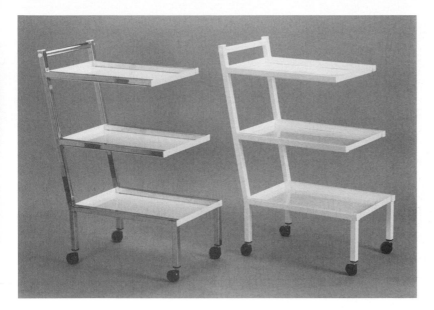

Figure 7.3 *Three-tier trolleys*

At least two shelves are needed to hold your epilator, products and consumables. Three shelves of course give more room and are useful for storing items that will not tip over, such as towels. Castors are essential for smooth running across the floor and from room to room, but if your treatment room is on an incline look for lockable castors.

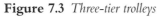

GOOD PRACTICE

A good trolley aids efficient and professional work.

Stool

This is an essential item as you spend a lot of your working day sitting on one. It is a matter of personal choice as to whether you have a back rest, but a deep and comfortable seat is vital. Try many before you buy. Castors are important as they help you to move about with ease when treating, and adjustable height is essential.

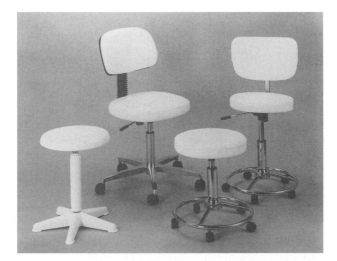

Figure 7.4 *Stools*

GOOD PRACTICE

If you are not comfortable, you cannot work well. Choose carefully.

Magnifying lamp

Electrolysis can be tiring on the eyes. It is therefore necessary to give your eyes as much help as possible. Help comes in the form of magnification and light, normally joined together in a magnifying lamp. They can sometimes take a little getting used to, but are well worth the effort.

Another means of providing magnification and light is magnifying glasses, used alongside a separate light source or with a built-in light. Which is best is a matter of personal choice, whether or not you like wearing glasses for example.

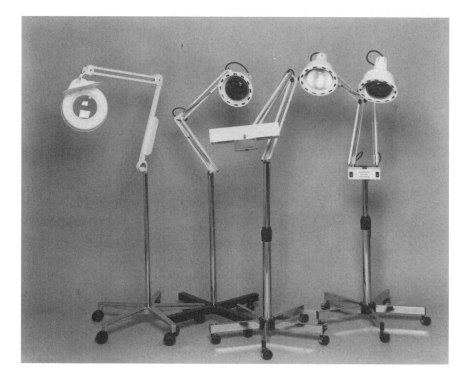

Figure 7.5 *The lamp on the left is a magnifying lamp*

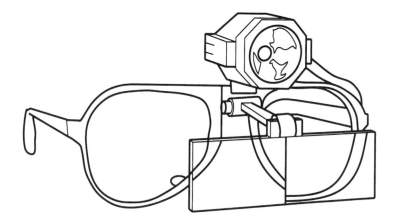

Figure 7.6 *Magnifying glasses*

Electro-epilation units

There are three basic types of epilator: diathermy, galvanic and blend.

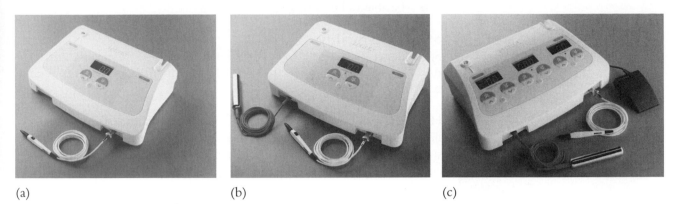

(a)   (b)   (c)

Figure 7.7 (a) *Diathermy*, (b) *galvanic and* (c) *blend epilators*

These units can be subdivided into finger button or foot switch control, timed or non-timed, manual or flash and computerised or non-computerised. The most popular type of epilator is manually controlled by a finger button for short-wave diathermy and a foot switch for blend.

Table 7.1 is a guide to the features available.

> **REMEMBER**
> Blend epilators are 'three-in-one' epilators offering short-wave diathermy, galvanic and blend treatment techniques.

Forceps

Diathermy	Galvanic	Blend
Finger control	Finger control	Finger control
Foot switch control	Foot switch control	Foot switch control
Timed	Non-timed	Timed
Non-timed	Non-computerised	Non-timed
Manual flash	Manual	Computerised/non-computerised (blend modality)
Computerised		Diathermy (as left column)
Non-computerised		Galvanic (as middle column)

Table 7.1 *Features available on electro-epilation units*

> **REMEMBER**
> The most popular epilators in the UK are manual and under finger button control for short-wave diathermy and foot switch control for blend.

A good pair of forceps is worth its weight in gold. Forceps are different from tweezers in that they are generally made of better quality materials, such as stainless steel. Forceps should:

- feel good in your hands
- not get in the way when you are working
- not be so long that they stick in the client

- not be so sharp that they break the hair when removing it from the follicle
- be able to be sterilised.

Sterilising facility

See Chapter 20. Autoclaving is the preferred method of sterilisation. Autoclaves are simple to use, do not take up much room and, although not cheap, last for a long time.

However, some materials do not autoclave well because of the extreme heat used. In this case an acceptable alternative is to use a cold sterilising solution such as activated glutaraldehyde. Activated glutaraldehyde is classed as slightly irritant to the skin and severely irritant to the eyes. Skin contact should be avoided and rubber gloves should be worn by those with sensitive skin. If any solution splashes into the eyes rinse thoroughly with running water and seek medical attention. Always use glutaraldehyde in a well-ventilated area and follow the manufacturer's instructions.

Figure 7.8 *Autoclave*

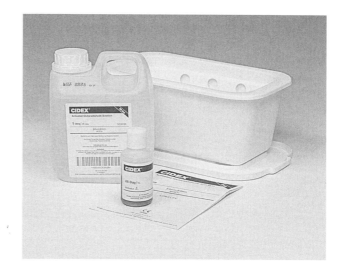

Figure 7.9 *Activated glutaraldehyde*

Sharps (needles) box

See Chapter 20. Too large a sharps box may be offputting to clients, particularly if it is similar to the type seen in the doctor's surgery or hospital. It should fit neatly onto the trolley near to where you are working so that you can dispose of your needles without fuss.

Waste bin

See Chapter 20. This should preferably be white as this looks better to the client. A covered lid and a foot pedal prevent hand contamination. Ideally the waste bin should fit under the treatment couch as long as it does not get in your way.

Other equipment

In addition to the equipment mentioned a whole range of products, consumables and stock items are necessary to carry out electrolysis treatment.

Products
- needles
- aftercare lotions
- skin cleansing products
- hand sanitising soaps.

Consumables
- cotton wool
- tissues
- paper couch roll
- disposable gloves
- disposable face masks
- disposable eye masks.

Figure 7.10 *Sharps box*

Stock items
- needleholders
- spare leads
- record card system
- aftercare leaflets
- skin and hair chart
- bowls
- kidney dishes
- jars for forceps
- blankets
- towelling couch covers
- towels
- client robe.

Stockists

There are a number of companies that supply electrolysis equipment, products and consumables, through cash and carry outlets, mail order and trade shows. There is a list of companies in the back of this book; look out for them at exhibitions and trade events.

Progress Check

1 List the essential equipment needed for epilation.
2 Which couch is most suitable for a newly qualified electrologist and why?
3 What are the requirements for a good electrolysis trolley?
4 What are the requirements for a good electrolysis stool?
5 Give two examples of magnification and light sources which are useful when treating a client.
6 State the three basic types of epilator available.
7 Give four examples each of products and consumables and eight examples of stock items.

NEEDLES

8

After studying this chapter you will be able to:

- list needle characteristics and types
- describe needle sizes
- understand how to insert a needle correctly
- recognise presterilised disposable needles
- describe sterilising methods.

The needle is the smallest piece of electrolysis equipment but the most important because its function is to both conduct and position the current.

The first needles used for electrolysis were adapted from existing medical ones. They were one piece and similar to sewing needles, and were honed down to a small diameter by the use of an abrasive stone.

Needles are sometimes referred to as probes, as the word 'probe' is considered to be less offputting than 'needle'.

Needle structure

There are two basic types of needle – one-piece and two-piece – both of which have three parts: the shank, the shaft and the tip.

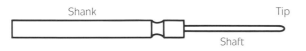

Shank | Tip
Shaft

Figure 8.1 *The electrolysis needle*

Shank
The shank is the part of the needle that is inserted into the needleholder. Most needles have a perfectly round shank, which fits easily into the rounded needleholder chuck; some are more triangular in shape and are not so easy to insert and discharge. The shank needs to be a good fit to ensure proper transfer of current.

Shaft
The shaft is the part of the needle that is inserted into the hair follicle. The shaft must be smooth and highly polished to aid insertion and to conduct the current evenly.

Tip
The tip is the part of the needle that first enters the follicle. The tip must be rounded, smooth and polished to ensure ease of insertion without tearing the delicate follicle walls.

> **REMEMBER**
> The shank must fit well to give proper current transference.

Needle materials

Needles have been made from a variety of materials. In the early days they were made from iron with a high carbon content (steel), but these had a tendency to rust. Other metals were then tried instead but none had all the essential properties. Copper, silver and gold were all tried without real success, and even platinum was used for a while but was found to be too soft. Iridium was added to make the platinum stronger and stiffer, but this alloy could not be polished to the necessary smoothness. Stainless steel, when developed, had two major benefits over other metals: it does not rust and it can be polished. Today the vast majority of needles used around the world are made from stainless steel.

Presterilised disposable needles

Before the introduction of presterilised disposable needles in 1980 it was normal for electrologists to spend a considerable amount of time caring for and maintaining their needles, which were straightened, refurbished and used over and over again.

The presterilised disposable electrolysis needle was first used in 1980, having been developed and manufactured in the UK by Englishman John Heath. The driving force for the development was the elimination of the risk of cross-infection, particularly from hepatitis B virus. (This was before the danger resulting from HIV infection and development of AIDS attracted considerable media attention and public concern.) Before Heath's pioneering work on disposable electrolysis needles, electrologists around the world would use one needle on many clients with only a wipe of surgical spirit in between. Thanks to his commitment electrolysis is a more hygienic treatment and clients are better protected from the risks of cross-infection.

> **GOOD PRACTICE**
>
> Always use presterilised disposable needles to prevent cross-infection.

Figure 8.2 *A presterilised disposable electrolysis needle*

There are now several different types of presterilised disposable needle available in the UK. There are certain criteria that a needle should meet for it to carry out the joint functions of conducting and placing the current. To ensure even conductivity and smooth insertions the needle must be smoothly polished with a rounded, not sharp, tip.

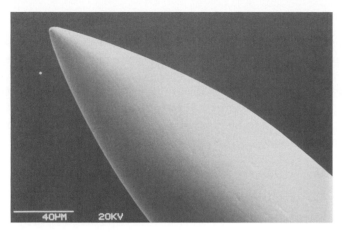

Figure 8.3 *Polished, rounded tip*

Needle diameter

The diameter of the needle should be equal to the thickness of the hair being treated. A narrow needle produces a very intense sensation for the client as well as a smaller treatment area. The larger the diameter of needle, the greater the treatment area and the more comfortable it is because the sensation is spread over a wider area. It makes sense therefore to use the largest needle that comfortably fits into the follicle.

GOOD PRACTICE

Use the correct size of needle for greater client comfort.

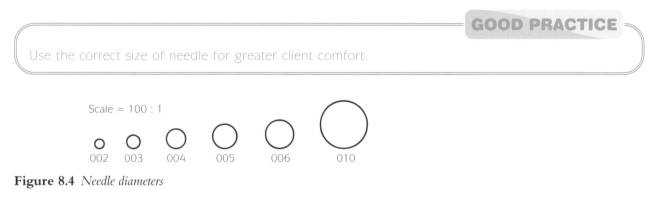

Scale = 100 : 1

002   003   004   005   006   010

Figure 8.4 *Needle diameters*

Most needles come in sizes 003, 004, 005 and 006. These are measurements of shaft diameter in thousandths of an inch – 003 being three thousandths of an inch.

Also available is an 010 needle, which is longer, thicker and more durable and is used in the treatment of warts and skin tags by those qualified to carry out these advanced, specialised treatments. Needle sizing can vary between needle types, making a direct comparison difficult.

004

003

002

Figure 8.5 *Increasing taper*

The increasing taper needle must be 002 at the tip, because when fully inserted the diameter of the widening taper at the follicle opening is 003/004.

Needle length

The needle should be long enough to reach the deepest follicle. The most common length in the UK is ³⁄₁₆ of an inch, denoted by the letter 'S' after the diameter size, i.e. 003S. The longer needle at ¼ of an inch is denoted by the letter 'R', i.e. 004R (R stands for 'regular', the popular size in the USA).

'Follicle feedback'

The insertion of a needle should never be rushed: time must be allowed to 'feel' into the follicle, while observing the surrounding skin and any movement of the needle. Insertions are not uncomfortable when correctly carried out, and good insertions are the only way to achieve effective, comfortable treatment. It is said that electrologists work 'blind', meaning that the area to be treated cannot be seen, but that the needle acts as the electrologist's 'eyes', indicating what is happening under the skin.

Bending of the needle is due to resistance either at the follicle base or on the follicle walls, requiring the electrologist to pull back or reinsert. 'Follicle feedback' from the needle is essential for trainee electrologists to develop their sense of touch, and to prevent future bad probing habits. Accurate probing is essential for treatment to be successful.

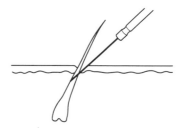

Figure 8.6 *Follicle feedback. Note slight flexing of the needle*

Types of needle

The two types of needle can be divided into five subtypes:

- two-piece straight
- two-piece tapered
- one-piece tapered
- insulated
- gold plated (two-piece and one-piece).

Two-piece straight needle

The two-piece straight needle consists of a shank through which a very fine, flexible wire is drawn, both parts being made from surgical grade stainless steel. The shaft is straight, i.e. the same size all the way up, and thus this type of needle does not exert any pressure on the follicle opening. The 'point effect' of the rounded tip keeps the current effect in the lower follicle. The two-piece straight needle is far more flexible than

Figure 8.7 *Two-piece straight needle*

any other type, giving the electrologist more feedback. (It was electrologists' desire for increased flexibility that led to the development of the two-piece needle, sometimes referred to as 'Ferrie' needles after their American originator, Joe Ferrie.)

Two-piece tapered needle

The two-piece tapered needle is manufactured in a similar way to its straight counterpart, the difference being that the shaft is tapered instead of straight. The taper is not as acute as in the one-piece tapered needle, and there is little, if any, risk of overstretching the follicle opening. However, flexibility is impaired because of the extra width.

Figure 8.8 *Two-piece tapered needle*

One-piece tapered needle

The earliest type of electrolysis needle, the one-piece needle, is ground down from a single piece of stainless steel. This design makes it extremely durable and hardwearing. The one-piece tapered needle offers the least level of flexibility because of its great strength and stiffness, therefore care must be taken when inserting because the needle does not offer the same feedback.

GOOD PRACTICE

Extra care is needed during insertion of one-piece needles.

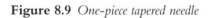

Figure 8.9 *One-piece tapered needle*

Insulated needle

Insulated needles have a coating covering the shaft of the needle, leaving only a small area near the tip exposed. The coating prevents current from treating the sides of the follicle so that only a very small part of the follicle is treated. This can be a drawback when dealing with curved or distorted follicles or any follicle with a large dermal papilla. There is increased sensation for the client as the current effect is over a very small and intense area. These needles are designed for use with electro-desiccation (flash technique) as the level of heat is much greater than that

Insulated part

Non-insulated part

Figure 8.10 *Insulated needle*

of electro-coagulation. Some electrologists use these needles for the blend technique, but there is concern that the very small contact area between the follicle and the uninsulated part of the needle prevents the wider and deeper action of the galvanic current which is instrumental in blend's effectiveness.

Gold needles

Gold needles are stainless steel needles with a gold coating applied to the whole of the needle surface. Manufacturers claim that gold needles are suitable for clients who are sensitive to stainless steel and that, as gold is a 'slippery' metal, the insertions are easier.

Figure 8.11 *Gold needle*

Understanding the needle packet

Each needle is individually packaged to keep it sterile until use. The red dot is the visual guarantee that the needle is sterile – when the dot is first applied it is yellow, turning red only when sterilisation by gamma radiation is complete.

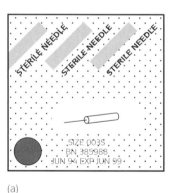

(a)   (b)

Figure 8.12 *Needle packet information*: (a) *gamma-irradiated packaging* (b) *ethylene oxide gas packaging*

The size number consists of two pieces of information: the diameter of the needle first, followed by the length, either S or R.

The batch number (BN) is the long number under the size/length information and from this the manufacturer can trace all components.

The two dates at the bottom of the packet refer to:

- date of sterilisation
- the expiry date (date by which the needle must be used).

The expiry date is 5 years after the date of sterilisation. The gamma-irradiated packs are opened by pulling down from the top unsealed part of the pack, and lifting out the needle by its protective cover, or by using the 'easy open' tear at the bottom of the pack. The ethylene oxide packs come in strips of 10. Pull away an individual needle pack and open it. Take care not to damage the needle when inserting it into the needleholder as there is no protective cover with which to hold the needle: it should be held through the pack until secure in the needleholder.

Sterilising methods

Virtually all needles used in the UK today are presterilised disposables.

There are two methods of sterilisation: gamma irradiation and ethylene oxide gas.

Gamma irradiation

The term gamma radiation is used to describe the very short-wavelength, very high-energy radiation associated with radioactive decay. The discovery of radiation is fairly recent. In 1896 Becquerel (pronounced Bek-er-el) found that a uranium compound affected a photographic plate wrapped in lightproof paper. Later Marie Curie called the phenomenon radioactivity. In the early 1900s physicists studied the atom and discovered its basic structure and developed theories to explain the three types of radioactivity observed: alpha, beta and gamma radiation.

The penetrating power of gamma rays makes them especially useful for irradiation sterilisation, as they are not only of high energy but can also penetrate a range of materials. The penetrative property of gamma radiation allows the product to be packed ready to use and then irradiated. In the case of needles, they are first packed individually, then put in boxes of 50, then into an outer transport case and then taken to an irradiation plant.

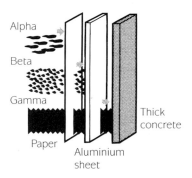

Figure 8.13 *Penetrating power of gamma-rays*

The most useful source of gamma rays is the radioactive isotope of cobalt 60. This radioactive isotope of cobalt decays, giving out gamma rays in the process. (An irradiation dose of 25 kGy is internationally accepted as being suitable for sterilisation of medical devices.)

Packaging

Single-use disposables (needles, hypodermic syringes, etc.) can be packed and boxed first and then the whole carton sterilised. This means that the goods can be despatched immediately after irradiation without further processing. Sterilising of needles by gamma irradiation is carried out in the UK by 'licenced medical irradiators' in accordance with national and international regulations.

Dosimetry

During the radiation procedure the dose of radiation emitted is monitored using plastic dosimeters in the load. These change colour very precisely depending on how much radiation they have received. Dosimeters are checked with calibrated light absorbance meters to verify the correct dose has been given. Approximately 90% of all needles used in the UK are sterilised in this way.

Ethylene oxide gas

A highly poisonous gas, ethylene oxide can be used for sterilising prepacked items. The molecules are very small and will penetrate the packaging to sterilise the contents. This method should be used only when no other method is practicable, and each sterilisation cycle should be monitored with suitable biological indicators.

Products are sealed in a chamber, which is then flooded with the gas. When sterilisation is completed time must be allowed for all the toxic gas to escape from the packs.

Progress Check

1 Why is an electrolysis needle the most important piece of equipment?
2 Name the parts of an electrolysis needle.
3 What shape was the first electrolysis needle?
4 Name the different types of electrolysis needle.
5 What effect does the diameter of an electrolysis needle have on the treatment area?
6 How do you choose the diameter of needle?
7 What benefits do flexible needles have?
8 List five pieces of information found on a needle packet.
9 Name the two methods of sterilising needles.
10 Why are disposable needles better than non-disposable?

Key Terms

You will need to know what these words and phrases mean. Go back through the chapter or check the glossary to find out.

- Batch number
- Conduction
- Cross-infection
- Disposable
- Dosimetry
- Electro-coagulation
- Electro-desiccation
- Ethylyne oxide gas
- Expiry date
- Ferrie needle
- Follicle feedback
- Gamma irradiation
- Insertion
- Insulated
- Presterilised
- Probe
- Shaft
- Shank
- Tip

Part III

Consultation and contraindications

CONSULTATION

9

After studying this chapter you will be able to:

◆   understand what a consultation is and when and how to conduct one
◆   welcome a new client
◆   distinguish between a potential client and a regular one
◆   position yourself and your client correctly
◆   answer potential clients' most common questions
◆   ask the questions necessary to carry out treatment
◆   fill in a record card.

What is a consultation?

The consultation is an appointment between you and a 'potential' client before any treatment is given. This allows you to give information about treatment, for your client to voice any queries and ask questions, and finally for you to ascertain if he or she is a suitable client for treatment by asking certain questions.

This confidential appointment should always be carried out in private. Some of the questions are of a personal nature and there may be people in the reception or within earshot who the client would not wish to overhear this often delicate conversation.

Consultations are always free of charge and should be offered without obligation. This means that potential clients coming into the salon or clinic can be confident that the consultation will cost nothing and that they can leave without treatment if they wish.

GOOD PRACTICE

◆   At the consultation clients are 'potential' clients only. This is the time to impress them by your manner and knowledge.
◆   Never embarrass a client by allowing others to overhear the consultation.

Welcoming the client

It is very important that potential clients are made to feel welcome, special and important. A friendly greeting, whether on the telephone or face to face, is absolutely vital in creating the right atmosphere and environment.

Never mention the word electrolysis in the reception area, as clients may be embarrassed. Keep the conversation general until you are in the private treatment room or cubicle.

The positioning of yourself and potential clients during the consultation has a direct bearing on their level of comfort with you and upon their decision whether or not to have treatment, therefore becoming a regular client.

Client–electrologist position

Where possible ensure that both you and the potential client are seated, preferably facing each other on one side of the couch.

However, if there is only one chair or stool you should sit on it; the potential client should then be seated on the couch (not lying) looking down at you.

Figure 9.1 *Correct client/electrologist position*

Try to keep your eyes at the same level as your potential client's. If this is not possible, you should be lower down. The consultation must never begin with the potential client lying on the couch. This can make him or her feel ill at ease and not in control: lying down before the decision to proceed with treatment has been made is inappropriate. At this stage potential clients are only seeking information.

GOOD PRACTICE

The potential client does not want to be laid out looking up at your face from the underside of a magnifying lamp.

As most potential clients have little or no understanding of electrolysis, it is important to give them the following information, but make sure you give them the opportunity to ask questions if they wish.

Questions a client may ask

What happens during treatment?

♦ Your skin is cleansed with an antiseptic lotion (show product).

- A new sterile disposable needle will be opened in front of you at each visit so you know there is never any risk of cross-infection (demonstrate removing needle from sterile pack).
- The needle size is chosen to match the size of the hair or follicle.
- The needle is inserted alongside the hair down into the hair follicle, which is a natural opening in the skin and as such does not involve any piercing of the skin (show on skin and hair chart).
- When the needle is in the correct position in the follicle, the epilator is used to treat the part of the follicle which produces the new hair (show on skin and hair chart).
- The treated hair is then removed from the follicle without being plucked with a pair of tweezers.
- Treatment action in the follicle gradually makes the hairs finer and finer until they no longer grow.

GOOD PRACTICE

Show client products. Explain terms clearly and listen carefully.

How many hairs can you remove in one treatment?
- There is no set speed I should work at and I could not give you a figure. I must stress that accuracy, which means effective treatment, is far more important than speed.
- Some areas are more difficult to work on, which can slow down the pace of work, while others are easily treated.
- Your skin reaction will also dictate how much work I can carry out in one area, as I will not overtreat the skin.

The answers to the following questions can only be answered after treatment has started.

How often will I need to have appointments?
- This depends how large the treatment area is and how well the skin heals between treatments.
- You must understand that this is a permanent method of removing hair and, as each follicle is treated individually, it does take time. However, as the hairs grow back finer, the length of time between treatments becomes longer.
- Regular appointments are vital in the early stages of treatment to ensure progress.
- The frequency of your appointments will reduce as your follicles respond to treatment.

How long will it take before the hair is removed permanently?
This is a very difficult question to answer as everyone responds differently. All I can give you is an estimate based on the following points:

- the treatment technique used
- how much hair is present
- how thick and dark the hair is
- the condition of your skin
- your skin's healing powers

- how frequently you can attend the salon/clinic
- how long the treatment sessions are
- results of previous treatment
- causes of the unwanted hair.

It is vital that the client understands that you are only estimating and that neither you nor any one else can give an accurate time scale.

Is the treatment painful?

Sensation is relative. Can I suggest that I treat one or two hairs for you now so that you can feel what it is like; it is always worth it because of the long-term benefits of being hair free.

How will my skin look after treatment?

- Immediately after treatment the area usually looks a little pink/red. However, special aftercare products will be applied to the treated area and, if you follow the aftercare procedures on the sheet I will give you, the reaction disappears quite soon, normally within the hour.
- Electro-epilation, when carried out properly, leaves the skin looking perfectly normal after the course of treatment has been completed.

How much will the treatment cost?

- The cost depends on the length of time the treatment takes. The price varies from salon to salon and in different areas of the country.
- You may like to pay for a number of sessions all at once, in which case I can do it a little cheaper for you (put on record card), or . . .
- You can pay for each appointment as you have it.

Other information to give

It is useful to impart the following extra information at the consultation, particularly at the beginning:

- history of electro-epilation in brief (to show that it is a tried and tested method)
- the fact that it is used in some hospitals (and thus has medical approval)
- how the treatment works (use a skin and hair chart to help)
- why electro-epilation is permanent (use a skin and hair chart to help)
- the fact that many women worry about unwanted hair
- the fact that most women remove hair from some part of their bodies
- the areas that can be treated.

Other information to obtain

Gently ask the potential client 'What area are you concerned about?' (always ask, never assume). This generally opens the floodgates of information, and tactful prompting helps you to fill in the record card, which is your means of recording information relating to that client, including name and address, specific medical particulars, treatment settings, duration, dates, etc.

Information to be obtained and written on the record card

Always ensure that the potential client can see what you are writing.

General information
♦ name
♦ address
♦ telephone number
♦ date of birth
♦ doctor's name
♦ doctor's address.

It is more polite to ask for the client's date of birth than to ask about age.

Information required to determine if the potential client is suitable for treatment

Ask about the following:

♦ any medication being taken (steroids/pill/HRT, etc.)
♦ recent scar tissue in the area being considered for treatment
♦ contagious skin diseases
♦ diabetes
♦ epilepsy
♦ heart condition
♦ pacemaker
♦ hepatitis
♦ endocrine disorders
♦ HIV or AIDS.

Medical history

Ask the following questions.

♦ Do you have children?
♦ When was your last pregnancy?
♦ Did everything go smoothly in the pregnancy?

EAST MIDLANDS COLLEGE
ELECTRO-EPILATION

UNITS _____   Name of Therapist: _____
ELEMENT _____   Date of Consultation: _____

Recommended Method: diathermy / blend / galvanic

Client's name: _____
(Mr/Mrs/Miss/Ms)

Client's address: _____

_____

Telephone No. (Home) _____ (Work) _____

Date of Birth: _____ Children / Ages: _____

MEDICAL HISTORY _____
Regular periods (last date): _____
Menstrual problems: _____
Any known hormonal problems: _____
Pregnancy: _____
Medication: _____
Recent operations: _____
Recent scar tissue: _____
Keloid scars: _____
Pigmentation problems: _____
Pacemaker: _____
Epileptic: _____
Diabetic: _____
HIV / AIDS / hepatitis B: _____
Haemophilia: _____
Any other illnesses: _____
_____

Treatment plan: _____
_____
_____
_____
_____
_____

Homecare advice: _____
_____
_____
_____
_____
_____

Figure 9.2 *Example of a consultation sheet*

◊ Is everything normal with your periods and menstrual cycle?
◊ When did you first notice the growth?
◊ Did anything trigger or start the growth off?

Previous methods of hair removal
Ask the following questions.

◊ Have you had electrolysis in the past?

If the answer is 'yes', ask the following.

◊ What method was used (short-wave diathermy, galvanic or blend)?
◊ How long ago was it?
◊ For what length of time?

Date	Time	Current	Needle	Comments	Therapist's signature

Figure 9.3 *Record card*

- How did the area react to treatment.
- Do you use temporary methods of hair removal (shaving, waxing, depilatory creams, tweezers, etc.)?

If the answer to the last question is 'yes', ask the following.

- How often do you remove the hairs?
- For how long have you used temporary methods?

The area to be treated
Ask the following questions.

- Which is the area of concern?
- How would you describe your hair growth (fine, medium, strong or coarse).

How would describe your skin condition?

How would you describe your skin healing?

CONFIDENTIAL
CLIENT RECORDS

Name: _____

Address: _____

_____

TREATMENT RECORD	
AROMATHERAPY	
BODY TREATMENT	
FACIAL	
ELECTROLYSIS	
RED VEIN	
SUNBED	
WAXING	

Tel: (Home) _____ Tel: (Work) _____

SPECIAL NOTES: (contraindications diabetes, allergy, etc. likes & dislikes)

_____

_____

_____

_____

_____

Ellisons
Client De-luxe Record System
Crondal Road, Exhall, Coventry, CV7 9NH. Tel: 0203 361619

EPILATION TREATMENT CARD

NAME:

ADDRESS:

TEL: (Work)   (Home)

NUMBER/AGES CHILDREN:

DOCTOR:

MEDICATIONS:

HEALTH:

MEDICAL HISTORY:

Diabetes/Hepatitis/Pacemaker/Other:

PREVIOUS EPILATION OR ELECTROLYSIS TREATMENT: (year)   (hours of work)

RESULTS OF PREVIOUS TREATMENT: SKIN REACTION:

PRESENT HAIR AND SKIN CONDITION: Normal Skin/Good Healing   Sensitive/Prone to Reaction

Oily & Blocked		Subject to Blemishes/Cysts		Prone to Pigmentation Patches		
Very Dry Skin		Erratic/Slow to Heal		Dilated Capillaries Present		Scars Present
Hair Growth On Lip		Hair Growth On Chin		Strong Hairs		Dense Fine Hairs
Other Areas:						

I confirm that I understand the treatment and contraindications, and that the above statements are true, knowing that the electrologist needs the information for correct treatment of my condition, and that the electrologist cannot accept any responsibility for any injury suffered by me attributable to my not having given full and true answers to the above questions.

Signature:...................................

PRINTED ON ENVIRONMENT FRIENDLY PAPER

EPILATION TREATMENT DETAILS:

Date	Time	Current Intensity	Needle Diameter	Area	Reaction	Date	Time	Current Intensity	Needle Diameter	Area	Reaction

Treatment Notes and Special Advice to the Client on Home Skin Care and Hygiene.
Products purchased for Home Care.

ETI   E.A.Ellison & Co. Ltd. • Birmingham • Coventry • Leicester

Figure 9.4 *Confidential wallet*

Any other relevant information

Although this comprehensive test covers the main questions that need to be asked during the consultation appointment, other factors specific to individual clients may become evident as you talk to them. This information must be recorded on the record card if it has any bearing on the treatment of the unwanted hair.

Record keeping

All record cards must be stored out of sight of other clients to ensure confidentiality, preferably in a lockable container. Each client's card should be removed before the appointment and returned immediately the latest treatment information has been recorded. When a record card is full, staple a new one to the back so that the name, address and telephone number are not obscured.

Technology is continually moving forward and assisting us in our work; the area of client information is no different. There are a number of computer software programs available specifically for record keeping. Care must be taken to ensure that the screen or printed reports are kept where only you can read the private information. There are also software programs for stock control, reception, retail sales, etc.

Some wholesalers sell confidential wallets. These are particularly useful for clients who have many types of treatment and/or if correspondence from a client's doctor or specialist must be kept with the record card.

Progress Check

1   What are the aims of a consultation?
2   What is the difference between a 'potential client' and a client?
3   How should you position yourself and a potential client during this appointment and why?
4   List at least six pieces of information that need to be explained to a potential client.
5   How do you answer the question 'Is the treatment painful?'
6   List five extra informative statements that give a potential client confidence.
7   Go through the consultation procedure with a person outside the training environment (i.e. family member) and fill in a record card.

After studying this chapter you will be able to:

◆   explain what a contraindication is

◆   give examples of and recognise contraindications

◆   understand why some conditions are contraindications to treatment.

A contraindication is anything which indicates that you should not carry out the treatment or should proceed with extreme caution.

Depending on the circumstances, you will have to decide whether to proceed with caution or ask the client to visit his or her doctor for a medical opinion. It is very important that you do not attempt to diagnose any condition you feel a client may have. It is not our place to diagnose medical conditions.

GOOD PRACTICE

A contraindication means you should not proceed with the treatment before consulting your client's GP.

Contraindications

The following conditions are relative or absolute contraindications to electro-epilation.

◆   Infections or contagious skin diseases (see Chapter 1).

◆   Hairy moles. If written approval is given by the client's GP, these may be treated in the same way as other hairs. However, you may find probing a little more difficult because of the soft tissue of the mole. When the hairs have been successfully treated, clients often find that the mole is less noticeable and it may appear to them to be smaller. Later in this chapter you will find a sample letter that may be sent to a client's GP asking for written permission to treat certain hairs or clients.

◆   Pregnancy. Avoid treatment of the abdomen and breasts in the last 3 months of pregnancy. These areas will be tender and hairs which have appeared during pregnancy often disappear after the birth of the child. Treatment in all other areas may continue with short-wave diathermy: facial areas can be treated with galvanic or blend.

◆   Emotional disturbance. Clients who are emotionally disturbed may find the discomfort of treatment too much to tolerate as their pain threshold is often low. Liaison with their medical carers is necessary. If treatment is permitted, the electrologist will find that extra time is required for explanations and reassurance during the treatment. Short frequent visits should be planned initially until the client gains confidence in your work. Ask to be kept informed of changes in the client's medication which may affect tolerance of electro-epilation.

- Age. Young people under the age of 16 should not be treated without the agreement of their GP. Young people's hormones are very active at this stage, and slight imbalances may correct themselves as maturity is reached. Between the ages of 12 and 16 girls are easily upset by comments from school friends, and if their upper lip hair is dark they may be subjected to thoughtless jibes. Asian schoolgirls in particular find that facial hair develops at this age and can become extremely disturbed by its presence. Therefore, in some cases electro-epilation is appropriate and may prevent the use of temporary methods of removal which could have a detrimental effect in the long term.
- Diabetes. In people with diabetes skin healing is often poor, but this can usually be compensated for by using a low current, increasing the distance between treated follicles and extending the time between treatments.
- Epilepsy is a contraindication but people with epilepsy can be treated with their GP's permission.
- Systemic disorders, e.g. haemophilia.
- Endocrine disorders which may affect hair growth.
- Heart disorders. Heart conditions seldom cause problems in treatment except that pacemakers are a definite contraindication to the use of high-frequency current. The speed of the pacemaker may be altered by treatment.
- Cardiovascular disorders. Treatment with anticoagulant drugs can adversely affect the success of electro-epilation, which depends on coagulation of the lower part of the hair follicle. Medical advice should be sought to establish the strength and effects of medication.
- Hepatitis, HIV infection and AIDS. In this case liaison with the client's GP is necessary because of the highly infectious nature of these diseases; they may be transmitted by contaminated blood. Electrologists must decide whether they are willing to treat clients with these conditions. If they are, all necessary sterilisation and hygiene precautions should be taken and gloves should be worn throughout treatment. It is recommended that all electrologists should be vaccinated against hepatitis B; this can be arranged through your own GP. In addition, care must be taken to ensure that infections are not transmitted to these clients, who are extremely susceptible to infection because of their immune system.
- Sensitive areas. Hairs inside the ears or nose, very close to the pubic region or on the nipple should not be treated.
- Drugs. It is worth contacting the GP if a client is taking any kind of medication. Electrologists cannot be expected to understand all the effects of every drug, and medical personnel usually accept your concern. Approached in a professional manner, doctors can provide you with information which will enable you to assess:
  a) the effect of certain drugs on hair growth, i.e. steroids
  b) the effect of some drugs on the effectiveness of electro-epilation, i.e. aspirin reduces coagulation of blood.
- Electronic implants and metal plates and pins. High frequency currents can affect the frequency of electronic implants. A galvanic or blended current can be attracted to metal in the body.

- Areas of inflammation, bruising, cuts, open wounds, psoriasis, eczema, dermatitis, dilated capillaries, varicose veins and recent scar tissue. Work around such areas or avoid them completely until the condition is healed.
- Asthma. Clients with asthma, if they have a nervous disposition, should be treated with care. If they are taking oral steroid medication, this could well be the cause of increased hair growth. Make sure that the client's upper body is slightly raised and that they are comfortable and relaxed. Allow extra time for reassurance.
- Black skin may be prone to keloid scarring and hyperpigmentation, therefore extra care should be taken to use as little heat as possible. Aftercare should also be fully explained and skin reaction monitored closely. It is generally accepted that

---

Dr............................   Date

Address..   Your name

                                                                 Address

Dear Dr............................

A patient of yours...wishes to have electro-epilation treatment

to remove hair on...Would you please indicate on the slip

below if treatment may commence. Also inform me of any medication which may be affecting hair growth

or have an effect on the treatment planned.

Yours faithfully

Name

Qualifications

- -

I have no objections to..having electro-epilation on

....

Signed

Dated

Figure 10.1 *Sample letter to a GP requesting approval for treatment*

galvanic or blend methods of epilation cause least damage to this type of skin and are also more effective in dealing with the problem of curved hair follicles.

- Asian skin is also prone to hyperpigmentation and if it persists treatment should be discontinued.

GOOD PRACTICE

A caution indicates that treatment should proceed carefully.

This list of contraindications and cautions appears to be formidable, but in fact very few clients can never be treated.

Figure 10.1 shows a sample letter that could be sent to a client's GP when seeking approval for treatment.

ACTIVITY

1 Check with your doctor on the procedure for vaccination against hepatitis B.
2 Write a sample letter to the GP of a client with epilepsy requesting advice on whether treatment should be carried out and details of any relevant medication.
3 In privacy, discuss with fellow students whether they would have any contraindications or cautions to treatment.
4 Complete a consultation sheet (Figure 9.2) for yourself.

Key Terms

You will need to know what these words and phrases mean. Go back through the chapter or check the glossary to find out.

- Asthma
- Diabetes
- Endocrine disorder
- Epilepsy
- Haemophilia
- Heart conditions
- Hepatitis B
- High/low blood pressure
- HIV positive
- Pacemaker

1   Which two half-sentences below best describe a contraindication?

Can never be treated ☐   If the doctor gives permission ☐

Can be treated with care ☐   Under any circumstances ☐

Can sometimes be treated ☐   If the therapist is confident ☐

2   List true contraindications.

_____

3   What would you say to a girl of 13 who was distressed about upper lip hair growth?

_____

4   List infectious or contagious skin conditions which would contraindicate treatment.

_____

Part IV

Treatments

Part IV

DIATHERMY NEEDLE EPILATION

After studying this chapter you will be able to:

- lay out an electro-epilation treatment room
- create the correct work environment
- comfortably position yourself for treating different parts of the body
- understand the needs of various types of client
- prepare and carry out a short-wave diathermy treatment
- select the most suitable level of diathermy current
- select the most suitable needle
- recognise possible problems that may arise with diathermy treatments and be able to solve them
- describe the basic differences between diathermy, galvanic and blend treatments.

Laying out an electrolysis treatment room

The correct layout of a treatment room makes your working life easier, as well as being more efficient. The treatment couch should be in the centre of the cubicle to give you access from all around. This is important as it allows you to position yourself correctly when treating the various parts of the body.

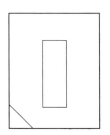

Figure 11.1 *Couch position*

GOOD PRACTICE

- Prepare the treatment room for your comfort in operating.
- Leave enough room to walk around the couch, with extra space at the top and side where you will be giving treatment.

If the central position is out of the question then the couch will need to go against a wall (a right-hand wall if you are right handed and a left-hand wall if you are left handed). However, if possible, leave room to work from behind the couch and at the bottom.

The trolley should be on the same side that you are working on, usually to the left of the couch for right-handed operators and on the right for left-handed operators.

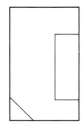

Figure 11.2 *Alternative couch position*

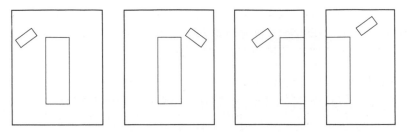

Figure 11.3 *Trolley positions*

Storage cupboards should be neatly out of the way. If the treatment room is quite large they can be floor standing, possibly housing the sink unit and any chemical sterilising system you may have. If the room is on the small side, wall units are best as they do not take up any floor space.

Retail/display units should be mounted on the wall so that the clients can look at them during treatment. Some clients will have their eyes covered during treatment if a magnifying lamp is being used, but they can still benefit from an attractive retail display.

Figure 11.4 *Example of a well laid out treatment room*

Creating the correct work environment

Creating the correct treatment environment for you and your clients is just as important as a correctly laid out cubicle. If you are working in the same room all day you will certainly not appreciate large, bold abstract designs or bare cold walls. And nor will clients: they want to relax and feel comfortable during their time with you.

Delicate pastel shades give a warm or fresh feel to a room while avoiding the 'surgical' or 'medical' look of pure white. A few plants and/or pictures make the room appear more homely and brighter colours can be introduced in the form of wallpaper borders or murals.

In some salons the colour schemes can be very bold or vivid, but for the electrolysis cubicle a more relaxing and welcoming look is far more appropriate, particularly for nervous or unsure clients.

GOOD PRACTICE

The treatment room should be welcoming yet maintain an atmosphere of professionalism.

Positioning yourself

GOOD PRACTICE

Positioning yourself comfortably enables you to work all day without placing strain on your back, shoulders and the rest of your body.

Positioning the equipment so that it is easy to reach and use is important, but so is how you position your body to carry out treatment. Working in the wrong position will cause all sorts of aches and pains, particularly in the lower back and shoulders.

To carry out treatments comfortably all day, try to ensure that your back is as straight as possible, you are not leaning over too much and that your shoulders are relaxed. This is achieved by making sure your stool is at the correct height for the length of your legs and the height of the couch.

GOOD PRACTICE

Move the client into a position that allows you to operate comfortably.

When working on different parts of the body it is necessary to change your position to remain comfortable and to achieve accurate insertions. It is almost impossible to insert a needle into a follicle accurately if you are positioned at the wrong angle.

GOOD PRACTICE

When treating a follicle, position yourself so that your wrist and elbow are in line with the direction of hair growth. This helps achieve the correct angle of insertion.

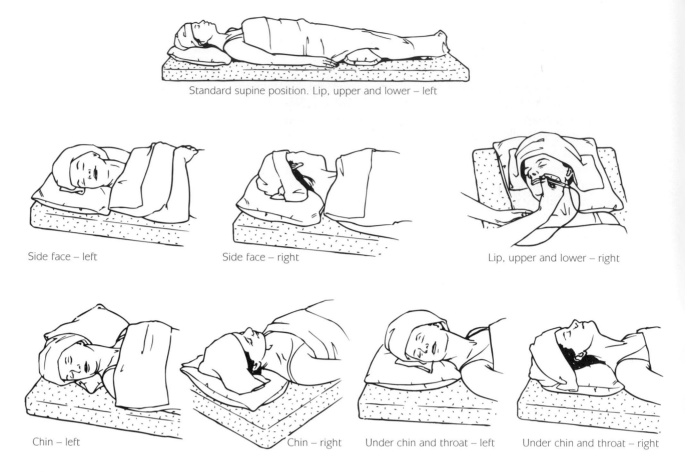

Standard supine position. Lip, upper and lower – left

Side face – left

Side face – right

Lip, upper and lower – right

Chin – left

Chin – right

Under chin and throat – left

Under chin and throat – right

Figure 11.5 *Correct facial working positions*

To avoid straining your shoulders you can rest your wrist or lower arm on the client.

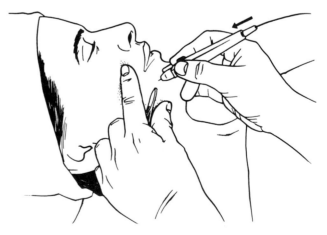

Figure 11.6 *Correct elbow and wrist position*

As a general rule clients do not mind you leaning lightly on them, but it is advisable to ask their permission to lean on the breast area, as they may have had a mastectomy or feel very uneasy about being touched there in general.

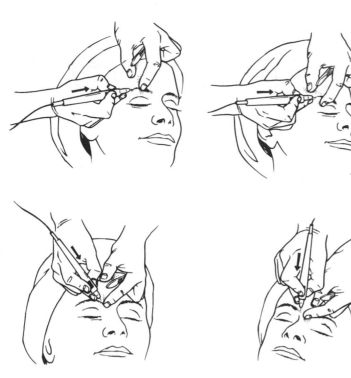

Figure 11.7 *Positioning for eyebrows*

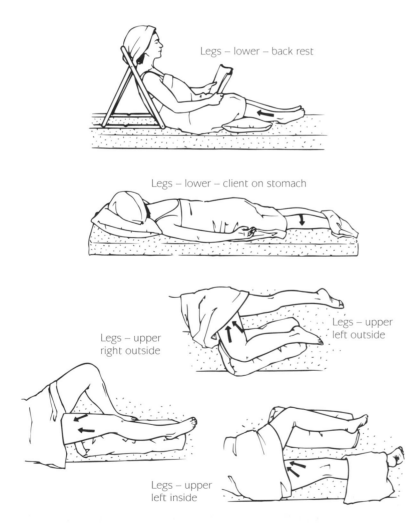

Legs – lower – back rest

Legs – lower – client on stomach

Legs – upper
right outside

Legs – upper
left outside

Legs – upper
left inside

Figure 11.8 *Positioning legs*

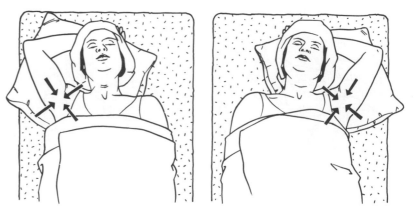

Figure 11.9 *Positioning for underarms*

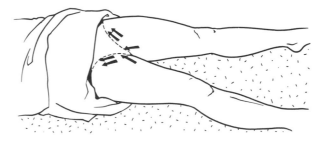

Figure 11.10 *Positioning for bikini*

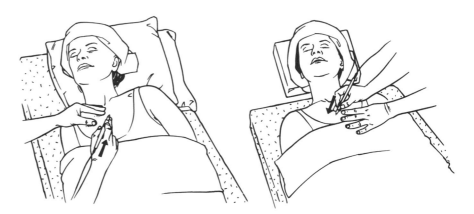

Figure 11.11 *Positioning for breast*

Types of client

It would be wrong to think that only women undergo electrolysis, and only post-menopausal women at that. Men and women will come to you for help, advice and treatment. In some cases you may not understand the need for treatment, but that does not make the patient's needs any less important.

The areas you may be asked to treat in women will include:

- abdomen
- bikini
- breast/nipples
- chin
- eyebrows
- fingers
- forearms
- hairline
- legs
- neck/throat
- sides of face
- toes
- underarms
- upper lip.

Previously the most common treatment area was the face, but as the public's awareness of electro-epilation and its benefits increased so more and more body treatments were carried out, particularly in the bikini line and underarm areas. Today virtually any area of the body can be treated with electrolysis. As a general guide, any area that can be treated by temporary methods of hair removal (i.e. waxing) can be treated with electro-epilation.

The treatments you may be asked to carry out on men will include:

- abdomen
- arms
- back
- beard area
- chest
- fingers
- hair implants (when the natural hair line has receded behind the implants it leaves a row or rows of isolated 'carrot tops')
- hair line
- legs
- lobes of ears
- tip of nose
- toes.

GOOD PRACTICE

Hair can be removed from parts of the face and body. If in doubt consult the client's GP.

Both men and women of all ages request treatment for many reasons. However, some men have specific needs. A number of men suffer from folliculitis (inflammation of the follicles). The only cure for this is to remove the hair. Black males are more likely to suffer from folliculitis because of their predisposition to ingrowing hairs. Folliculitis can be particularly severe in the beard area, leading to unsightly lumps and bumps.

Sportsmen have for years shaved parts of their bodies to decrease water or wind resistance. Do not be surprised if a sportsman arrives at the clinic wanting his leg or chest hair removed. Body builders may request removal of body hair so that the definition of their hard-earned muscles can be displayed to best advantage.

Male to female transsexuals also need treatment prior to surgery to remove 'masculine pattern' hair, i.e. on the beard area, chest, etc. It is particularly rewarding to treat such clients.

Professional appearance

GOOD PRACTICE

Always look and act professionally and ensure that hygiene standards are as high as possible.

Having prepared your treatment room and ensured that all equipment is ready for use, be sure you are prepared to receive your client. Make sure that you look professional, that your clinic dress or overall is clean and bright (not dingy from too many washes), that your tights/stockings are freshly laundered and not laddered, that your hair is off your face and neat and tidy, that your nails are unvarnished and short and that your personal hygiene is of the highest standard.

Electrologists are not medical practitioners, and we should not look and act as if we are. To do so would be offputting to clients. However, the practice of electrolysis requires a high level of hygiene, skill and professionalism and members of the public must have confidence in electrolysis and our ability to give effective treatment.

GOOD PRACTICE

Always appear professional.

Progress Check

1   What is the best position for a couch in a treatment room?
2   Design a treatment room layout.
3   Create three different colour schemes.
4   What should you remember to help position your body correctly?
5   Draw the correct position of the needleholder and needle in relation to eyebrows, underarms and breast.
6   List 10 different areas of the body which can be treated.
7   Explain why more men are seeking electrolysis.
8   Discuss the correct appearance for an electrologist.

Procedure for electro-epilation treatment

Order of procedure
1   Greet the client.
2   Escort the client to the treatment area.

3 Carry out the consultation or review progress.
4 Prepare the client for the treatment.
5 Position the lamp.
6 Wash your hands.
7 Wear appropriate personal protective equipment to avoid cross-infection i.e. gloves and masks.
8 Load the needle and switch on the lamp.
9 Commence the treatment.
10 Carry out and explain the aftercare.
11 Explain to the client when the next appointment should be.

Preparation for electro-epilation treatment

Prepare the work area
1 Cover the bed with bed roll.
2 Put a pillow under the bed roll for the client's comfort if it is not going to get in the way.
3 Place two stools under the bed.
4 Cover both shelves of the trolley with tissue.
5 Place the following items on your trolley:

Top shelf:
- epilation machine
- needleholder
- selection of needles
- tweezers in a pot of Steritane or antiseptic
- sharps box

Bottom shelf:
- antiseptic skin cleanser
- cosmetic skin cleanser
- aftercare lotion
- cotton wool
- tissues
- disposable gloves
- mirror
- bowl for jewellery (to be removed for galvanic or blend)
- consultation card and pen
- hand towel.

6 Place a waste bin protected by a bin liner underneath the trolley, ready for any waste. The bin should have a lid on it so that the waste is covered.

Figure 11.12 *Antiseptic solution*

Prepare the client
1 Ask the client to remove clothing if necessary and hang it up out of the way.
2 Offer the client a gown, if applicable.
3 Help the client onto the couch.

4   When the client is in position protect clothing with towels or tissue, then assess the hair and decide the needle size.
5   Position the lamp.
6   Wash your hands.
7   Wipe over the area to be treated with a square of cotton wool soaked in skin cleanser/Steritane, then blot the area dry with a tissue. Have a fresh piece of cotton wool for each area.
8   Wipe the needleholder with Steritane/antiseptic.

Load the needle

1   Select a suitable needle.
2   Loosen the chuck on the probe.
3   Unwrap the needle without touching it.
4   Using the wrapping or plastic cap, place the needle in the probe.
5   Tighten the chuck until it is gripping the needle tightly.
6   Remove the plastic covering over the needle with the tweezers.

You should have two pairs of tweezers: one for loading the needle, the other for working with.

Disposing of the needle

1   Loosen the chuck at the end of the treatment.
2   Tip the probe into the sharps box allowing the needle to fall into the box. If the needle does not fall out, gently remove it using your used tweezers and place it in the sharps box.

Do not touch the needle, and never try to use it on anyone else.

Ideally the chuck cap should be sterilised between clients. Several chuck caps will be required if treatment is continuous throughout the day.

Procedure for diathermy treatment

1   Turn the machine on to a low current.
2   Probe the follicle and apply the current for about 2 seconds depending on the strength of hair growth and the condition of the skin.
3   Stop applying the current and remove the needle from the follicle.
4   Try removing the hair from the follicle with the tweezers.
5   If the hair cannot be removed easily, probe the follicle again.

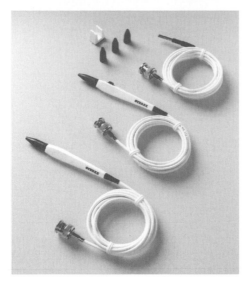

Figure 11.13 *Needleholders*

6 Again try to remove the hair with the tweezers. If it comes out after the second probe then you will know that you only need to increase the current a little to achieve the right level for treatment.

7 If the hair will not come out after the second probe then a third probe should be attempted, again applying the current for a longer period of time. This should allow the hair to be removed with the tweezers. Increase the current for treating other hairs. (If at this stage in the treatment the hair will still not come out then it should be removed with the tweezers and the current increased enough for the next hair treated.)

8 The current should now be at the right level for working on the area, although there will be times when strong hairs require either further treatment or an increased current.

GOOD PRACTICE

♦ The current should be as low as is necessary to enable you to remove the hair without pulling.

♦ You should always seek to achieve effective treatment with the lowest level of current over the shortest time.

NB. Whether you probe a maximum of two or three times into a follicle is a debatable point. The electrologist must decide whether the client's skin will tolerate a third probe without damage.

Factors affecting treatment effectiveness

Needle size
The needle diameter should equal the hair diameter. The effect of treatment depends on the diameter of the needle: with a 003 needle the area affected is smaller but the effect is more intense than with a larger needle.

Imagine the needle as a hosepipe and the current as water.

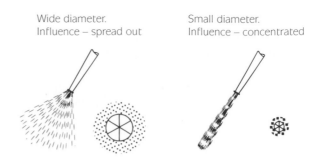

Wide diameter.
Influence – spread out

Small diameter.
Influence – concentrated

Figure 11.14 *How needle diameter affects current flow*

Type of needle
The type of needle used depends on the personal preference of the electrologist, unless the client has an allergy to a specific type of needle. See Chapter 8 for further information.

Current strength
The correct current is the lowest needed to remove the hair without causing skin damage or unnecessary discomfort to the client.

GOOD PRACTICE

Always start with a low current and increase the intensity a little at a time. This ensures that you never overtreat.

Effects of current on the follicle
Diathermy (alternating current)
Alternating current produces heat, causing quick tissue destruction.

Galvanic (direct current)
Direct current produces chemicals that cause thorough tissue destruction.

Blend (combined current)
With blend the production of chemicals and warmth combined results in fast and thorough tissue destruction.

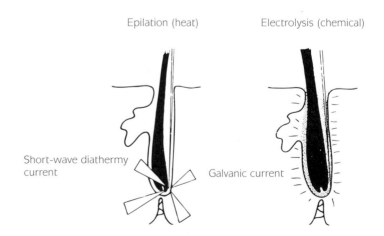

Epilation (heat)

Electrolysis (chemical)

Short-wave diathermy current

Galvanic current

Figure 11.15 *Comparison of the areas of tissue destruction when using diathermy and galvanic currents*

Effective treatment

Effective treatment occurs when the correct amount of current is discharged in the correct position for the correct length of time.

Needle insertion into the follicle

By using a magnifying lamp or glasses it is possible to see exactly where the hair enters the skin. The needle should be lined up with the hair and slid into the follicle just under the hair itself. The insertion must be slow and precise so that it is possible to feel the base of the follicle to know when to stop the insertion.

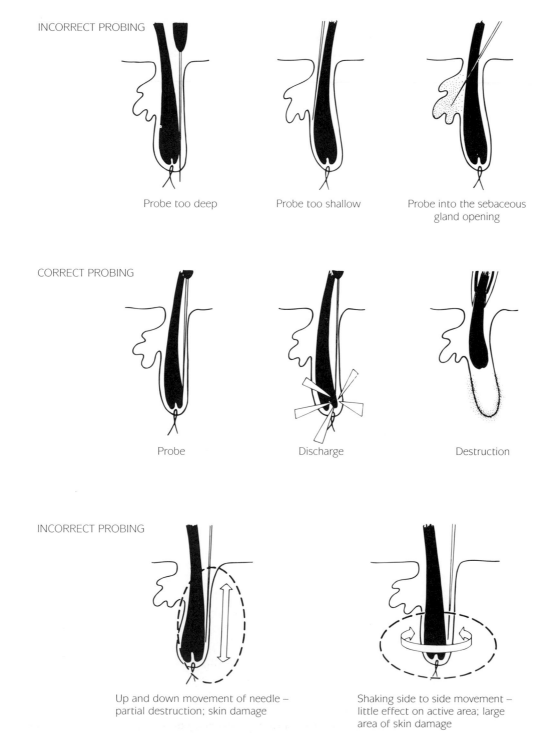

INCORRECT PROBING

Probe too deep Probe too shallow Probe into the sebaceous gland opening

CORRECT PROBING

Probe Discharge Destruction

INCORRECT PROBING

Up and down movement of needle – partial destruction; skin damage

Shaking side to side movement – little effect on active area; large area of skin damage

Figure 11.16 *Comparison between correct and incorrect needle insertions*

Angle of needle

The angle of hair growth varies in different parts of the body. For example, the hairs on the legs insert at a much shallower angle than the hairs on the chin. With short hairs which have regrown after shaving it is very difficult to determine the true angle under the skin. The section of the shaft closest to the skin gives an indication of the likely angle of the root under the surface. If the angle of the follicle and insertion of the needle do not match exactly the needle will not enter the follicle easily and the probe will hurt the client.

Skin stretch

Stretching the skin slightly will allow the needle to enter the follicle more easily. The skin must not be overstretched as this will be uncomfortable for the client and make insertion less accurate.

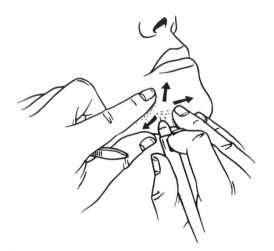

Figure 11.17 *Three-finger skin stretch*

Applying current

Press either the finger button or foot pedal to transmit the current into the follicle. The needle must be kept perfectly still while this is being done. The lower the level of current, the longer the current will need to be applied. When you have used enough current, make sure that you release the finger button or foot pedal before removing the needle gently from the follicle.

Position of operator

The electrologist should work in a comfortable position, with the back straight and not bent. The height of the stool should be adjusted so that the operator is able to reach the treatment area easily and without strain. Then the trolley and equipment should be positioned on the electrologist's working side, so that the flex does not trail across the client. Fidgeting and repositioning during application must be avoided. Uncomfortable positioning often results in inaccurate probing, damage to needleholders and needles, physical and mental fatigue, eye strain and a slow rate of work.

(a) Probe

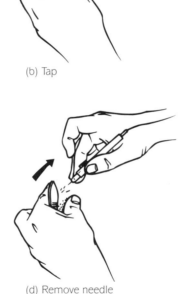

(b) Tap

(c) Pause

(d) Remove needle

Figure 11.18 *Tapping and probing sequence*

Position of client

The client should be made as comfortable as possible without inhibiting the operator. The client should be asked to move into the best position for the work to be carried out. Pillows can be used for extra client support.

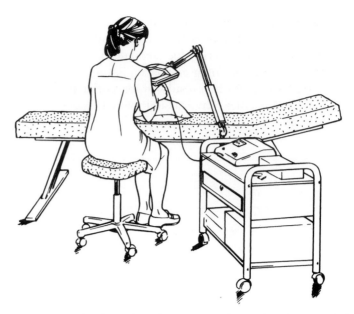

Figure 11.19 *Example of a good working position for an electrologist and of equipment layout*

Probing problems

- If the electrologist's hand is not steady the current will not reach the dermal papilla or matrix of the hair and the desired destructive effect will not be achieved.
- Movement of the needle may cause too much current to seep through to surrounding skin tissue, leaving too little to treat the dermal papilla. This can result in a burn or even scarring.
- If too fine a needle is used it may pass through the follicle wall or base of the follicle, thus making the probe inaccurate. The operator's sense of touch and the client's reaction give the guidance as to whether the insertion is accurate.

GOOD PRACTICE

Always watch the surface of the skin very closely when probing.

What should be done if the hair will not come out after treatment?

1　Ensure equipment and accessories have been set up correctly.
2　The follicle should be treated again, checking that:
   - probing is accurate
   - the level of current is suitable
   - the length of current application is suitable
   - the needle did not move while in the follicle.
3　On the second insertion the current should not be turned up, but should be applied for a longer period of time. If this does not remove the hair a third treatment can be applied.
4　The third treatment should be the last one. The hair should be removed with tweezers after three treatments because to leave it in the follicle could cause infection and cause so much trauma to the

skin that the follicle cannot be probed again. This is a definite indication that the current is too low. (A third probing must not be a common occurrence. It should be necessary only when finding the correct level of current.)

5   The current should be increased to remove the remaining hairs successfully.

Opinion differs as to whether the maximum number of insertions should be two or three. The authors suggest that you come to your own decision, bearing in mind the skin type of each client.

Factors affecting the heating pattern

Length of current time

The longer the current is left on, the larger the heating pattern becomes, so destroying more of the follicle. Care must be taken to avoid destroying parts that should not be treated. The stronger the hair, the higher the current will have to be.

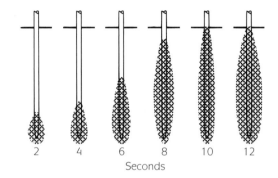

Seconds

Figure 11.20 *Effect of time on heating pattern*

Strength

Lower currents will take longer to reach all parts of the follicle, while higher currents will act more quickly. However, if the current is too high this will overtreat the follicle and disfigure the skin. The strength of the current and the length of time for which it is applied must be considered together.

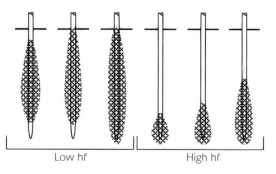

Low hf   High hf

Figure 11.21 *Effect of intensity on heating pattern*

Small needle

Larger needle

Figure 11.22 *Comparison of effects of needle diameter on field intensity; same current flow*

Needle diameter

The smaller the diameter of the needle, the denser the heating pattern. A small area of more intense heat is suitable for treating finer hairs. If the diameter of the needle is less than the diameter of the hair the treatment will not be effective. For the most successful treatment the needle diameter must equal the hair diameter.

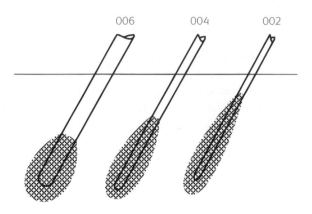

Figure 11.23 *Effect of needle diameter on heating patterns*

Depth of insertion

Unless the insertion is completely accurate the current will not reach the correct path of the follicle and treatment will not be totally successful. If insertion is too shallow the current may spread out over the surface of the skin, causing burning. If insertion is too deep the heat may be too low to treat the correct part of the follicle.

The typical angle of hair growth

Hairs grow at an angle to the skin. The size of the angle varies in different parts of the body. Here are some general examples as a guide.

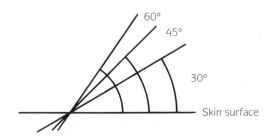

Figure 11.24 *Angle of hair growth: 60° on the point of the chin; 45° on most of the body and face; 30° on the neck and throat*

1   Why do you think waste bins should have lids?
2   Show how the heating patterns are different for a large 006 size needle and a small 003 size.
3   Why is the position of the operator important to the success of the treatment?
4   What factors affect whether a hair comes out successfully after one treatment?
5   Briefly describe the different shapes of hair follicles.

Summary of procedure for diathermy

1   Conduct consultation/examination.
2   Position client.
3   Drape/cover client.
4   Position light.
5   Apply antiseptic to client.
6   Disinfect light, machine and probe.
7   Wash hands/put gloves on.
8   Load needle.
9   Begin work/work for recommended period of time.
10   Dispose of needle.
11   Aftercare.
12   Complete record card and make next appointment.

Coagulation

The blood circulating through the dermal papilla coagulates (turns to jelly) when exposed to a certain amount of heat. This process is called electro-coagulation, and is achieved by the high-frequency current used in diathermy treatment. The heat from the diathermy current can also cause the tissue of the hair follicle to desiccate or dry out, but much more heat is needed to cause desiccation than coagulation. Thus, desiccation is more likely to occur with the flash technique as the temperature reached in this technique is much higher.

Flash technique

This is a method that can be used when working with a diathermy current. It involves the application of a very short flash of a high-intensity current. The aim of the flash technique is to cause destruction to the base of the hair follicle with the least amount of distress to the surface of the skin.

A study conducted in Canada and reported in the journal *Cosmetic and Medical Electrolysis and Temporary Hair Removal* found that regrowth with the flash technique was 'disappointingly high'. For this reason it was recommended that the technique is used only on fine hairs for which the area of treatment is very small.

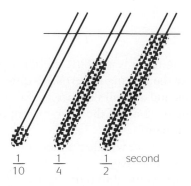

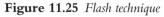

$\frac{1}{10}$ $\frac{1}{4}$ $\frac{1}{2}$ second

Figure 11.25 *Flash technique*

1　Indicate the order in which the following steps could be carried out.

　　♦　Load the needle and switch on the lamp.
　　♦　Position the lamp.
　　♦　Greet the client.
　　♦　Carry out and explain aftercare.
　　♦　Prepare the workplace.
　　♦　Wash your hands.
　　♦　Commence the treatment.
　　♦　Prepare the client for the treatment.
　　♦　Carry out the consultation or review progress.
　　♦　Explain to the client when the next appointment should be.
　　♦　Escort the client to the treatment area.

2　Where should the needle be placed after the treatment?

　　a)　The bin.
　　b)　The yellow box.
　　c)　The sharps box.
　　d)　The incineration box.

3　How many times can a follicle be probed?

　　a)　One.
　　b)　Two.
　　c)　Three.
　　d)　Four.
　　e)　Any other.

4　Match the type of treatment with the correct definitions.

Galvanic	Heat	Direct current
Blend	Chemical	Alternating current
Diathermy	Heat and chemical	Direct and alternating combined

5　Choose the correct definition of an effective treatment.

　　a)　The strongest current the client can stand in the correct position for the correct length of time.
　　b)　The correct current in the correct position for the shortest possible time.
　　c)　The correct current discharged for an effective period of time.
　　d)　The correct amount of current discharged in the correct position for the correct length of time.

GALVANIC ELECTROLYSIS

After studying this chapter you will be able to:

◊ understand how the process of galvanic electrolysis works
◊ describe the process of galvanic epilation
◊ explain how direct current works
◊ carry out a galvanic electrolysis treatment.

REMEMBER
Galvanic electrolysis uses direct current only.

Galvanic electrolysis uses direct current. Direct current is often called galvanic current after Luigi Galvani, who discovered it. Galvanic electrolysis was the first method of permanent hair removal and dates back to 1869. The first experiments were carried out by Dr Charles E. Michel, an ophthalmologist from St Louis, Missouri, USA, who treated ingrowing eyelash hairs (trichiasis), Michel reported his findings in the *St Louis Clinical Record* in October 1875. Electrolysis had begun.

Definitions

Electrolysis by definition is the process by which a chemical substance in solution is decomposed by the passage of an electric current through that solution.

An electrolyte is a chemical in solution, often referred to as an electrolytic solution. The passage of a direct current through an electrolytic solution causes chemical changes to take place at the electrodes.

Figure 12.1 *Galvanic epilator*

REMEMBER
Cathode, negative charge; anode, positive charge.

The electrodes are the two wires at which the current enters and leaves the electrolytic solution. Each wire is attached to a different pole. This makes one negatively charged (called the cathode) and the other positively charged (called the anode).

Positively charged ions (particles) move towards the negative electrode and negatively charged ions move towards the positive electrode.

A positively charged ion is called a cation and it moves toward the cathode, which is negative. A negatively charged ion is called an anion and it moves towards the anode, which is positive.

Figure 12.2 *Movement of ions*

How galvanic electrolysis works

When a direct current (galvanic current) is passed through an electrolytic solution, such as saline (salt water), the salt and water break up into their constituent chemical elements, and then rearrange themselves to form completely different substances.

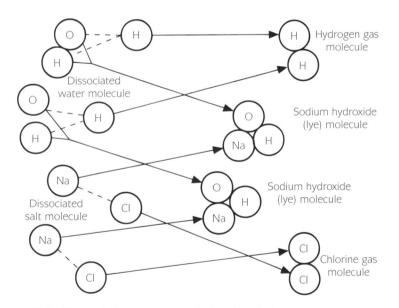

Figure 12.3 *Chemical change occurring during electrolysis*

The water consisting of two atoms of hydrogen (H) and one atom of oxygen (O), separates and forms ions (electrically charged particles):

1 a hydroxyl ion (OH$^-$), which is a negative anion
2 a hydrogen ion (H$^+$), which is a positive cation.

The salt, consisting of one atom of sodium (Na) and one atom of chlorine (Cl), separates and forms a sodium ion (Na$^+$), which is positively charged, and a chloride ion (Cl$^-$), which is negatively charged.

As these ions are unstable, they immediately rearrange themselves. At the positive electrode the negative chloride ions unite to form chlorine gas (Cl_2). At the negative electrode the positive hydrogen ions unite to form hydrogen gas (H_2).

The positive sodium ion (Na^+) combines with the negative hydroxyl ion (OH^-) to form sodium hydroxide ($NaOH$) around the negative electrode. This is the destructive caustic agent of direct current, referred to as caustic soda or lye.

The amount of lye produced is proportional to the amount of current flowing and the length of time for which it flows, i.e. the amount of current × the length of time it is flowing = the amount of lye.

The electrochemical formula demonstrating galvanic electrolysis is:

$$2\,NaCl + 2H_2O = 2NaOH + H_2 + Cl_2$$

The amount of lye produced is referred to as units of lye.

Tenths of a milliamp × time in seconds = units of lye.

$\frac{1}{10}$ milliampere flowing for 1 second = 1 unit of lye

$\frac{2}{10}$ milliampere flowing for 1 second = 2 units of lye

$\frac{5}{10}$ milliampere flowing for 1 second = 5 units of lye

And so on.

However, when the time of current flow is increased the amount, or units, of lye is increased.

$\frac{1}{10}$ milliampere flowing for 10 seconds = 10 units of lye

$\frac{2}{10}$ milliampere flowing for 10 seconds = 20 units of lye

$\frac{3}{10}$ milliampere flowing for 10 seconds = 30 units of lye

$\frac{4}{10}$ milliampere flowing for 10 seconds = 40 units of lye

$\frac{5}{10}$ milliampere flowing for 10 seconds = 50 units of lye

$\frac{6}{10}$ milliampere flowing for 10 seconds = 60 units of lye

$\frac{7}{10}$ milliampere flowing for 10 seconds = 70 units of lye

$\frac{8}{10}$ milliampere flowing for 10 seconds = 80 units of lye

$\frac{9}{10}$ milliampere flowing for 10 seconds = 90 units of lye

Direct current as an electrical epilation technique

Hair follicles, like the body, contain a lot of salt ($NaCl$) and water (H_2O). This saline is an electrolytic solution. The negative electrode (needle) passing the direct current into the hair follicle causes the water and salt to change into sodium hydroxide, chlorine gas and hydrogen gas. Sodium hydroxide is the destructive agent in galvanic electrolysis.

The practical application of galvanic electrolysis

The positive electrode (indifferent or passive electrode and lead) is connected to the positive outlet of the epilator.

The negative electrode (needle, needleholder and lead) is connected to the negative outlet of the epilator.

When the direct current is applied to the follicle the reaction does not occur immediately, i.e. lye is not produced instantly. The process takes time. Nor, however, does the reaction stop immediately the current is no longer applied and the needle is withdrawn.

REMEMBER
The production of lye takes time and continues after the needle is withdrawn.

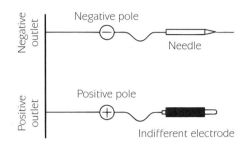

Figure 12.4 *Connection of electrolysis electrodes*

We have seen that the amount of lye produced depends on current intensity and the length of time for which current flows; however the production of lye is also dependent upon the level of tissue fluids or moisture.

Direct current is available along the complete length of the needle shaft, but it will only produce lye in the presence of moist tissue.

Moisture plays a crucial role in galvanic electrolysis, and this works to the electrologist's, and client's, advantage. There is a moisture gradient in the skin and follicle. The lower parts of the follicle situated deeper in the skin are the most moist, the follicle becoming drier the closer it is to the skin surface. This is most noticeable beyond the sebaceous gland.

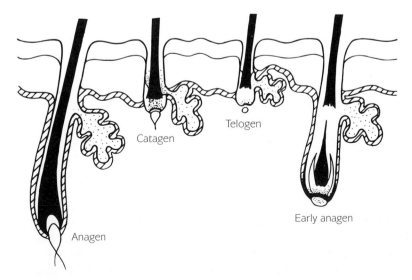

Figure 12.5 *Moisture gradient*

REMEMBER
No moisture, no effect. The greater the moisture the greater the effect.

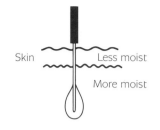

Figure 12.6 *How moisture affects electrolysis action*

The action of the lye is greatest at the moister, lower, part of the follicle. There is little, if any, lye production in the upper levels of the follicle because there is too little moisture. Thus the likelihood of causing superficial skin damage is reduced.

However, because of the lack of moisture and therefore lack of current action and lye development in the upper follicle, electrologists may prefer to use short-wave diathermy to treat very shallow hairs.

The level of intracellular moisture plays a vital role in the production levels of sodium hydroxide (lye), therefore an awareness of your client's tendency to water retention is vital. Water retention should be queried at consultation and recorded on the record card. This is one of the factors to consider when deciding on the modality to use.

Anaphoresis and cataphoresis

Direct current has other uses in electrolysis, as a preparatory treatment and as an aftercare procedure.

Anaphoresis

In anaphoresis a carbon roller instead of a needle is used as the negative pole. The roller is covered with clean lint soaked in a saline solution (and changed after each client). The effect on the skin is to open the pores, increasing erythema and relaxing the tissues, all of which help to make insertions easier.

Cataphoresis

In cataphoresis the positive pole is used as the active electrode, i.e. the electrode that creates the action. The positive electrode, also usually a carbon roller, is applied over the skin after treatment and has the effect of closing the pores, reducing erythema and soothing the nerves. In addition, the formation of hydrochloric acid is said to neutralise the sodium hydroxide.

Anaphoresis and cataphoresis treatments, although available, are not widely offered, probably because of the extra time and cost involved. Salons that do offer this extra service usually offer cataphoresis only as an aftercare treatment.

Direct current source

Dr Michel would not have plugged his epilator into a wall socket as we do today; his source of direct current was a wet cell. A wet cell is composed of two dissimilar metal plates, usually copper and zinc, both of which are submerged in a 'wet' electrolytic solution (electrolyte) which contains both positive and negative ions. The wet cell creates a flow of direct current through the wires attached to the two plates, as the positive ions continually move towards and collect around the copper plate and the negative ions move to and collect around the zinc plate.

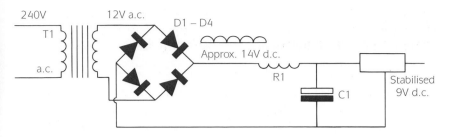

Figure 12.7 *Alternating current (a.c.) to direct current (d.c.). Voltage regulator or equivalent electronic circuit set to adjust final voltage to that required. T1, transformer; D1–D4, rectifying diodes; R1, current-limiting resistor; C1, current-smoothing capacitor*

Today we plug galvanic epilators into the wall socket, where alternating current (a.c.) is available. The alternating current is changed into direct current within the epilator by rectification. This process involves:

- a transformer which alters voltage. Step-up transformers increase voltage while step-down transformers decrease it
- a rectifier which rectifies or changes a.c. to d.c. by redirecting the reverse alternations so that they flow in the same direction
- a capacitor which smoothes the pattern of impulses created by the rectifier
- a rheostat which controls the amount of current flowing through the circuit.

A meter/visual display is only an indicator of how much direct current is flowing.

The direct current passes through the needle (negative electrode) into the tissues of the hair follicle then takes the shortest possible route to the indifferent electrode (positive) and back to the epilator. All of the current action takes place at the needle electrode when it comes into contact with the moisture of the follicle.

Frothing

During galvanic electrolysis a frothy substance can sometimes be seen at the follicle opening.

The froth consists of released hydrogen gas mixed with dissolved tissue fluids which escape from the follicle opening; it is not lye coming out of the follicle. In the early days of electrolysis Michel actually looked for this frothing as an indication of correct treatment. Today frothing merely indicates that the follicle is more moist, and therefore producing more destructive lye, than those previously treated.

The chlorine gas released at the positive electrode is dispersed over the electrode's large surface area. Some of the gas combines with body surface water to form hydrochloric acid, but this too is dispersed over the large surface area of the electrode and is not normally irritating.

Figure 12.8 *Frothing*

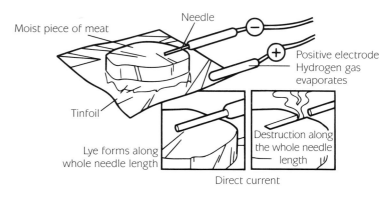

Figure 12.9 *Experiment to demonstrate the action of the lye*

Galvanic treatment procedure

1 Prepare as for short-wave diathermy (p. 169).
2 Pass the indifferent electrode to the client to hold.
3 Choose and insert needle as for short-wave diathermy (p. 170).
4 Switch on the epilator and set the current to minimum.
5 Probe the follicle and apply current.
6 Gradually increase the current intensity for each follicle until the client's tolerance has been reached or hairs are removed without traction.
7 Remove the treated hair from the follicle.
8 Keep to that current setting while treating the same type of hair in the same area.
9 Reduce the intensity and time when changing areas or hair type and repeat the above procedure.
10 Apply aftercare as for short-wave diathermy (p. 200).

As the intensity of current is variable, time should be a constant factor. Ten seconds is a suitable length of time to begin with. All clients are different. Increase the current intensity until an effective level is just achieved. If the client's tolerance is reached, keep the intensity the same and increase the time of application or follow the guide shown in Table 12.1.

Units of lye (u.l.)	Hairs
15 units	Fine hairs
45 units	Medium hairs
60 units	Coarse hairs
80 units	Very coarse hairs

Table 12.1 *A guide to the units of lye needed to give effective treatment*

The aim is to achieve an effective treatment as quickly as possible with the minimum amount of discomfort, at the lowest intensity and in the shortest time.

Some clients will prefer a very low current for a minute or longer; others will prefer a higher current for 10 seconds or so.

The phrase 'units of lye' is often shortened to u.l.; 45 units of lye will be expressed as 45 u.l. or 45 u.l. value.

REMEMBER
Tenths of a milliampere × time in seconds = units of lye or 1/10 milliampere flowing for 1 second = 1 unit of lye.

Progress Check

1 How is sodium hydroxide formed?
2 What is meant by lye and units of lye?
3 Why does galvanic electrolysis take longer than diathermy?
4 What is the electrochemical formula for galvanic electrolysis?
5 Why is moisture important?
6 Explain what the moisture gradient is.
7 When would you use anaphoresis and cataphoresis?
8 Describe the various processes which create d.c. from a.c.
9 What is frothing?
10 Describe a galvanic treatment procedure.
11 Carry out the experiment and record your findings.

You will need to know what these words and phrases mean. Go back through the chapter or check the glossary to find out.

- Anaphoresis
- Anode
- Cataphoresis
- Cathode
- Chlorine gas
- Galvanic
- Hydrochloric acid
- Hydrogen gas
- Indifferent electrode
- Ions
- Lye
- Moisture gradient
- Passive electrode
- Rectification
- Saline
- Sodium hydroxide
- Wet cell
- Frothing

BLEND EPILATION

After studying this chapter you will be able to:

- demonstrate how blend electro-epilation works
- understand the workings of a blend epilator
- understand the various treatment techniques
- explain the benefits of blend electro-epilation.

Definition

Blend literally means a combination or blend of direct current and short-wave, high-frequency, alternating current.

Background

Blend was developed in San Francisco during the late 1930s by an American electrologist, Henri St. Pierre, and Arthur Hinkle, who at that time was a service engineer with General Electric Company (he later became an electrologist and wrote *Electrolysis, Thermolysis and the Blend*).

Up until this time electrologists were using either the older, slower, but reliable method of galvanic electrolysis or the newer, quicker (in the follicle) but less reliable short-wave, high-frequency epilators.

Both modalities (types) had benefits, i.e. the effectiveness of galvanic and the speed (in the follicle) of short-wave diathermy, but both also had drawbacks, i.e. the slowness of galvanic and the higher regrowth rate of short-wave diathermy.

St. Pierre and Hinkle developed a combined current epilator and in 1945 applied for a patent, which was granted in 1948. They created an epilator and techniques which gave electrologists the best of both worlds: effective, quick treatment.

The blend method is gaining popularity around the world, having a firm foothold in the USA (mainly on the west coast), Japan, Canada, Australia, New Zealand, the Netherlands and in some Scandinavian countries.

In the UK blend is now practised widely, although it was slow to impress when foreign units were first introduced in the early 1980s. Blend really took off when representatives of the Institute of Electrolysis and the British Association of Electrolysists, journalists from the consumer press and electrologists from up and down the country were introduced to the British-designed Sterex blend epilator in early 1988 through a national programme of workshops, press launches and hands-on presentations.

> **REMEMBER**
> Blend is a combination of a.c. and d.c.

After 1988 blend quickly caught on as its benefits became obvious to electrologists who had previously used short-wave diathermy only: regrowth occurs more slowly and the regrown hairs are finer; clients are cleared of hair much sooner; distorted follicles can be treated successfully; and clients prefer the sensation and the choice of treatment techniques.

Blend theory

When high-frequency, alternating current and direct current are combined, the effects of each modality, i.e. the chemical destruction of sodium hydroxide caused by direct current and the coagulating heat of short-wave diathermy, are combined in the follicle.

The two currents are superimposed and are both available at the needle at the same time.

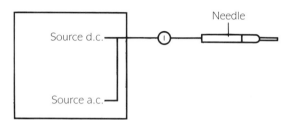

Figure 13.1 *Both currents available at the needle*

As the method involves direct current, the circuit from the client back to the epilator is completed by an indifferent electrode.

The effect in the follicle of the blend method is one of short-wave diathermy quickening the action of the sodium hydroxide created by direct current. This is achieved as follows.

- The short-wave diathermy warms the lye, which is produced by the direct current, thereby increasing the lye's caustic effect.
- The short-wave diathermy coagulates any tissue with which it comes into contact, making it spongy and porous, thereby increasing the tissue absorption of lye.
- The short-wave diathermy warms the lye, which makes it turbulent and agitated. The agitated lye rushes around, entering every nook and cranny of the lower follicle.

The aim of blend treatment is to achieve total destruction of the dermal papilla and lower follicle more effectively and in less time that the other modalities. In addition, blend offers more treatment choice and a greater level of comfort for the client.

The working point for blend epilation can be established in two ways.

- Set the intensity of both types of current to the minimum level. Increase the intensity of the galvanic current until the desired effect is achieved, i.e. the working point. Do not increase the intensity of the short-wave diathermy. This method follows the simple procedure of increasing the current each time a follicle is treated until the hairs are destroyed.

♦ Find the point at which the short-wave diathermy will loosen the hair (the intensity will be lower than that used in treatment with short-wave diathermy only, but the application time will be longer). Divide the time taken (in seconds) by the units of lye required to treat the follicle (see p. 189). This will give the direct current setting in milliamperes.

$$\frac{\text{Seconds of diathermy}}{\text{units of lye}} = \text{d.c. milliamperes (mA)}$$

For example:

$$\frac{5 \text{ seconds}}{20 \text{ u.l.}} = 0.4 \text{ mA}$$

Short-wave diathermy timing		Units of lye guide	Direct current in tenths	Milliamperes
5	divided into	15	$\frac{3}{10}$	0.3
6	divided into	30	$\frac{5}{10}$	0.5
10	divided into	30	$\frac{3}{10}$	0.3
15	divided into	30	$\frac{2}{10}$	0.2
5	divided into	45	$\frac{9}{10}$	0.9
6	divided into	60	$\frac{10}{10}$	1.0

Table 13.1 *Quick reference conversion chart*

There are many treatment options with blend and we shall be looking at them later in this chapter. However, there are two main techniques which influence the levels of short-wave diathermy.

♦ The first technique uses very low levels of short-wave diathermy, i.e. minimum or just above. This is known as the 'face technique' as there is little or no chance of surface skin damage because very little heat is involved. The duration of the currents' flow can be anything up to 20 seconds or even more depending on the treatment option chosen.

♦ Slightly higher levels of short-wave diathermy may be used on areas of the body where clients are less concerned about skin reaction. This technique is known as the 'body technique' and enables the electrologist to work more quickly as the application time may be as low as 4 seconds.

Direct current is the working current, i.e. creating the effect that treats the follicle. Short-wave diathermy whips the already mobile destructive lye into a frenzy of action, ensuring quicker, more effective, treatment.

True blend is when both currents are available at the needle simultaneously, however there is a variety of techniques which can be used in treatment depending on client sensitivity and skin reaction. The traditional method will be considered first and then some other treatment options will be described.

Traditional method

In this method the two currents are available at the needle together. However, when starting treatment the short-wave diathermy will come in immediately to the preset level, whereas the galvanic gradually builds or ramps up to its preset level. The ramping of the direct current allows the short-wave diathermy to be active first, warming the follicle so that the lye is produced in a warmed environment. In addition, by first stimulating the nerve endings, the short-wave diathermy reduces awareness of the galvanic sensation.

The direct and high-frequency currents finish together.

Treatment options
Aftercount method

Apply direct current and short-wave diathermy simultaneously as with the traditional method, but allow the direct current to continue to flow into the follicle for 5 seconds. This is known as an aftercount.

Using the aftercount method the follicle is flooded with lye, giving an even more effective and thorough treatment. It is, however, used mainly with a technique not familiar in the UK, in which the hair is held by forceps with the electrologist occasionally exerting a slight tension on the hair until such time as the hair comes out without traction. This technique is known internationally as the 'two-handed technique'.

The needle stays in the follicle and the direct current aftercount is applied. This method is used in all countries where blend is prevalent and the two-handed technique is used.

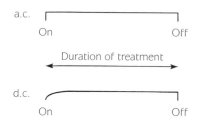

Figure 13.2 *Direct and alternating currents flowing simultaneously*

GOOD PRACTICE

Using the aftercount technique gives a more thorough treatment.

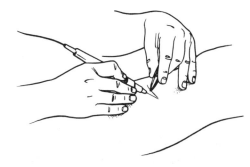

Figure 13.3 *Hand positioning in the two-handed technique*

Pulsing

This method begins with the two currents together. The short-wave diathermy goes off for a few seconds, then back on for 1 or more seconds, then off, then on again and so on. This is known as 'pulsing'. Pulsing of short-wave diathermy during the continuous flow of direct current can take many forms, e.g. a 1-second pulse of short wave every 4 seconds or a ½-second pulse of short wave every 3 seconds or a very high, very short blast of diathermy every 2 seconds could be used.

Other techniques

- Both currents may be applied for exactly the same length of time, but this technique does not have the advantage of the 'prewarming' of the follicle by the short-wave diathermy in the early part of the follicle's treatment.
- Short-wave diathermy is applied first then discontinued after a few seconds. Next the direct current is introduced for a few seconds, joined by the short-wave diathermy again for a 'proper' blend towards the end of the follicle's treatment.
- Begin and end with the direct application, using short-wave diathermy in the middle of treatment.

The variety of options is extensive.

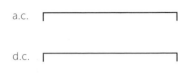

Figure 13.4 *Constant direct current with pulsed diathermy*

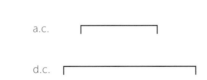

Figure 13.5 *Simultaneous a.c. and d.c. flow without d.c. ramp*

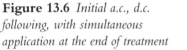

Figure 13.6 *Initial a.c., d.c. following, with simultaneous application at the end of treatment*

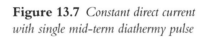

Figure 13.7 *Constant direct current with single mid-term diathermy pulse*

> **REMEMBER**
> When both currents are flowing at the same time the benefit of prewarming is lost.

Whichever treatment technique is used, it must be remembered that at no time should high levels of short wave be used because too much heat would merely dehydrate the follicle and inhibit the production of lye.

> **REMEMBER**
> The short wave is used only to increase, encourage and quicken the action of the galvanic.

Note that, although some techniques do use very high levels of short-wave diathermy, it is usually applied in pulses for fractions of a second. This is known as flash blend. In the past both currents were activated by separate foot switches, one for each current; now most epilators have just one foot switch. The more advanced epilators have no foot switches at all but have sensors instead. These sensors detect when the needle has been inserted and, after a preset time delay which allows for insertion adjustment, the currents are applied.

Blend was designed to help electrologists who have a good understanding of both galvanic and short-wave diathermy give better, more comfortable, treatments.

There are three modalities to offer your client. Be aware that your client's emotional needs as well as physical needs must be met. For example it may be appropriate to treat a large area of facial hair with diathermy initially and treat the regrowth with blend. Combining modalities has the benefit of clearing an area as quickly as possible and then treating the regrowth with a more effective blend technique.

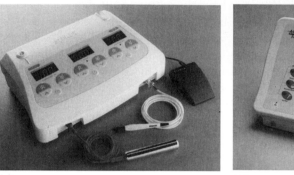
(a)

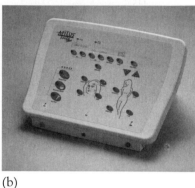
(b)

Figure 13.8 (a) *UK-designed blend epilator* (b) *American blend epilator*

Diathermy	Blend	Galvanic
Alternating current; short-wave high-frequency current	Alternating current and direct current	Direct current
Produces heat in the skin	Produces warmth and chemicals in the skin	Produces chemicals in the skin
Allows quick removal of hair, but this is thought to be the least thorough of the methods	Allows hair to be removed in a medium length of time with thorough results	Hair removal is very slow but this is a very thorough process
The sensation felt is a sharp quick sting	The sensation is a quite mild sting for a medium amount of time	The sensation is mild for a relatively long period of time
The skin reaction varies with each individual, but there may be a lot of redness	The skin reaction varies with each individual, but is milder than with diathermy alone	The skin reaction varies with each individual, but is usually the least of all three modalities
Treatments can be as regular as the skin will allow provided that complete healing has occurred	Treatments can be as regular as the skin will allow, but as the method is more thorough than diathermy alone fewer treatments are usually required	Treatments can be as regular as the skin will allow; usually many treatment sessions are needed as only a few hairs can be worked on each time

Table 13.2 *Comparison of different methods of electro-epilation*

Experiment to demonstrate blend action in the follicle.

Set up the experiment in the same way as the experiment to demonstrate the action of galvanic current (p. 188).

1 Treat with galvanic (p. 188).
2 Move the needle about 2 cm and treat with short wave.
3 Move needle another 2 cm and use the same galvanic intensity as in step 1 and the same short-wave intensity as in step 2.
4 Treat with both currents ensuring that short wave comes in first.
5 Note the difference in speed of liquefaction compared with galvanic and the quicker production of froth and bubbles.

Note that in the skin the action of the turbulent lye does not reach as far up in the follicle as in the experiment because of the skin's natural resistance to the galvanic effect resulting from the moisture gradient.

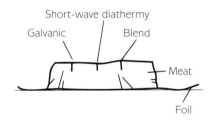

Figure 13.9 *Experiment to compare the different actions of the three modalities*

Blend gives a thorough and effective treatment, and with the many techniques available there is always at least one that will suit every client's needs and every electrologist's aims.

Progress Check

1 What is combined to make 'blend'?
2 How does blend work in the follicle?
3 Why is blend more effective?
4 How does blend benefit the electrologist?
5 How does blend benefit the client?
6 What is the action of the galvanic when blending?
7 What is the action of the short-wave diathermy when blending?
8 Which methods are most popularly used to establish the blend working point?
9 Describe a treatment procedure on a first-time client.
10 Describe three other treatment techniques and explain why you would choose them.
11 How do the face and body techniques differ?

The following assignment is reproduced with kind permission from the Confederation of International Beauty Therapy and Cosmetology (CIBTAC).

ACTIVITY

Assignment brief

Select a client who requires a course of electrical epilation treatments. Plan and carry out a course of treatment (minimum of six) which meets the client's requirements. Keep a record of the programme from consultation to completion. Present the information in project form, using a neat and logical format.

Criteria

1   Carry out a consultation. Elicit and record relevant information and complete a record card. Include the following:
    - previous treatment of hair (temporary, permanent, areas treated)
    - other relevant previous/present treatments, e.g. skin care
    - possible causes of hair growth
    - the client's psychological attitude to the hair growth.
2   Summarise and evaluate the information gathered. Justify your findings.
3   Plan and carry out a course of electro-epilation treatments which meet the client's requirements and consider any financial and time constraints.
4   Describe additional appropriate complementary treatments, e.g. temporary hair treatments, skin care.
5   Keep a diary of treatments, recording all relevant information including:
    - duration and frequency of treatments
    - area treated
    - technical details – probe size, intensity level, current duration
    - client's psychological and physiological response to treatments
    - adjustments to original treatment programme plan, giving reasons.
6   Monitor and evaluate the effectiveness of the treatment programme. Draw conclusions and justify your findings.
7   Outline an appropriate maintenance programme for the client.

All the above criteria must be fulfilled in order to successfully complete this assignment.

Key Terms

You will need to know what these words and phrases mean. Go back through the chapter or check the glossary to find out.

- Alternating current
- Blend
- British Association of Electrolysists
- Caustic effect
- Circuit
- Coagulation
- Direct current
- Distorted follicles
- Flash method
- Galvanic
- High frequency
- Institute of Electrolysis
- Lye
- Modalities
- Regrowth
- Short-wave diathermy
- Working point

After studying this chapter you will be able to

◊ provide and explain aftercare for electro-epilation

◊ recognise normal and abnormal skin reactions following electro-epilation treatment

◊ understand why abnormal reactions have occurred and will know how to treat them and prevent them in the future

◊ describe the factors that affect regrowth.

Instructions to client

◊ Do not have any hot baths or showers for the next 24 hours.

◊ Do not use any perfumed products such as

perfumed soaps/cleansers
perfumed creams
perfumed sprays
perfumed bubble baths
perfumed shower gels
perfumed talcum powder

for the next 24 hours.

◊ Do not sunbathe or use sunbeds for the next 24 hours.

◊ Avoid wearing tight clothing that might rub or chafe.

◊ Do not use deodorant or antiperspirant on the treated area for the next 24 hours.

◊ Try to avoid touching the area.

◊ Do not have a sauna or any form of heat treatment for the next 24 hours.

Electro-epilation irritates the skin and all the above may increase that effect.

GOOD PRACTICE

It is a good idea to give your client written as well as verbal aftercare instructions.

Aftercare procedure

GOOD PRACTICE

Never apply aftercare products with your fingers. Always use clean cotton wool.

Apply witch hazel or an antiseptic cream with a swab of clean cotton wool. Advise the client that the redness will fade within a short time and that any slight swelling should disappear within an hour. Cooling, calming, slightly antiseptic preparations can be used as necessary by the client over the next 24 hours. Tinted preparations are available, providing some camouflage.

GOOD PRACTICE

Advise clients not to further irritate the treated area for 24 hours.

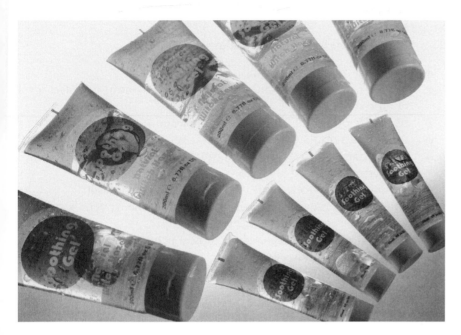

Figure 14.1 *Witch hazel*

Normal skin reaction after epilation

The following reactions are normal:

- pink or red colouring of the skin
- very slight swelling around the mouth of the treated follicles.

GOOD PRACTICE

Abnormal skin reactions need thorough investigation and changes in technique to prevent them recurring in future.

Abnormal skin reaction after epilation

Swelling

The most common causes of swelling are overinsertion, too much work in one area or an allergy to the treatment. Antiseptic creams and ice packs soothe and cool the area, which will reduce the swelling.

Bleeding

This is caused by incorrect insertion, i.e. the needle is inserted either too far or at too steep an angle, piercing the follicle wall and causing bleeding and possibly bruising.

Crusts/scabs

If blood or lymph accumulates in an area and then dries out, a crust or scab may form. These should be left to fall off in their own time. Picking scabs may cause a temporary scar.

Scarring

This may be caused by one of the following:

- operating too quickly and not taking enough care
- using a faulty machine and not being able to control the exact level of current
- using a bent or blunt needle (current accumulates at this point)
- using a current that is too strong, so overtreating the skin tissue
- concentrating the treatment too much in one area, again resulting in overtreatment
- probing at the wrong angle, so piercing the follicle wall
- entering or removing from the follicle while the current is still on, burning the surface of the skin
- not giving the skin long enough to heal between treatments, so overtreating the skin
- failure of the client to follow the aftercare instructions, resulting in an infection.

Bruising

This may be caused by using a needle which is too big for the follicle, or by poor insertion that results in piercing of the follicle wall or base and damage to a blood capillary. Too much finger pressure in an area can also cause bruising.

Types of scars caused by electro-epilation

- keloid scarring
- pitting
- hyper- or hypopigmentation.

Keloid scars

This is an unusual overgrowth of the skin due to enlargement and multiplication of its constituent cells. It is a skin reaction caused by damage or injury, and is a permanent lesion which will occur only in certain individuals who have an inherited predisposition to keloid. The operator should take care if this type of scar is already present, as overtreatment of their follicles may result in keloid scars. Negroid skin can be prone to keloid scars; if some are already present before treatment the client should be advised that treatment or later infection may cause more. Proceed with caution on a small area and monitor the skin reaction.

Pitting

This is a form of scarring caused by overtreatment and damage to the dermis that causes the skin to dip below the surface level of the rest of the skin. It is usually caused by overtreating a follicle, but similar damage can also result if the client has persistently picked scabs.

Hyperpigmentation/hypopigmentation

Hyperpigmentation occurs when extra pigmentation develops in the area that has been worked on. Diathermy, and to a lesser extent galvanic, is likely to cause this type of reaction, particularly in Negroids and Asians. Hypopigmentation occurs when the area of skin being treated loses its colour.

Condition	Symptoms	Cause	Outcome
Honey-coloured scab/crust	Lymph or plasma seeps through capillary walls and accumulates in the follicle	Mild overuse of current or overtreatment in area	Fluid eventually hardens and soon drops off, leaving perfect skin
Reddish scab/crust	Slow seepage of blood into follicle, causing disintegration of large sections of skin	Overuse of current Overtreatment Inaccurate insertions	Scab should not be picked off or a pit may result, taking a number of months to heal. If the scab is left to fall off the skin will appear pink, but will revert to normal in time
Pustule	Inflammation, heat, swelling and pain	Bacteria invading the follicle after treatment	If the body does not destroy the bacteria pus will develop, forming a pustule. This disappears after 1–2 days, leaving a honey-coloured crust. If the crust falls off naturally, the skin will be normal; if the crust is picked off, a pit will be left behind and will take longer to heal
Folliculitis	Large pockets of pus in the skin. Superficial folliculitis is found under the stratum corneum. Deep folliculitis affects the entire follicle	Secondary infection of the follicle	Heals without any mark. Often leaves a pit upon healing
Gas/vapour blister	Hydrogen-filled gas blister or hydrogen- and water-filled vapour blister which develops quickly, usually at one side of the needle	Possible result of galvanic or blend treatment	On removal of the needle the blister is pressed with a sterile tissue so that it will go down and not cause any problems. Care must be taken to prevent bacteria entering and causing a pustule
Vapour blast	Extreme heat quickly converts moisture in the tissue to vapour. Sometimes the tissue can be seen to move	High-intensity diathermy current	If the epidermis does not turn white owing to over-treatment, no harm will be done to the tissue; if it does the condition is called blanching, which will take much longer to heal and may result in a pitted scar

Table 14.1 *Adverse skin reactions which can occur after electro-epilation (cont. over)*

Bruising	A blue/black discoloration that may swell. Usually appears upon insertion	Incorrect insertion Oversized needle	Tissue will heal perfectly
Pitting	Formation of crust Region of damaged tissue that sits below the level of the surrounding skin	Overtreatment of follicle Picking crusts	Pitted scar which will improve with time depending on the degree of damage
Keloid scarring	Raised scar with a shiny stretched appearance	Some people, particularly Negroids, have a pre-disposition to keloid scars. In epilation the damaged tissue would result from inaccurate probing or overtreatment	Fibroblasts proliferate in the dermis, resulting in overhealing of the tissue and formation of a raised scar
Hyper- and hypo-pigmentation	Changes in the pigmentation of the skin. Black skins show the colour change more, with either very dark or very light areas	Inaccurate probing Excessive diathermy current	Excess skin colour or loss of skin colour in the area just around the follicle which will not fade

Table 14.1 *Continued*

Recording scars

If any of these conditions occurs, further treatment should be discussed with the client and the outcome noted and confirmed by the client's signature on the record card.

Regrowth hairs

These are hairs which grow after epilation has taken place and partial destruction of the follicle has occurred. These hairs are finer than the original hairs, paler in colour and lie nearer the surface of the skin.

The effect of abnormal hormone imbalance on regrowth

Abnormal hormone imbalance or steroid therapy may make regrowth more persistent, sometimes making further medical advice necessary. The client and the electrologist need to know what other factors are affecting the hair growth besides the treatment so that they have a good idea of what to expect.

Previous treatments affecting regrowth

Any previous temporary treatments will affect the rate of regrowth. Any distortion of the follicle affects the accuracy of probing and thus the success of the treatment. If previous methods have involved a certain amount of topical stimulation, the results will also be slower to occur (see pp. 211–13). As plucking is regarded as a form of topical stimulation, the client must not pluck out hairs during the course of treatment as this will reduce the effectiveness and speed of treatment. Advise the client to clip regrowth hairs with scissors to shorten them.

Regular treatment is essential for successful permanent removal of hair. Regrowth time should be explained to the client with the aid of a chart showing the hair growth cycle (see Figure 2.19, p. 42). At this stage form a treatment plan with your client depending on the area to be treated, the strength of hair and amount of money available for treatment.

Example 1: female aged 18

This client has fine upper lip hairs and has had no previous treatments.

The type of hair will take the longest time to return, if it does so at all. Treatment is simply a matter of gradually thinning out the area until the client is satisfied with the appearance. Treatment time must be short as you will be working in a small very sensitive area.

Treatment plan

Use short-wave diathermy for 10 minutes every 2–4 weeks depending on the client's financial situation.

Example 2: female aged 58

This client has strong hairs on chin and neck which have been regularly plucked. The client had successful electro-epilation on chin and lip at age 20–25.

Women who have had unwanted facial hair previously may find that the problem recurs to a lesser degree after the menopause. Plucking will exacerbate this problem and permanent removal may again be sought. Remembering that a plucked hair will take approximately 4 weeks to return, you must try and establish how many are plucked out each week in order to estimate the time required for removal.

Treatment plan

Use short-wave diathermy for 15–20 minutes every week initially, reducing to every other week then further reducing in frequency and time as treatment progresses, plus 20–30 minutes blend each week.

Example 3: female aged 26

This client has previously shaved her lower legs weekly. This hair is likely to be strong and will take some time to remove.

Treatment plan

Use short-wave diathermy for 1 hour every week and blend for 1–1.5 hours every week.

Example 4: gender change client

This client has the full male pattern of hair growth on the face and shaves daily.

This client will not wish to discontinue shaving between treatment, therefore start on a small area, say the chin, and when that is under control progress gradually to other areas. Shaving may be continued on areas not being treated with electro-epilation.

Treatment plan

Use short-wave diathermy for 1 hour every week and blend for 1–1.5 hours every week.

Length of treatment

The question of how long it will take to permanently remove the unwanted hair is always asked, but it is impossible to give an accurate answer. Small areas can take up to 4 years. This may appear daunting to the client, but explain that treatment will not always be weekly but will reduce to once every 2, 3,4 or even 6 weeks as the strength of the hair is reduced. The length of each treatment period is also reduced over time. Weekly treatment and constant regrowth are very difficult for clients to cope with. Encourage and support them through this period.

Electro-epilation is still the most popular method of permanently removing unwanted hair and successful treatment is well worth the time and effort required. Whether you use short-wave diathermy, galvanic or blend is a matter of preference. Although it takes longer to treat each hair with blend than with short-wave diathermy, regrowth should be less. Operators who use galvanic, particularly for facial hair, are convinced that, although treatment initially progresses very slowly, regrowth is so slight that the time spent on each follicle is worth it. Many experienced operators use a combination of all three treatments, choosing the most suitable method for each particular client depending on personal experience.

Progress Check

1 Briefly explain why the aftercare instructions must be followed.
2 What is a crust and why might it appear on the skin?
3 List the adverse skin reactions that can follow a treatment.
4 Once electro-epilation treatments have begun why is it advised that the client discontinues all temporary methods of hair removal?
5 What factors affect how often the client can have electro-epilation appointments?

Key Terms

You will need to know what these words mean. Go back through the chapter or check the glossary to find out.

- Bleeding
- Bruising
- Hyperpigmentation
- Hypopigmentation
- Keloid scars
- Pitting
- Swelling

1   What is the cause of bruising?
   a)   Overuse of current.
   b)   Incorrect insertion.
   c)   Overtreatment of the follicle.

2   Indicate whether the following statement is true or false.
   Exposure to sunlight immediately after electro-epilation is not advisable.
   True   False
   ☐   ☐

3   Which of the following is true of the normal skin's reaction to electro-epilation?
   a)   Pink or red colouring.
   b)   Bleeding.
   c)   Blanching.
   d)   Scabs.
   e)   Minor swelling.

4   Fill in the blank.
   Keloid scars are caused by _____
   a)   Having black skin.
   b)   Bacterial infection.
   c)   Having a predisposition to the condition.
   d)   Picking scabs.

5   Which of the following factors affects how hairs respond to electro-epilation?
   a)   The client having a bad diet.
   b)   The client plucking hairs in between appointments.
   c)   The client cutting the hairs in between appointments.
   d)   A hormonal imbalance such as pregnancy.

6   Indicate whether the following statement is true or false.
   Pigmentation is more likely to change in white skins than in black skins.
   True   False
   ☐   ☐

7   Why is it important to monitor the skin's reaction to treatment?

   _____

8   Why should reactions be noted on the record card?

   _____

9   Explain why a client should understand the treatment plan at the beginning of the treatment course.

   _____

10 How would you plan a course of treatment for a student with medium to strong hair growth on chin and upper lip?

   _____

After studying this chapter you will know more about:
- reducing telangiectasia
- removing skin tags.

Diathermy can be used to reduce telangiectasia and remove skin tags and warts. However, students of electro-epilation should not concern themselves with carrying out these invasive procedures until they are qualified and experienced electrologists.

Telangiectasia

The technique of reducing telangiectasia is simple to learn, but the underpinning knowledge and experience needed is considerable. It is the opinion of the authors that they should not lay out a 'how to do' section in this book. We advise practising electrologists to seek out experienced tutors who offer the appropriate training courses that are recognised for insurance purposes. Ask your professional associations for details of tutors and their membership and insurance requirements.

The treatment of facial veins is generally most successful and there is great public demand. The results on the legs can be disappointing and we would recommend that the legs are not treated with this method. Veins on the legs respond much better to sclerotherapy which involves the introduction of a chemical by injection into the superficial vessel causing an irritation. This in turn causes disintegration of the vessel. Medical personnel usually carry out treatment but limited training is available to advanced electrologists. Contact all the beauty associations for details of trainers accepted by their insurers.

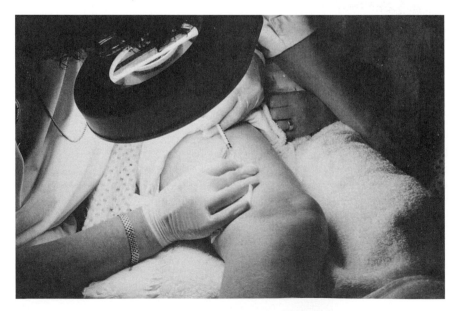

Figure 15.1 *Sclerotherapy injections for the reduction of leg telangiectasia*

The consultation for treatment is more in depth than for hair removal and causes and contraindications to treatment must be thoroughly investigated. It is also vital to the outcome that the client is aware of her responsibilities regarding home care, and time must be scheduled into the consultation to stress this point. Clients must also be given realistic expectations of the result.

Telangiectasia are often called:

- broken capillaries
- broken veins
- blood spots
- Campbell de Morgan spots
- dilated capillaries
- red veins
- spider naevi
- thread veins.

Causes are many and varied and can include:

- allergies/sneezing
- genetic predisposition
- giving birth
- wearing glasses
- harsh exfoliation
- physical trauma to the area
- skin sensitivity
- sun damage.

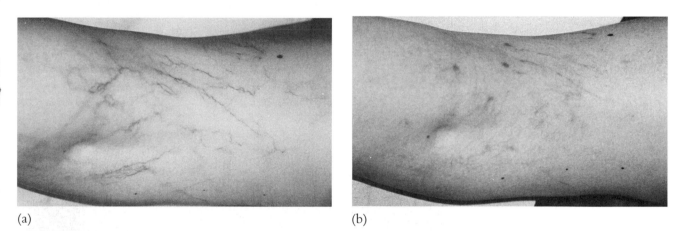

(a)   (b)

Figure 15.2 (a) *Before and* (b) *after removal of thread veins in the leg by sclerotherapy*

The authors still consider diathermy the best method of reducing facial telangiectasia. The blend method has been used in America for a number of years but we believe diathermy is most beneficial and least traumatic to the client. Lasers and pulsed light machines are also used and are very successful in reducing severe cases or generalised redness. However, for individual veins diathermy is accurate, effective and inexpensive.

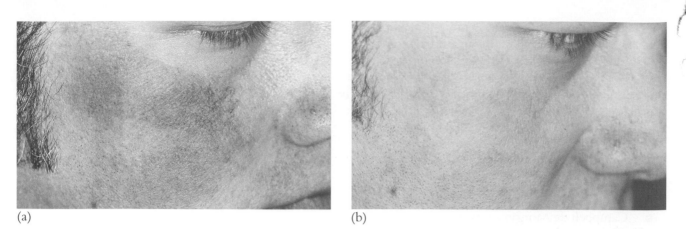

(a)   (b)

Figure 15.3 (a) *Before and* (b) *after facial telangiectasia reduction by photoderm pulsed light*

Prior to carrying out this procedure you must ensure additional insurance cover which is usually separate to your standard electro-epilation insurance.

Skin tags

These small growths are commonly found around the neck and areas of friction such as armpit or groin. They can be removed by diathermy simply and without scarring.

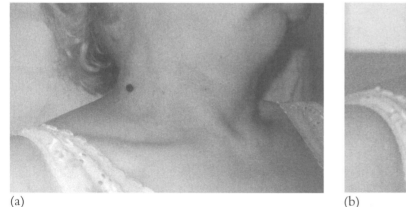
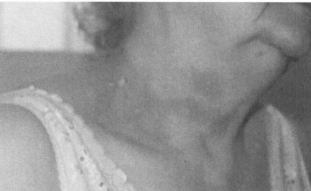

(a)   (b)

Figure 15.4 (a) *Before and* (b) *after skin tag removal by diathermy*

Written approval from a medical doctor is required before treatment by most insurers. Check with your insurance company prior to treatment.

Training

Combined courses of training are available which cover the theory and practice of these two treatments but always check with your association on their requirements. You may have to have worked longer as an electrologist to treat skin tags than to treat telangiectasia.

Warts

We do not recommended the removal of viral warts by diathermy as the area is extremely prone to infection after treatment. Most general practitioners now remove these within their surgery.

ALTERNATIVE METHODS OF HAIR REMOVAL

After studying this chapter you will be able to:

◊ understand the alternative methods of hair removal

◊ compare the advantages and disadvantages of alternative methods of hair removal.

Bleaching

Bleaching is an effective method of disguising unwanted hairs, by removing the colour in the hair. A powder and a cream are mixed together immediately before use, applied to the hair, then removed thoroughly after 5–20 minutes according to the manufacturer's instructions. The effect lasts for up to 4 weeks. Bleaching does not affect hair growth and is an ideal way of disguising fine dark hair on the face and arms.

Chemical ingredients
Bleach contains 3% hydrogen peroxide.

Reactions which can occur to bleaching
Reactions to bleaching include burned skin, irritation and redness. A spot test should be carried out on a small area before treatment.

Chemical depilation

Chemical depilators are creams or pastes applied to the skin which dissolve the hair above the level of the skin. The cream is applied to the hair and left for the length of time stated in the instructions for use. The stronger the hair, the longer it will take to dissolve. Creams should then be rinsed thoroughly from the skin. Regrowth will be visible after a few days. Chemical depilation does not affect hair growth but may irritate the skin and is to be avoided during electro-epilation.

Chemical ingredients
Hydrogen sulphide is very effective and was commonly used in the past. However, this chemical has an unpleasant odour which is difficult to disguise. For this reason, most sulphides have been replaced with salts of thioglycolic acid, which take longer to act but have a more attractive smell and are less irritating to the skin.

A typical depilatory cream contains calcium thioglycolate, calcium carbonate, calcium hydroxide, cetyl alcohol, sodium lauryl sulphate, water and a strong perfume.

Reactions which can occur to depilatory creams
These creams may cause skin irritation and ingestion can lead to gastrointestinal irritation.

Shaving

Shaving involves removal of hair at skin level by cutting it off with a blade. This is the most popular method of temporary removal of body hair and in theory should not affect the hair growth. However, many electrologists and clients will tell you that hair seems to be stronger after regular shaving. The results last only a few days. Shaving is not recommended during electro-epilation treatment.

Equipment required
A razor and shaving cream are required for a wet shave, or an electric shaver for a dry shave.

Reactions which can occur to shaving
The skin can appear grazed and red or may develop a temporary rash.

Cutting

Cutting involves removal of hair at skin level using scissors. This is the only method of temporary removal recommended for clients to use between electro-epilation treatments. Cutting the hair simply removes the length, making the hairs less noticeable. However, clients should not cut hairs just before treatment as they will not then be long enough to grasp with tweezers.

Equipment needed
The only equipment required is a pair of scissors.

Reactions which can occur to cutting
There are no adverse reactions unless the skin is cut by accident.

Plucking

Plucking involves removal of hair at root level by pulling out with tweezers. Successfully plucked hair will take 4–6 weeks to regrow, but constant plucking stimulates growth and once electro-epilation starts must be discontinued. Machines such as 'Epilady' pluck hairs more quickly than tweezers.

Equipment needed
The technique requires tweezers or an electrically driven hand-held machine.

Reactions which can occur to plucking
Small spots can occur in the follicle (folliculitis). If any dirt enters the follicle. The skin is also slightly red after plucking.

Waxing and sugaring

With these techniques hair is removed at root level by applying either hot or cool wax or sugar paste. Both methods are another form of mass plucking and should not be used once electro-epilation treatment has commenced. They are good methods of temporary removal for large areas such as legs and the effects last for 4–6 weeks. A salon treatment performed by a trained therapist will be more effective than home kits because better technique will be used to apply and remove the product. Waxing, like plucking, can stimulate hair growth and is unlikely to reduce growth, as some manufacturers imply.

Equipment needed

The equipment required includes a wax pot, hot or cool wax, spatulas, strips for removing cool wax, before and after use products, prewaxed strips or sugar paste.

Reactions which can occur to waxing

The skin will turn pink or red immediately after the treatment, but this will usually fade within 24 hours. Some clients are prone to ingrowing hairs as a result of waxing; they should then use a loofah and moisturiser or body exfoliant. If ingrowing hairs persist then another method of removal is advised. Sugar products usually cause less skin reaction.

Very occasionally a particular product, either the wax itself or a before or after wax product, may cause an allergic reaction. The reaction will be temporary, and soothing antiseptic products only should be applied. When the client returns for waxing carry out test patches of all products 24 hours before treatment and proceed with caution if no further adverse reaction is observed.

Threading

Threading involves removal of hair at root level by twisting a thread over the hair and plucking. This method is popular in the Middle and Far East and requires a highly skilled operator.

Equipment needed

Thread is the only equipment needed.

Reactions which may occur to threading

Reactions to threading are the same as the reactions that may occur after plucking.

Abrasion

Fine hair can be removed by rubbing it with a pumice stone or abrasive surface, but the results may be patchy. The method is not commonly used these days but was one of the earliest methods of hair removal, apparently being used by the ancient Egyptians and perhaps even earlier.

Equipment needed

An abrasive stone/pad is all that is required.

Reactions which may occur to abrasion

Adverse reactions are similar to those for shaving.

Tweezer epilation

Both electrically powered machines for home use and salon equipment are available. The hair is held in tweezers while a high-frequency current is passed down the hair. Hair is a poor conductor of electricity and lacks moisture above the skin, and in clinical tests carried out many years ago by the British Association of Electrolysists (BAE) the method was found to be ineffective. The BAE successfully appealed to the Advertising Standards Council to have the word 'permanent' removed from advertisements for these machines.

Microlysis is a technique that uses conductive gel on the skin which, the manufacturers claim, is carried down to the dermal papilla weakening and destroying the hair.

This and other new developments should be investigated, and we can only recommend that the electrologist keeps an open mind about different treatments and takes any opportunity to carry out personal trials and record the results prior to purchase.

Lasers and pulsed light machines

The industry has seen a huge growth in the use of these machines, which appears to be continuing. They are both used to reduce hair growth by the method of photothermolysis. The advantages are that they can cover a large area relatively quickly and are non-invasive. The disadvantage is the high cost of treatment, however clients should see this reducing as more and more clinics offer this treatment.

Lasers produce a fixed beam of light that is fired at the hairs either targeting follicles or covering a fixed area of skin with the result that the hairs 'go up in a puff of smoke'.

Pulsed light machines use selected rays from the light spectrum, cover a fixed area of skin and fire the light in short very fast pulses, building up sufficient heat to shatter the hair within the follicle without damaging surrounding skin tissue.

Both treatments require short hair to reduce wastage of energy outside the follicle and need pigment in the hair to differentiate between hair and skin. Consequently, white hair does not respond to treatment.

It is possible with suitable insurance cover and medical supervision for electrolysists to operate these machines. The use of lasers requires the premises in which they are located to be approved by the local health authority.

Side-effects of alternative methods

Alternative methods of hair removal may cause distortion of the follicle and/or stimulation of growth.

Distortion of the hair follicle

This causes difficulty when probing during electro-epilation because the needle cannot reach the dermal papilla in a curved or distorted follicle.

Distortion of the follicle can be caused by plucking, threading, waxing and sugaring. If the hairs are pulled out of their follicle at an incorrect angle the follicle may become curved or twisted.

Stimulation of growth

It has been suggested that growth may be stimulated by plucking, threading, waxing or sugaring. When a hair is repeatedly removed by these methods it is thought that the germinative cells may be stimulated into overaction.

Shaving is also reported by some to cause growth stimulation, perhaps as a result of the pulling action just before cutting. This is a highly controversial area, however, and there is no clinical proof that any method of hair removal causes growth stimulation. Students should merely be aware of the debate.

Progress Check

1   Compile a chart comparing the advantages and disadvantages of all temporary methods of hair removal.
2   What makes some temporary methods of hair removal last longer than others?
3   Which are the cheapest methods of hair removal at present?
4   Which of the temporary methods of hair removal cause the least amount of skin reaction?

ACTIVITY

Ask all the students in your class what methods of hair removal they have used and how long the results lasted.

Collate the results to show which are the most popular methods and the average time each method lasted.

Key Terms

You will need to know what these words and phrases mean. Go back through the chapter or check the glossary to find out.

- Abrasive stone
- Bleaching
- Chemical depilation
- Cutting
- Electrical epilation
- Plucking
- Shaving
- Sugaring
- Threading
- Tweezer epilation
- Waxing

1   The main ingredient of chemical depilatories

    is _____ _____ (fill in the blanks)

2   What strength of hydrogen peroxide is used in bleaching creams?

    a) 2%.
    b) 3%.
    c) 4%.
    d) 5%.

3   Which of the following methods take the hair out from the root?

    a) Waxing.
    b) Shaving.
    c) Cutting.
    d) Plucking.
    e) Electrical epilators.
    f) Chemicals.
    g) Electro-epilation.
    h) Sugaring.

4   Match the treatments with the reactions they cause.

    a) Bleaching
    b) Cream depilatories
    c) Electro-epilation

    Skin goes red.
    Skin develops hives.
    Irritation to the skin.
    Skin temporarily looks paler.
    Likely to cause allergies.

Part V

Professional practice

PROFESSIONAL ETHICS

After studying this chapter you will be able to:
- understand the meaning of professional ethics
- list the details that give a professional image
- liaise with other professionals.

Collins dictionary gives the following definitions.

- Professional: a person who engages in an activity with great competence.
- Ethics: set of moral values held by an individual or group.

In order to present a professional image to the general public you should make sure that your personal presentation is in line with public expectations. The clinic/practice also must present a picture of clean orderliness, and any promotional material should be well written and present information clearly.

Electrolysists are classed as paramedics, and members of the public have the same expectations of them as of medical personnel. Remember also that your client is paying for your time and should therefore receive your complete attention and the highest possible standard of treatment. This brings us to ethics.

GOOD PRACTICE

Treat others as you would wish to be treated yourself.

We all have our own standards of honesty and value which we should apply consistently. In addition when you join a professional organisation you must follow its codes of practice.

Personal professionalism applies to your:
- appearance
- attitude/behaviour
- care and attention
- body language
- qualifications.

Clinic professionalism applies to your working environment:
- layout
- decor
- hygiene
- sterilisation
- equipment
- records
- insurance.

Professionalism in promotion applies to:

- quality of literature
- accuracy of text
- confident authoritative approach.

Ethics

The medical profession

If a client is receiving medical treatment you may need to liaise with his or her GP regarding electro-epilation (see Figure 10.1, p. 156). If permission is given for treatment to commence keep in touch with the GP regarding progress.

(see Figure 10.1, p. 156)

GOOD PRACTICE

Continue to keep in touch with medical personnel involved with your client's treatment.

Other electrolysists

It is not professional to discuss other electrolysists with clients. Some clients may change their operator because they are dissatisfied with their treatment. You must not comment on this as you will not know all the facts.

If a client is moving to another area then put him or her in touch with a local operator and provide information on the progress of your treatment.

Your professional association

When you become a member of a professional body you will receive a copy of its rules and regulation. These have been laid down to maintain standards within the profession and should be adhered to. The association will promote its members and will also investigate complaints from the public. The association exists for your benefit and will assist with any problems you may have. Most operate a 'helpline' and can keep you informed of new developments.

Progress Check

1. How can you ensure that your treatment provides value for money?
2. What are the differences between an electro-epilation treatment and a high-quality electro-epilation treatment?
3. What does honesty mean to you?

ACTIVITY

Draft a letter to another electrolysist outside your area transferring a client for treatment because of relocation.

Key Terms

You will need to know what these words mean. Go back through the chapter to find out.

- Authoritative
- Confident
- Liaison
- Quality
- Value

After studying this chapter you will:

◊ be aware of customer requirements within your area
◊ be familiar with safety and first aid in the salon
◊ have started to think about salon resources.

Core units project

An understanding of and the ability to participate in the function of running a salon/clinic/leisure centre is required by most awarding bodies.

ACTIVITY

Answer the following questions in as much detail as possible, relating each question to your work placement or industrial salon/clinic within college. If a satisfactory system is already in place simply explain the current procedure. Otherwise give details of systems/procedures you think cover legal/health/good practice requirements.

Services and operations

1 Are you providing a satisfactory service at the correct treatment charge to the customer?
2 How would you decide on which treatments your salon/clinic should offer?
3 What considerations are necessary when fixing treatment charges?
4 Detail procedures/systems for ensuring that the quality and safety of treatments are consistent in a salon where there are several therapists.

Safety at work

1 Does your salon/clinic need to be registered with your local authority? If so what is the procedure?
2 Do you personally need to be registered with your Environmental Health Inspectorate? If so, for what reason?
3 Do you know what a business safety policy should specify? Give an example.
4 Why should an employer have employer liability insurance?
5 Why should an employer have public liability insurance?
6 Why is it necessary to display in a salon/clinic public/employer liability insurance cover?
7 Is it necessary to have a trained first aider in a salon/clinic? How often is refresher training required?
8 What details have to be entered in an accident book?
9 What is a notifiable accident?
10 Who has to be contacted following a notifiable accident?
11 What fire-fighting equipment is required in a salon/clinic?

12 When would you use a water fire extinguisher?
13 When would you use a CO_2 extinguisher?
14 When would you use a foam extinguisher?
15 How often does fire-fighting equipment have to be checked?
16 Who should be aware of the fire evacuation procedure and assembly point?
17 What signs are required for fire escape routes?
18 Legally how often should all your electrical equipment have a safety check?
19 Who can carry out this safety check?
20 What essential information does a Health and Safety Law poster give?
21 Where should this be displayed at work?
22 What are COSSH regulations?
23 List items related to the module(s) you are studying that are covered by COSSH regulations.
24 What should your salon first aid box contain?
25 Outline the first aid treatment and advice for:
- asthma attack
- dry heat burn
- scald
- chemical burn
- electrical burn
- overexposure to infrared heat
- overexposure to ultraviolet rays
- cramp
- cuts
- diabetic coma
- insulin coma
- dislocation and fracture
- electric shock
- epileptic shock
- chemical in the eye
- faint
- fall
- graze
- headache
- heart attack
- heat exhaustion
- hysteria
- inhalation of fumes
- nose bleed
- shock
- sprain
- sting
- swallowing chemicals
- swelling and inflammation
- unconsciousness
- winding.
26 Describe the recovery position.
27 When would you use the recovery position?
28 Describe the procedure for artificial respiration.

Control of resources

1 Provide photocopies of your work placement appointment book and explain why work rotas, equipment availability and timing are taken into consideration when making a booking.
2 Alternatively, show your own planned appointment sheet explaining the above variables.
3 Given £500 to promote a treatment or product what would you choose and how could the money be used to best effect?
4 Suggest procedures for monitoring and evaluating the results of promotion.
5 Suggest ways to link product sales with treatments.
6 How will you keep up to date with changing client demands and new treatments/products when you have finished studying?
7 How do you feel your present work placement's turnover could be increased? If you are not in a work placement visit a local salon/clinic, look around, speak to therapists, collect a treatment list and discuss what changes you would make. (This question should be answered in considerable detail.)
8 How would you introduce your ideas for the above changes to the salon/clinic owner/manager?

Useful publications

The following list of government publications will be useful and can be acquired from government authorised bookshops.

- *COSHH A Brief Guide to the Regulations* ISBN 07176 24447
- *RIDDOR Explained: Reporting of Injuries, Diseases and Dangerous Occurrences Regulations* ISBN 07176 24412
- *5 Steps to Successful Health and Safety Management* ISBN 07176 0425X
- *Essentials of Health and Safety at Work* ISBN 07176 0716X
- *Employer's Liability (Compulsory Insurance Act 1969)* ISBN 010 545 769 8
- *Guide for Employers* ISBN 0 11 079725 6
- *First Aid at Work* ISBN 07176 10748
- *Health and Safety at Work Act Advice to Employers: Management of Health and Safety at Work Regulations* ISBN 07176 15650
- *5 Steps to Risk Assessment* ISBN 07176 15650
- *Manual Handling: Solutions You Can Handle* ISBN 07176 06937
- *Electricity at Work (safe working practices)* ISBN 07176 0442X
- *Electrical Safety and You* ISBN 07176 12074
- *Maintaining Portable Electrical Equipment in Offices and Other Low Risk Environments* ISBN 07176 12724

BUSINESS CONSIDERATIONS

After studying this chapter you will:

- know who to contact for advice and assistance
- have examples of books to read before starting to plan your venture.

This book is about electro-epilation. Business and salon management is another subject entirely. We cannot hope to give you sufficient information to start your own business in a few pages. Therefore in the bibliography you will find three books listed which we recommend you read before planning your own clinic/practice.

Today there is a wealth of help available, and listed below are local and national contacts.

Sources of advice

Local
Look in your local telephone directory for numbers.

Local advice centres
Organisations offering financial and business advice within your area may have a variety of names. These organisations will advise on funding for your venture. Assistance is also given on forming a business plan, obtaining a bank loan and dealing with the bookkeeping. They also often run free courses in promotion, sales and marketing.

- Small Business Advisory Service
- Business Venture
- Business Link.

Your local chamber of commerce can usually direct you to the local advisory service most suited to your needs.

Bank
Your bank manager can give you advice on obtaining a bank loan.

Environmental health office
This is usually part of the local city/town council and its officers will advise on health and safety requirements.

Fire prevention officer
The fire prevention officer at your local fire station will give advice regarding fire safety and regulations.

Crime prevention officer
The crime prevention officer at your local police station will give advice regarding personal and business crime prevention, i.e. security of doors and windows, burglar alarms, etc.

Insurance broker

The cheapest form of treatment insurance can usually be obtained through a professional association such as the British Association of Electrolysists (see address under Professional Associations, p. 250). Often the association's brokers will be able to extend your cover to include public liability, building and contents cover, etc.

Accountant

A small business owner is usually able to keep simple business accounts which can be submitted to a local chartered accountant at the end of the trading year. The accountant will then prepare the accounts for submission to the Inland Revenue and you will be advised of your income tax and national insurance liability. If your income is below a certain level you may be able to submit your own accounts directly to the Inland Revenue. Local tax officers will assist you in completing the relevant forms.

GOOD PRACTICE

Reserve sufficient money to pay your income tax at the end of each financial year.

VAT office

Contact your local VAT office to find out the current VAT threshold. If you do not expect your turnover to reach the threshold you do not have to register for VAT and you may not wish to do so.

Estate agents

Estate agents will look for suitable properties and give advice on fair rents and rates.

Solicitor

There will be times, when trading, that you require legal help. The professional association that you belong to will have a legal advisor who can usually be consulted without charge initially. Otherwise, personal recommendation is the best way of finding a local solicitor or the chamber of commerce will recommend a local firm.

National

The following organisations may be useful:

Advertising Standards Authority
Brook House
2–16 Torrington Place
London
WC1E 7HN

For queries on wording of advertisements or business literature.

Data Protection Registrar
Springfield House
Water Lane
Wilmslow
Cheshire
SK9 5AX
website www.dataprotection.gov.uk

If you use a computer database to hold records of clients you may have to register this.

Contact checklist

- chamber of commerce
- bank manager
- estate agents
- environmental health office
- fire prevention officer
- crime prevention officer
- insurance broker
- Inland Revenue office
- VAT office.

ACTIVITY

1. Contact your local chamber of commerce to find out what financial assistance is currently available to new business ventures and what free or subsidised training is available.
2. If you are seriously considering starting your own business we suggest that you form a detailed business plan. This helps to focus your mind on all the items that need to addressed before commencing the venture.

GOOD PRACTICE

Assistance in completing a business plan can be obtained from your local business venture advisor. Contact the chamber of commerce.

After studying this chapter you will be able to:

♦ define and understand the terms relating to health and hygiene
♦ list a variety of products and equipment relating to health and hygiene
♦ decide on the most appropriate methods of maintaining health and hygiene
♦ understand bacteria, virus and fungi
♦ explain AIDS and hepatitis B
♦ understand immunity.

Every electrolysis salon must register with and be approved by its local environmental health office. Contact yours for local requirements in the salon and to obtain a 'Certificate for Skin Piercing'.

Sharps boxes and contaminated waste must be removed by an approved refuse collector. Contact your local council refuse department, which will arrange regular collection. Sharps boxes can be purchased from your local hair and beauty wholesaler.

Hygiene procedures

It is necessary to keep all working surfaces disinfected, any working implements sterilised and any areas of the body that you will be working on sanitised.

Sterilisation

Sterilisation is the complete destruction of all microbial life, including spores. A sterile object or environment is free of all living organisms.

Disinfection

Disinfectants are chemicals that destroy the growing forms of micro-organisms, but not the spores. When the effect of the disinfectant wears off the bacteria regrow from the spores. (Disinfectants should not be used on the skin.)

Some examples of disinfectants are as follows.

♦ Halogens: bleach (hypochlorite) for work surfaces; iodine for the skin.
♦ Acids and alkalis: phenol, for walls as in carbolic acid; diphenols (soap) for the skin.
♦ Quaternary ammonium compounds: centrimide, chlorhexidine (Steritane).

GOOD PRACTICE

Disinfectants are typically diluted to 70% strength and antiseptics to 40% strength.

Antiseptics

Antiseptics are chemicals which are similar to disinfectants but are safe to use on living tissues. Again they kill bacteria and fungi completely, but not the spores.

Some examples of antiseptics are:

- methylated spirits (ethyl alcohol)
- soap
- hydrogen peroxide.

Other definitions

Sanitation

A sanitiser is a substance which reduces micro-organisms to a level considered safe by the Public Health Administration. Disinfections and antiseptics are sanitisers.

Bacteriostatic

Anything which kills growing forms of bacteria.

Asepsis

This is the opposite of sepsis and means the absence of disease.

Methods of sterilisation/sanitisation

There are many such methods:

- alcohol
- autoclaves
- glass bead sterilisers
- boilers and steamers
- UVC sanitisers
- chemicals (formaldehyde).

Note that complete sterilisation can only be achieved in the salon using the following methods:

- autoclave
- glass bead steriliser
- formaldehyde.

Complete sterilisation is required for tweezers and chuck caps. Needles should always be of the presterilised disposable type.

Alcohol

Alcohol, or a suitable alcohol-based disinfectant (e.g. chlorhexidine/alcohol), can be used in certain circumstances to sanitise or disinfect but not to sterilise. The recommended concentration is 70%. When used for instruments care should be taken that:

- only one or two instruments at a time are disinfected
- the alcohol covers the instruments completely
- period of immersion is as recommended by the manufacturer
- the alcohol is discarded after one use.

Containers used for disinfecting with alcohol should be washed regularly with hot water and detergent, rinsed thoroughly and left to dry. Commercially available alcohol-impregnated wipes are recommended.

Discard used alcohol down the sink in running water.

Autoclaves

An autoclave is a machine that uses steam at high pressure to sterilise instruments and other articles. Boiling alone cannot be used for sterilisation. The procedure requires the correct temperature (higher than boiling) and pressure (higher than atmosphere) to be applied for the correct length of time (varying from 15 minutes at 121°C to 3 minutes at 134°C). An autoclave is highly recommended for salons. It is still the most efficient method of sterilising objects. All metal objects as well as some plastics can be sterilised in this way. Autoclaves are easy to use and cheap to run.

Glass bead sterilisers

These are small inexpensive gadgets that use the dry heat method of sterilisation. They can be used as an alternative to the boiling method provided the instruments are inserted for the correct length of time. They take time to warm up after being switched on (usually about 20–30 minutes), so all timings must be measured from at least 30 minutes after switching on. The higher the temperature, the shorter the time period required for sterilisation, but instruments are more likely to be damaged or blunted at high temperatures. Only the parts covered by the glass beads can be considered sterilised. The following conditions for dry heat sterilisation comply with the European and British Pharmacopieia criteria (times after load has reached the required temperature):

- 160°C for 60 minutes
- 170°C for 30 minutes
- 80°C for 120 minutes.

It is best to sterilise each instrument separately, rather than to put several in together. Increase these times if more than one instrument is being sterilised at any one time.

Boilers and steamers

Boiling water or steam does not sterilise, it only disinfects. However, these instruments are useful for reducing the risk of spreading infection. The unit should be heated by electricity and should be equipped with a lid, a perforated removable shelf for raising and lowering instruments and an automatic timer. Instruments should be boiled or steamed for 10 minutes and then removed with clean forceps; for boilers timing should commence from the point at which the water begins to boil after the instruments have been immersed in it. Clean distilled or deionised water should be used and replaced completely once a day.

UVC sanitisers

Ultraviolet light has disinfectant properties only. It is not recommended that this method should replace any of the methods described above. The cabinet can be used for storing presterilised instruments.

Chemicals

The utensil must be immersed in the chemical for at least 20 minutes. The container holding the chemical and implements should be covered to prevent further particles infecting it, and the chemical must be changed at regular intervals according to the manufacturer's instructions. Bear in mind that the more implements put into the chemical the sooner it will require changing.

Progress Check

1 What is a 'sharps box'?
2 Define sterilisation.
3 Compare disinfectants and antiseptics.
4 Name and explain any three methods of sterilisation.
5 Define the term 'bacteriostatic'.

Surfaces, chairs and floors

Keep basins clean using any proprietary cleanser. Other surfaces may be wiped with 70% surgical spirit or a similar alcohol-based disinfectant wipe three or four times a day. These surfaces should also be washed at the end of each day with a solution of household detergent in hot water. Floors and chairs should be kept clean with a regular wash down but need no special treatment.

Blood spill

In the event of a blood spill, pour neat household bleach on to the blood, leave for 1 minute, then wash off with plenty of hot water and detergent. Be sure to wear disposable gloves. Neat bleach should not be used on the skin; a 10% dilute solution with water can be used on the skin if no alternative antiseptic is available.

GOOD PRACTICE

Always protect your hands with rubber gloves when dealing with chemicals or blood.

Types of micro-organisms

Bacteria
Bacteria are single-celled organisms with no nucleus. There are many types of bacteria, which are usually classified according to shape.

Bacteria are well protected by their outer rigid wall and sometimes by an outer jelly capsule. Bacteria contain DNA, but since there is no nucleus it is distributed throughout the cell.

Some bacteria can exist in two forms: the vegetative form is the normal form of bacteria which are easily destroyed; the other form, spores, are thick-walled and more difficult to kill. Bacterial spores have nothing to do with reproduction, they are a form of protection for the bacteria when the environment is not conducive to normal existence and functioning.

Vegetative forms can change into spores and back again whenever necessary.

Types of bacteria

A spherical bacterium is called a coccus, e.g. *Staphylococcus, Streptococcus.* A bacterium in the form of a straight rod is called a bacillus. Curved or spiral bacteria include the genera *Vibrio* (common shape), *Campylobacter* and *Spirillum*. Spirochaetes have a long flexible spiral shape.

Alternative definitions

Autotrophs	Bacteria that can live in an inorganic environment (without carbon); these are not a medically significant type of bacteria.
Heterotrophs	Bacteria that need organic material to grow.
Commensals	Bacteria that are considered as normal inhabitants of the body; they do not cause disease.
Facultative anaerobes	Bacteria that can live with or without oxygen.
Anaerobes	Bacteria that can only live without oxygen.
Strict or obligate aerobes	Bacteria that must have oxygen to live.
Pathogenic bacteria	Disease-causing bacteria; they usually grow and reproduce best at body temperature, 37°C.
Non-pathogenic bacteria	Bacteria that do not cause disease, harmless to the body.

Table 20.1 *Alternative definitions of bacteria*

Bacteria and disease

The ability of bacteria to cause disease is called pathogenic virulence. Pathogenic bacteria enter (invade) another organism called the host and multiply there. Their effects are due to the production of substances called toxins which can harm or destroy the tissues of the host.

Viruses

Viruses are minute infective particles that can survive outside another organism or host but are only active when inside the cells of a host.

Once inside the host cell a virus uses the machinery of the cell to reproduce itself. When it has done so, the cell bursts open, releasing the new virus particles, or virions, into the bloodstream of the host. The virions are then able to infect other host cells. The time when the virus is reproducing is called the incubation period.

Viruses are much smaller than bacteria, some being only one-fiftieth of the size of bacteria. Viruses usually contain either RNA or DNA; some contain both. Viruses are classified according to their shape and structure but are named after the disease they cause.

All viruses are antigenic, and to neutralise and inactivate the virus the host needs to produce antibodies against it. Some viruses can cause cancer.

Viruses are very resilient organisms. They can change their characteristics through a process known as mutation. Mutation may result in altered antigenicity or virulence (disease-causing capacity) of the virus.

AIDS (acquired immunodeficiency syndrome)

AIDS is caused by a virus known as HIV (human immunodeficiency virus). Not all people who are infected with HIV have AIDS, but it is thought that most of them will develop AIDS eventually. A very small number of people who have been found to be infected with HIV later have a negative test, showing that they have fought off the virus.

AIDS is generally considered to be always fatal. HIV enters its host's 'T-helper cells', a specific type of white cell essential for immunity to infection. The virus will either kill the cells or lie dormant, becoming active later, making the sufferer susceptible to infections and cancers.

For testing purposes HIV can be found in blood, semen, saliva, tears, nervous system tissue, breast milk and female genital tract secretions. Only semen and blood have been proved to transmit the virus. HIV cannot be transmitted by hugging, touching or by sharing items such as cutlery and crockery. Transmission of infection can be prevented by practising safe sex, wearing gloves when coming into contact with any body fluids and taking care with any sharp instruments.

The initial symptoms of AIDS include lymph gland enlargement, diarrhoea and weight loss, fever, skin disorders and oral thrush. In the more severe cases the affected individual will suffer from chronic herpes simplex infections, shingles, tuberculosis, salmonellosis and a variety of disorders of the neurological system including dementia. People with full-blown AIDS may suffer from Kaposi's sarcoma, lymphoma of the brain, thrombocytopenia (an autoimmune disease) and various infections.

At present there is no cure for AIDS; antibiotics can be used to alleviate some of the symptoms, and the antiviral drug AZT has in some cases been shown to slow the progression of the disease, but AZT is known to have serious side-effects.

Hepatitis B

Hepatitis B, sometimes called serum hepatitis, is also caused by a virus. Hepatitis B is a highly contagious virus that has an incubation period of anything from 40 to 150 days.

Blood transfusions used to be the main route of transmitting the hepatitis virus, but now it is mainly transmitted sexually or via accidental inoculation of contaminated blood.

During the early stages of the infection the sufferer may show no symptoms or develop a flu-like fever followed by jaundice.

The hepatitis B virus attacks the liver as its primary target, and in many cases symptoms persist for years after the initial infection, leading to a chronic form of hepatitis, liver cirrhosis or liver cancer. Approximately 10% of hepatitis sufferers go on to develop chronic hepatitis.

There is no cure for hepatitis, although it is recommended that everyone who is at high risk of infection because of either their lifestyle or the nature of their work should be inoculated against the virus.

Fungi

There are three different types of fungi:

- yeast and yeast-like fungi
- filamentous fungi
- dimorphic fungi.

The presence of bacteria will often prevent fungal infection, but any reduction in the normal level of bacteria in the body may allow fungal infection to develop, e.g. on the skin and in the gut.

Yeast and yeast-like fungi

Yeasts have round or oval bodies and reproduce by budding. Generalised infections due to this type of fungi are rare, although they can cause some more severe infections.

Yeast-like fungi are similar to yeasts but can form chains or filaments of elongated cells. They also reproduce by budding. *Candida albicans* and *Malassezia furfur* are fungi in this group. *Candida albicans* is commonly found in the mouth and throat, causing thrush, and in the vagina, causing vaginal inflammation. In some people this fungus can cause an intractable infection of the skin, nails, mouth and/or lungs. *Malassezia furfur*, another fungus in this group, causes the condition pityriasis versicolor.

Filamentous fungi

Filamentous fungi grow in filaments and reproduce by forming spores. These spores do not have a protective function like the spores previously mentioned. This group of fungi includes:

- dermatophytes, which infect the keratin in the skin and nails, resulting in tinea and ringworm
- *Microsporum*, which causes ringworm of the hair and skin
- *Trichophyton*, which attacks the skin, hair and nails
- *Epidermophyton*, which attacks only the skin and nails.

Dimorphic fungi

Dimorphic fungi can, as the name suggests, live in two forms. The filamentous form exists at lower temperatures and is saprophytic, i.e. it lives off dead matter. A yeast form is active at body temperature and is parasitic, i.e. it lives off and at the expense of another organism or host.

Immunity

The body has an innate (inbuilt) protection against some forms of infection without having to have been previously infected with the disease. Organs involved in the immune system include the skin and the blood plasma, the fluid part of the blood.

If the body is naturally infected by an organism it can fight it by developing a specific antidote to the infection. If the body is artificially exposed to infection by inoculation with a weakened strain of the micro-organism then again it can develop a specific antidote. This is the principle of vaccination. The antidote the body makes is called an antibody. Each antibody is specific, which means that it reacts with only one type of micro-organism or antigen.

All bacteria and viruses are unique antigens; thus, unless there exists innate protection or antibodies as a result of a previous infection, the body will always become infected until it can find a way of defending itself by producing a new antibody.

Progress Check

1. What action should be taken in the event of a blood spill?
2. Why is the same chemical sometimes called a disinfectant and sometimes an antiseptic?
3. What is the smallest infectious particle?
4. What types of organism live off a host?
5. How are bacteria classified?
6. In what circumstances does a spore reproduce?
7. Is there a cure for hepatitis B?
8. Why is the immune system affected by HIV and AIDS?
9. What are the different ways of developing immunity?

Key Terms

You will need to know what these words and phrases mean. Go back through the chapter to find out.

- AIDS
- Antiseptic
- Autoclave
- Disinfection
- Glass bead steriliser
- Hepatitis B
- Sanitiser
- Sterilisation

1 The certificate required to perform electro-epilation is called:

  a) 'Certificate for skin piercing'.
  b) 'Certificate for electro-epilation'.
  c) 'Certificate for skin treatments'.

2 Which of the following is the definition of sterilisation?

  a) A chemical that destroys the growing forms of infection and infectious microbes.
  b) The absolute destruction of all microbial life, including spores.
  c) A process that reduces microbes to a level considered safe by the Public Health Administration.

3 Place each disinfectant in the correct group.

  Halogens   Phenol
  Quaternary ammonium compounds   Bleach
  Acids and alkalis   Chlorhexidine

4 Match the method of sterilisation with the description (one does not fit).

  Alcohol
  Chemicals
  Autoclave
  Glass bead steriliser

  a) Steam pressure reaching temperatures of 121–134°C.
  b) Dry heat to sterilise.
  c) Ultraviolet light.
  d) Immersion for 20 minutes.
  e) 70% strength fluid, recommended immersion time 30 minutes.

5 What does AIDS stand for?

  a) Auto-immunodeficiency syndrome.
  b) Acquired immunodeficiency syndrome.
  c) Acquired immunity deficiency syndrome.
  d) Auto-immune disease syndrome.

GLOSSARY

Acne
A chronic skin disease caused by inflammation of the sebaceous glands of the skin, characterised by pustules and blackheads on the face. It is common in adolescents.

Acromegaly
A chronic disease characterised by enlargement of the bones of the head, hands and feet. It is caused by excessive secretion of growth hormone by the pituitary gland.

ACTH (adrenocorticotrophic hormone)
A hormone secreted by the anterior pituitary which stimulates the production and release of certain corticosteroid hormones by the adrenal cortex.

ADH (antidiuretic hormone/vasopressin)
A hormone secreted by the posterior pituitary gland which causes water reabsorption from the kidneys back into the body/blood.

Adrenal glands (suprarenal glands)
Small endocrine glands, one on the upper pole of each kidney. They have two parts: the medulla, which secretes adrenaline and noradrenaline; and the cortex, which produces various corticosteroid hormones.

AIDS (acquired immunodeficiency syndrome)
A complex syndrome caused by a virus (HIV) with as yet no known cure. The immune system is compromised, leading to increased susceptibility to fatal opportunistic infections and malignant disease. Intravenous drug users, homosexuals and those who have received transfusions of infected blood/blood products are particularly at risk.

Allergy
Sensitivity to a particular foreign protein, for example certain foods, animal fur and pollens. Allergic conditions include asthma, hayfever, urticaria and eczema.

Alternating current (a.c.)
An electric current that reverses direction with a frequency independent of the characteristics of the circuit through which it flows.

Amenorrhoea
Absence of menstruation. Amenorrhoea occurs during pregnancy, and may occur in certain endocrine disorders.

Ampere
The basic unit of electric current.

Anagen
The first active stage in the hair growth cycle, during which the hair is fully attached to the blood supply.

Anaphoresis
The chemical/electrical change that occurs at the anode when a galvanic current is flowing.

Androgens
A group of steroid hormones, e.g. testosterone, which produce the male secondary characteristics. They are secreted by testes, the adrenal and to a lesser extent the ovary.

Anorexia nervosa
A serious psychological condition characterised by a refusal to eat, self-induced vomiting and the use of laxatives. It is commonest in young females and may be associated with a fear of becoming obese and an obsession with thinness.

Antiseptic
A substance opposing sepsis by arresting the growth and multiplication of micro-organisms.

Apocrine gland
A specialised sweat gland found in the axillae and genital regions. Apocrine glands only become active at puberty.

Arrector pill
Muscle fibres around the hair follicles which on contraction produce 'goose bumps'.

Aseptic
Free from pathogenic micro-organisms.

Autoclave
An apparatus for sterilising by steam under pressure.

Axilla
The armpit.

Bacteria
Microscopic unicellular organisms widely distributed in a variety of different environments. They may be pathogenic (disease-producing) or non-pathogenic; some serve a useful function in humans, e.g. the production of an environment hostile to pathogens. Non-pathogens may become pathogenic if they move from their normal site in or on the body.

Blend epilation
Simultaneous use of direct current and short-wave diathermy current to treat a hair follicle.

Capillary
A tiny blood vessel communicating with arterioles and venules. The walls are one cell thick and allow transfer of substances between blood and the body cells.

Carcinogen
An agent that causes or predisposes to cancer, e.g. certain chemicals, viruses.

Catagen
The second changing stage of the hair growth cycle, during which the hair is moving up the hair follicle.

Cataphoresis
The chemical/electrical change that occurs at the cathode when a galvanic current is flowing.

Caustic
Capable of burning or corroding by chemical action.

Cauterise
To burn or sear body tissue with dry heat or a caustic agent.

Cell
The structural unit of any living organism. The basic unit of life.

Club hair
A hair that has a clubbed end and is usually in the catagen stage of hair growth. The shape is due to the bulb having disintegrated.

Coagulate
To cause a fluid such as blood to change into a soft semisolid mass.

Comedone
An accumulation of sebaceous secretions in a hair follicle, commonly called a blackhead.

Conductor
A substance, body or system that conducts electricity and heat.

Connective tissue
Supporting or packing material consisting of a fibrous gel made up of collagen and elastin fibres as found in the dermis.

Contraindication
A reason not to carry out a treatment or a reason to take very special care.

Cortex
The outer layer of an organ and the outer section of a hair.

Crust
A thick scab-type accumulation of cells on the surface of the skin.

Cushing's syndrome
Syndrome caused by an elevated level of corticosteroids resulting from oversecretion or as a side-effect of therapeutic corticosteroids. The syndrome is characterised by the typical appearance of moon face, fat redistribution, muscle wasting and weakness, purpura and hirsutism. There is also hypertension, glycosuria, osteoporosis and mental disturbance.

Cuticle
The external, often protective part of a structure, e.g. the cuticle around the outside of the hair.

Depilate
To remove superfluous hairs from the body.

Dermal cord
A string of cells that connect the hair follicle to the dermal papilla (blood supply) in the catagen and telogen stages of hair growth.

Dermal papilla
Blood supply to feed the bottom of the hair follicle.

Dermis
The true skin that lies below the epidermis.

DHT (dihydrotestosterone)

A derivative of the hormone testosterone that is 20 times more effective.

Diabetes mellitus
A common condition due to deficiency or reduced effectiveness of insulin. The body is unable to use glucose, resulting in hyperglycaemia, polyuria, glycosuria, hyperglycaemia, polydipsia and abnormal fat and protein metabolism.

Diathermy
The passage of a high-frequency electric current through tissue. The electrical resistance of the tissues causes heat to be generated.

Direct current (d.c.)
Continuous electric current that flows in one direction only.

Disinfectant
A chemical used to remove micro-organisms potentially harmful to humans.

Eccrine gland
A type of sweat gland occurring all over the body but particularly numerous on the feet and hands.

Electrode
A conductor through which an electric current enters or leaves an electrolyte, an electric arc or an electronic valve or tube.

Electro-epilation
A permanent method of hair removal involving the use of an electric current.

Endocrine
The term used to describe the ductless glands which produce the hormones controlling many functions. They include the pituitary, thyroid, parathyroids, adrenals, gonads, pancreas (also exocrine) and the placenta. Many links exist between this system and the nervous system.

Epidermis
The outer layer of the skin.

Epithelium
The tissue which forms the outer layer of the skin and lines tubes and cavities. The different types are classified by their structure and function.

Erythema
Redness of the skin.

Flash technique
A technique used in short-wave diathermy whereby a stronger current is used for a very short space of time.

Folliculitis
Inflammation within the hair follicle due to the entry of bacteria.

Formaldehyde
A substance used as a disinfectant and for the preservation of pathological specimens.

Frothing
Escape of hydrogen and chloride gases from the follicle as a result of treatment with galvanic or blend epilation.

FSH (follicle-stimulating hormone)
A hormone secreted form the anterior lobe of the pituitary gland.

Fuse
A protective device for safeguarding electric circuits, It contains a wire that melts and breaks the circuit when the current exceeds a certain value.

Galvanic current
Direct electric current.

Gamma irradiation
Electromagnetic rays of extremely short wavelength emitted by certain radioactive isotopes. Used to sterilise.

Gender dysphoria
A feeling of being ill at ease with one's sex; experienced by transsexuals.

Germinative layer
The lowest layer of the epidermis, sometimes known as the basal layer. It is responsible for production of epidermal cells.

Gonadotrophin
A hormone which stimulates the gonads, e.g. FSH, LH.

Haemophilia
An inherited bleeding disease in which factor VIII, the anti-haemophilic globin, is deficient. It is a genetic disorder that affects only males.

Hair bulb
The bottom of the hair where cell reproduction and keratinisation occur.

Hair cycle
The growth, change and rest phases of the life of a hair.

Hair follicle
A little pit in the skin in which the root of the hair is fixed.

Hair germ cells
The cells in the skin that initiate the formation of new hair.

Hair matrix
The inner part of the hair.

Hair shaft
The visible part of the hair above the surface of the skin.

High-frequency current
Alternating current with a high number of oscillations per second.

Hirsutism
A condition in which a female exhibits the male pattern of hair growth.

HIV (human immunodeficiency virus)
A retrovirus, previously known as LAV or HTLV III, which attacks helper T lymphocytes, causing immunodeficiency.

Hormone
A chemical substance which affects the functioning of structures distant from its source, e.g. growth hormone.

HRT (hormone replacement therapy)
Treatment with artificial oestrogen and progesterone recommended for menopausal woman to replace the hormones they lack.

Hyperpigmentation
An area of skin darker than the surrounding skin resulting from a high level of pigmentation.

Hyperthyroidism
Oversecretion of thyroid hormones causing an increase in metabolic rate.

Hypertrichosis
Excessive growth of hair, or growth of hair in unusual places.

Hypopigmentation
An area of skin lighter than the surrounding skin resulting from a low level of pigmentation.

Hypothalamus
An area of grey matter at the base of the brain which has links with other parts of the nervous system and pituitary gland.

Hypothyroidism
Undersecretion of thyroid hormones causing a decrease in metabolic rate.

Hysterectomy
Surgical removal of the uterus.

Impetigo
A highly contagious skin disease caused by bacteria.

Indifferent electrode
The positive pole that the client holds during blend or galvanic epilation.

Infection
The communication of a disease from one person to another.

Inflammation
The reaction of living tissue to injury or infection characterised by heat, swelling, redness and pain.

Ingrowing hair
A hair which has grown abnormally into the flesh covered by adjacent tissue.

Inner root sheath
The innermost part of the tissue found surrounding the bulb of the hair known as the root sheath. The inner root sheath is made up of these layers:

1. cuticle of inner root sheath
2. Huxley's layer
3. Henle's layer.

Insulin
A popypeptide hormone produced by the beta cells of the pancreas.

Islets of Langerhans
Small areas of specialised cells in the pancreas which have endocrine functions.

Keratin
A fibrous protein found in tissues such as the outer layer of skin, nails and hair.

Lanugo hair
The downy growth of hair which grows on the unborn child from about the fourth month of gestation.

Lesion
Any structural change in a bodily part resulting from an injury or disease.

LH (luteinising hormone)
A hormone produced by the pituitary gland.

Lye
Another name for sodium hydroxide, formed when the salts of the body separate and reform when in contact with d.c.

Lymph
Fluid in the lymphatic system derived from tissue fluid, similar in composition to blood plasma.

Medulla
The central part of various organs.

Melanin
A pigment derived from tyrosine, found in the skin, hair, eye and other sites.

Menopause
The period during which a woman's menstrual cycle ceases, normally between the ages of 45 and 50.

Menstruation
The discharge of blood and endometrium from the uterus. This occurs on a cyclical basis approximately every 28 days from menarche to the menopause except during pregnancy.

Metabolism
The sum total of chemical processes that occur in living organisms, resulting in growth, production of energy and elimination of waste material.

Milliampere
One thousandth of an ampere.

Mitosis
Cell division in non-gametes resulting in daughter cells which are identical to the original cell and have the same number of chromosomes/genes.

Modality
Type or method of electro-epilation, e.g. galvanic modality.

Mole
A dark pigmented area on the skin.

Nerve
A cord-like bundle of fibres that conducts impulses between the brain or spinal cord and another part of the body.

Oedema
Swelling due to excess fluid in tissues.

Oestrogen
A steroid hormone produced by the ovaries and which is responsible for the development of female genital organs and the female secondary sexual characteristics. Small quantities can be found in the adrenal cortex.

Outer root sheath
The outer part of the tissue found surrounding the bulb of the hair, known as the root sheath.

Ovaries
The female gonads. Two small structures situated either side of the uterus. Under the influence of pituitary hormones they produce ova and hormones.

Pancreas
A large elongated glandular organ situated behind the stomach that secretes insulin and pancreatic juice.

Pancreatic hormones
Hormones produced by the pancreas that regulate the blood sugar level.

Papillary layer
The layer of the dermis which lies directly beneath the epidermis.

Parathyroid glands
Four small endocrine glands normally situated on the posterior surface of the thyroid.

Pitting
Small pitted scars caused by overtreatment of the follicle and which will improve in time depending on the degree of damage.

Pituitary gland
The master endocrine gland attached by a stalk to the base of the brain. Its two lobes secrete hormones affecting skeletal growth, development of the sex glands and the functioning of the other endocrine glands.

Polycystic ovary syndrome
A disease in which there is increased ovarian and/or adrenal secretion of androgens, causing hirsutism, obesity, menstrual irregularity, infertility and multiple follicular ovarian cysts.

Pore
A minute opening, such as those on the skin, which discharges sweat onto the surface.

Pregnancy
The period of being with child; the gestation period in the female human lasts about 9 months or 280 days.

Progesterone
A steroid hormone produced by the corpus luteum and placenta which influences the endometrium, cervix and breasts during the menstrual cycle and pregnancy. Also produced in small amounts by the adrenals and testes.

Prolactin
The hormone produced by the anterior pituitary which stimulates milk production.

Psoriasis
A genetically determined abnormality of keratinisation producing skin lesions consisting of raised red scaly areas.

Puberty
The period at the beginning of adolescence when the sex glands become functional. Also called pubescence.

Radiofrequency
Another term for high-frequency current.

Regrowth
Hair that regrows after electro-epilation has been performed.

Ringworm
Tinea or dermatophytosis. A fungal disease affecting the skin, hair or nails.

Rosacea

A chronic disease of unknown cause, characterised by diffuse facial erythema with inflamed papules and pustules. The skin appears shiny because of lymphoedema.

Scab

An encrustation formed over a wound.

Sebaceous glands

Glands found in the skin which open out into the hair follicle, secreting fatty material called sebum.

Sensory nerve

An afferent nerve which carries sensory impulses from the peripheral nerve endings to the central nervous system.

Skin stretch

Stretching of the skin by an electrologist to allow easier entry into the hair follicle.

Sodium hydroxide (NaOH)

See Lye.

Spider naevus

A central dilated blood vessel with small capillaries radiating from it like the legs of a spider.

Staphylococcus

A spherical bacterium, usually found in clusters, which causes boils, infection in wounds and septicaemia.

Stein-Leventhal syndrome

See Polycystic ovary syndrome.

Sterilise

To render instruments, equipment, etc. free from micro-organisms by the use of heat, chemicals or radiation.

Stress

Any factor which adversely affects physical and/or mental well-being.

Subcutis

A layer of adipose fat found beneath the dermis.

Superfluous hair

An excess of normal downy hair.

Sweat gland

An exocrine gland which excretes a mixture of urea, salt and water mainly for the purpose of reducing the body temperature.

Synapse

The gap between the axon of one nerve fibre and the dendrites of another nerve fibre or the nerve and another cell type.

Telangiectasia

A group of dilated capillaries.

Telogen
The third and final stage of hair growth, during which the hair is at complete rest.

Terminal hair
The strongest and deepest type of hair growth found on the scalp, axilla and pubic region.

Testosterone
An androgen. A steroid hormone responsible for the male sexual characteristics. It is produced by the interstitial cells of the testes.

Thermolysis
American term for short-wave diathermy.

Thymus gland
A glandular organ of vertebrates consisting in the human of two lobes situated below the thyroid. It atrophies with age and is almost non-existent in the adult.

Thyroid gland
An endocrine gland consisting of two lobes, one on either side of the trachea. It secretes three hormones: triiodothyronine, thyroxine and calcitonin.

Unit of lye
American measurement for the amount of lye produced.

Urticaria
Also known as nettle rash and hives. An allergic reaction to certain foods, e.g. shellfish, characterised by wheals and erythema.

Vellus hair
The downy hair found over most regions of the body.

Virilism
The appearance of masculine characteristics in the female.

Vitiligo
Also known as leucoderma. Patchy areas of depigmentation occurring in the skin.

Volt
The unit of electromotive force.

Wart
Small horny tumour of the skin due to a viral infection.

Watt
The unit of electrical strength.

Archer P. (1994) *How to Run a More Profitable Beauty Salon*. Wakefield Associates, Derby

Baillière's Nurses Dictionary. Baillière Tindall, London.

Forster A. and Palastanga N. *Clayton's Electrotherapy*. Baillière Tindall, London.

Gallant A. (1983) *Principles and Techniques for the Electrologist*. Nelson Thornes, Cheltenham.

Greenblatt R.B. (1978) *The Hirsute Female*. Sudonna, Westwood, NJ, USA.

Hinkle A.R. and Lind R.W. (1994) *Electrolysis, Thermolysis and the Blend*. Arroway, California.

Levene G.M. and Calnan C.D. (1986) *A Colour Atlas of Dermatology*. Wolfe Medical Publications, London.

Mahler A.Y. and Mahler H.C. (1986) *Principles of Electrology and Short Wave Epilation*. The Instantron Company, East Providence, RI, USA.

Mieske A. (1994) *Hair and Beauty Business Management*. Blackwell Science, Oxford.

Pickering T. and Howden R. (1977) *Grays Anatomy*. Churchill Livingstone, Edinburgh.

Richards R.N. and Meharg G.E. (1991) *Cosmetic and Medical Electrolysis and Temporary Hair Removal*. Medric Ltd, Toronto.

Rigazzi-Tailing J. (1994) *Creating an Excellent Salon*. Hodder & Stoughton, Sevenoaks, Kent.

Sims J. (1993) *A Practical Guide to Beauty Therapy for NVQ2*. Nelson Thornes, Cheltenham.

Soloman E.P., Schmidt R.R. and Adragna P.J. (1990) *Human Anatomy and Physiology*, 2dn edn. Harcourt Brace, Orlando, FL, USA.

Wilson K.J.W. (1990) *Ross and Wilson's Anatomy and Physiology in Health and Illness*. Churchill Livingstone, Edinburgh.

USEFUL CONTACTS

Wholesalers of electrolysis goods

Adel
Alan Howard
Aston and Fincher
Barkers
Belitas
Capital
Chris & Sons
E A Ellison and Co. Ltd
G Choppen & Sons
Haselocks
Hairdressing and Beauty Equipment Centre
House of Famuir (HOF) (needles)
Ogees
Pompadour
Salon Services
Sterex

Consult your local yellow pages under Hair and Beauty Supplies to locate these and/or other wholesalers.

Equipment manufacturers

Look in trade magazines and attend trade shows for information on the variety of equipment available. We suggest you obtain as much technical information as possible and make a comparative study.

Awarding bodies – electrolysis and beauty therapy

City & Guilds of London Institute
46 Britannia Street
London
WC1 9RG

Confederation of Beauty Therapy and Cosmetology (CIBTAC)
BABTAC House
70 East Gate Street
Gloucester
GL1 1QN

Edexcel
Stewart House
32 Russell Square
London
WC1B 5DN

Hairdressing and Beauty Industry Authority (HABIA)
2nd Floor
Fraser House
Nether Hall Road
Doncaster
DN1 2PH

International Therapy Examination Council (ITEC)
10–11 Heathfield Terrace
Chiswick
London
W4 4JE

Qualification and Curriculum Authority (QCA)
83 Piccadilly
London
W1J 8QA

Vocational Training Charitable Trust (VTCT)
Unit 11
Brickfield Trading Estate
Chandlers Ford
Hants
SO53 4DR

Awarding bodies and professional associations – electrolysis only

British Association of Electrolysists (BAE)
40 Parkfield Road
Ickenham
Middlesex
UB10 8LW

Institute of Electrolysis
27 Bottesford Close
Emerson Valley
Milton Keynes
MK4 2AF

Other professional associations

British Association of Beauty Therapy and Cosmetology
BABTAC House
70 East Gate Street
Gloucester
GL1 1QN

Guild of Professional Beauty Therapists
PO box 310
Derby
DE23 6ZT

Federation of Holistic Therapists (FHT)
3rd Floor
Eastleigh House
Upper Market Street
Eastleigh
Hants
SO50 9FD

Trade magazines

Health & Beauty Salon Magazine (electrolysis and beauty)
Quadrant House
The Quadrant
Sutton
Surrey
SM2 5AS

International Hair Route (electrolysis only)
121 Lakeshore Road East
Suite 207
Mississauga
Ontario
Canada
L5G 1E5

Professional Beauty
Broadway House
2–6 Fulham Broadway
London
SW6 1AA

INDEX